Economic Growth and the Common Good
From Crisis to Sustainable Development
Bernard Berendsen (ed.)

Economic Growth and the Common Good

From Crisis to Sustainable Development

Bernard Berendsen (ed.)

KIT Publishers – Amsterdam

Economic Growth and the Common Good. From Crisis to Sustainable Development.
Bernard Berendsen (ed.)

KIT Publishers
Mauritskade 63
P.O.Box 95001
1090 HA Amsterdam
The Netherlands
E-mail: publishers@kit.nl
www.kitpublishers.nl

Mixed Sources
Productgroep uit goed beheerde bossen
en andere gecontroleerde bronnen
www.fsc.org   Cert no. SGS-COC-006507
© 1996 Forest Stewardship Council
FSC

This publication was supported by the Society for International Development (SID).

Economic Growth and the Common Good. From Crisis to Sustainable Development is also the title of the lecture series organised by SID in partnerschip with The Ministry of Foreign Affairs, Clingendael, Socires and the Dutch National Committee for International Cooperation and Sustainable Development (NCDO).

Editing: Joyce Armstrong, Amsterdam, the Netherlands
Production: Bariet, Ruinen, the Netherlands

ISBN 978 94 6022 102 6
NUR 754

Contents

Preface

T he Netherlands Chapter of the Society for International Development (SID) has a reputation for putting items on the agenda long before they are broadly perceived as relevant to the debate surrounding international cooperation. The lecture series we presented about the emergence of a global risk society is one such example. When we first discussed the plans for the series, for instance, the terrorist attacks of 9/11 had not yet taken place. What's more, during one of the lectures the speaker was called away because of a supposed outbreak of the avian flu!

This time, the planning of the 2008-09 lecture series coincided with a change of events that was unprecedented and predicted by very few. The original idea for the series was based on the thesis of strong growth in the economy in both rich and poor countries, and the central question was whether that growth could be pro-poor, inclusive and whether it could go hand in hand with sustainability and poverty alleviation. The presupposition was growth, rather than a lack of growth. The Society for International Development decided, on the basis of that starting point, to question the quality and the direction of the presumed economic growth. Two years ago, this concern still stood central in the overall debate about development and was reflected in the original title of the lecture series, 'Economic Growth and the Common Good'. The first lecture of the series, however, coincided almost exactly with the demise of Lehman Brothers Holdings and, at the concluding Senate Conference eleven months later, the title of one of the last lectures was 'Lessons from the crisis'. It was therefore determined that the subtitle of the whole series would become 'From Crisis to Sustainable Development'.

This publication is a landmark document about the unfolding of the shattering events of the last two years: from optimism about economic growth and achieving the Millennium Development Goals, to a certain panic about the uncontrollable collapse of the worldwide financial system, and to the conclusion that the crisis offered an opportunity, even a compelling need, for far-reaching institutional reforms in the international financial system. More important still was the realization that a moral and ethical crisis was the underlying cause of the economic calamity. What is clear now is that both throughout the crisis and in its aftermath, the poorest of the world pay the highest price for the failings of the richest. This reality was apparent immediately in the decline of world trade and the credit crunch, and later as the poor became the primary victims of severe cuts in funding for international assistance and the shrinking of remittances and foreign investments. In chapter after chapter of this volume, in contribution after contribution, we seek to understand the unforeseen course of events, the dramas, the challenges and the eventual solutions and new approaches.

That we are able to present this publication now is thanks in large part to the willingness of so many to contribute to the series and to the Senate Conference: from a Nobel Prize Winner to high-level financial and economic policy makers, from outstanding academics to innovative bankers, politicians and development practitioners. And for once it seems appropriate to underscore that all of the speakers were willing to contribute to this series without requiring a fee. Thanks are also due to the board members of SID and to the staff of this organization and of its twin institute, Socires, whose out-of-the-box methods allowed us to come up with an innovative approach to our work.

The cooperation between SID and FMO, its director Nanno Kleiterp and its staff in the production of this series was also very fruitful, both in terms of ideas and financial contributions. Additionally, the synergy resulting from the Worldconnectors Round Table provided great relevance, inspiration and orientation to this endeavour. As in previous years, the financial assistance provided by the National Committee for International Cooperation and Sustainable Development (NCDO) was indispensable. In the publication of this book, KIT Publishers provided for the third time productive and cordial cooperation.

Most of all, I would like to thank Ambassador Bernard Berendsen who, also for the third time, contributed endless energy, intellectual input and tenacity to what deserves to become an indispensable collection of observations, analyses and recommendations concerning one of the most severe economic shock waves of our times.

At the time of publication of this collection, a new concern is becoming apparent. The fear is that emergent signs of recovery will tempt old and new economic and political actors to revert back to pre-crisis conditions, which were marked by the perversity of short-term, extravagant remunerations and the acceptance of the overexploitation of the earth, rather than to seek systematic institutional reform and more ethical ways of thinking. May this book with its richness of contributions and reflections contribute to that alternative approach. Only when we fully implement the lessons of these past two years will we be able to avoid another, even more disastrous collapse of the international financial system, irreversible setbacks for the poor and irreparable environmental catastrophes.

Jos J. van Gennip
President
Netherlands Chapter of the Society for International Development, Worldconnector

Introduction

Bernard Berendsen

S ince the end of the cold war and the downfall of communism, the merits of the free market mechanism have been widely acknowledged but at the same time heavily contested. The fall of communism in Eastern Europe and the former Soviet Union had convinced many that a free market economic system provided the best safeguards for economic growth, and that economic growth was a crucial factor for poverty reduction. But in development circles, neo-liberalism had become a dirty word. Nowadays it is the market that is blamed, not only for increased poverty and income inequality, but also for the dismantling of public services and ecological destruction. Yesterday's solutions have become today's problems. Liberalization and privatization have left people and the environment at the mercy of the free market. The mightiest are reaping the benefits while the weakest are footing the bill. Meanwhile, the global economy is being hit by one crisis after another: the financial crisis, an energy crisis, a food crisis, and of course the poorest countries and people are affected the most.

The other side of the story is that those countries that have liberalized their economies and substituted inward looking strategies for export orientation have achieved the highest annual growth rates. They have been able to attract foreign direct investments, to make use of new technologies and to capture a strong competitive position in the world market. In the last twenty years, they have not only multiplied their share in the world economy but have reduced poverty drastically – sometimes by more than 50 percent – within their borders.

So we may ask, where do we now stand? Can economic growth be made more inclusive? Can capitalism be made to serve the common good, and what roles are there for the market and the state? With those questions in mind, the Netherlands Chapter of the Society for International Development decided to devote its 2008-09 lecture series to the subject of economic growth and the common good.

In the lectures that follow, current insights and difficult policy dilemmas are identified, and their implications for the policies of organisations and institutions in the field of international cooperation are explored. The lectures focus on what governments can do to promote inclusive growth – including measures to make markets work, to maintain macroeconomic stability and to preserve monetary and fiscal discipline – as well as to provide social and political stability, to take care of public services like education and health care and to provide infrastructure for transportation and communication.

Governments are supposed to take measures to enhance the competitiveness of national enterprises vis-à-vis foreign companies, while at the same time catering for societal needs that are not addressed directly by the market. This includes needs in the areas of the biophysical environment, climate change and biodiversity (planet), employment and social cohesion (people) and democracy, security and law and order (power). The way in which business and the economy are run has a tremendous impact on the biophysical, social and governmental spheres. Conversely, the planet, people and the dynamics of power all have a decisive influence on the economy and on the possibilities for sustained economic growth.

This book is organized in two parts. The first part presents a series of lectures that focus on economic growth and the ways in which economic growth can be made more inclusive and can cater for social needs. The second part deals with the chosen subject for the closing conference of the lecture series: the ways in which developing countries have dealt with the consequences of the current economic crisis and, particularly, what lessons can be learnt for their future macroeconomic management and for the creation of a more sustainable way of banking and financing for development.

The lectures

The lecture series started at the same time as the financial crisis was turning into a full-fledged and unprecedented global economic downturn. As an inevitable result, the lecturers devoted some of their attention to what might be the consequences of this negative economic spiral on the prospects of developing countries. For example, Rick Van der Ploeg, in his opening lecture, drew attention to the negative consequences of increased volatility of prices and exchange rates on the economic prospects of developing countries. Additionally, he looked at the resource curse in a historical context and pointed out that, while natural resources can be bad for you, under the right circumstances they can also be good for you. Van der Ploeg also introduced the concept of genuine savings as being positive if a country has used up less, or if it has invested more, than what it has taken out of the national economy. So what you see is that countries that have positive genuine savings – like China, Botswana or Ghana – are the big growers while those with negative savings – like Nigeria, Venezuela and Angola – are slow growers.

Michael Spence, in his lecture, elaborated on the outcomes of the report of the Growth Commission of which he is the chairman, but also looked at the financial crisis and the considerable damage it has already done and its effect on major financial institutions. He spoke of tough but manageable headwinds for developing countries in the form of a food and energy price shock, food emergencies for the poor, a major inflation issue which may later be abated, the temporary Balkanization of agricultural markets and a general decrease in global demand.

One of the immediate problems of the financial crisis has been the spread of damaged balance sheets from the United States and Europe to developing countries, which require increasing amounts of capital for solvency and capital adequacy reasons. As a result, the currencies of some emerging economies such as India, Brazil and South Africa started to depreciate in the summer and fall of 2008. This has caused considerable problems in those countries, because that kind of volatility is difficult to deal with and can be very damaging to the economy. Still, looking at which developing countries would weather the financial crisis best, Spence concluded that those ideally situated for such a crisis are those with a balanced budget, a modest trade deficit at most and preferably a mild surplus, and a lot of foreign reserves.

On the basis of earlier experiences with financial crises, Martin Wolf expected a flight from risk worldwide and therefore also a flight from emerging economies. The countries that are worse hit are those with large current account deficits, booming property sectors and large inflows of net capital financed by banks. The lesson that emerging economies drew from earlier crises is that it is much safer to go back to export-led growth and run current account surpluses to insure themselves against the next crisis. Somebody in the world has to run deficits, and it will very likely be the US again.

The panel discussion that followed focussed on the responsibility of the US as the dominant economic and financial power in the world to provide for economic, financial and monetary stability. The problem, according to Wolf, is not so much with the US but with the design of the Bretton Woods arrangement with the US dollar as international reserve currency. Moreover, instead of blaming the US, Wolf places more of the blame on countries like China for running colossal current account surpluses.

In their roles as panellists, Sylvester Eijffinger and Hans Schlaghecke concluded that the key questions are how to create stability in the international financial system and what role countries and institutions could or should play to achieve this. According to Schlaghecke, there is a mismatch between the requirements of the international system on the one hand and sovereign states with their own rules and moral systems on the other.

According to Wolf, we might be moving towards a more block-type world with probably three core countries or unions and their currencies – the US, the European Union and China – providing reserves to peripheral countries in a crisis, thus stabilizing their smaller neighbours.

In his lecture, Edgardo Campos drew attention to the mechanism of shared growth that was introduced in South Asia and East

Asia in the last century. Countries in those regions experienced a sense of urgency in the 1960s and 1970s due to a permanent threat of communist takeover. They had political leadership with a vision and a strategy to promote and sustain a shared growth process, and a mechanism in the form of institutions to implement these policies. Key institutions included deliberation councils that connected the government and the private sector, welfare sharing mechanisms that formed a kind of implicit contract between the government and the population, and a functional and competent bureaucracy.

The idea is that the shared growth principle might actually be beneficial to growth: East Asian countries have had more equal income distributions and have, over the last decades, been growing faster than countries with less equal income distributions. And the Asian crisis has proven that Asian countries are not likely to fall back. The lesson for Africa might be that fairly progressive leadership might be able to move countries forward and manage the politics of change better.

With regard to economic growth, Diane Elson asked several questions: does it really increase or deplete resources, and how equitable is the kind of growth we see today? Her main focus, however, was the relationship between gender equality and economic growth. Three studies were reviewed, one suggesting that economic growth might benefit women even more than men (Arthur Lewis), one that posited that gender equality promotes economic growth (Stephan Klasen) and a third that, on the contrary, speculated that gender inequality promotes growth (Stephanie Seguino). Elson doubted the conclusions of each of the three studies reviewed, and went on to question whether discrimination against women in the labour market would be in compliance with the human rights obligations of governments, and whether it is possible at all to have growth compliant with human rights. She argued that this required well-regulated markets, monetary and fiscal policies that focus on the provision of decent work, industrial policies that provide high productivity jobs, respect for the rights of workers to organize themselves and last but not least, the taxation and expenditure to provide public services and to redistribute income.

Geske Dijkstra presented her own argument for gender equality, arguing that allocative efficiency in the economy would improve if there would be less segregation in the workplace, if men would do more of the unpaid work and if the division of labour in the household would be more equally distributed.

Luc Soete, in his lecture on the technological divide, looked at the historical context of technological development. Industrial research and development (R&D) started with the industrial revolution and was modernized by growing in scale, by the way it was organized and by the instrumentation and equipment used. R&D became a factor in determining national competitiveness in a global context, and became a well-established process whereby new technologies must be developed on a small scale before being turned over to industrial production on a large scale. Nowadays, the role of users becomes more important in that users can interact, provide feedback and tell you what works and what does not.

This reality has also led to a shift from industrial technology to innovation policies. What results is a picture of global research and local innovation, or 'research on the move'. There is a role for local communities of practice. As a consequence there is a need to increase and broaden the scope of research activities. Instead of the old model of introducing new products and quality features, there is now a pursuit to find products that are standardized but with a major innovation element. Developing markets appear to produce the most motivation research and raise the most innovation challenges: autonomy, simplicity of use and lacking maintenance and repair. According to Soete, global access to knowledge is crucial to solve the current crisis, which depends on technological transfer and access to knowledge.

Vijay Paranjpye underlined the importance of agriculture for reaching the Millennium Development Goals (MDGs) and questioned the current policies of Europe and the US to promote the use of food grains for producing biogas. He pointed toward alternatives, and particularly to the use of straw instead of food grains in the production of biogas, a process that has been practised with success in India, noting that creating energy from biomass can be done without losing organic material or fertilizer. India has been successful because it never derailed agriculture from its central position. When international markets moved up or down, the Indian people did not lose. The Indian economy with its slow growth has been resilient. It also still had a lot of organic farming. Within these observations, there is a solution for Africa too: make the farmer independent by allowing him or teaching him to produce his own fertilizers and seeds, to generate his own power and to harvest his own water on his land. At the same time, we should try to achieve the MDGs by attacking them as if they were one goal, and get agriculture back onto the main stage. Then we will be able to show that we are serious about the African food crisis.

Cor van Beuningen agreed, but also drew attention to the changing international environment resulting in geo-politicization and a multi-polar world system wherein governments are again into the power game. This poses an additional challenge of how to deal with new scarcities in food and energy, and related problems such as climate change and biodiversity.

Ad Melkert considered it a challenge to explore the value side of the past and future of globalization against the backdrop of the G7 setting the global agenda and the resurgence of the recognition of public interest (or the common good) and the necessary role of the state. What is needed is recognition of the values that, in the post-war reconstruction phase of Europe, have glued countries together around the notion of responsibility of the state. It is also necessary to recognize and support, in an inclusive manner, the social rights and aspirations of all citizens based on the principle of equality. The current crisis offers an opportunity to foster a more inclusive type of society.

Melkert also believes that there is abundant evidence that an inducive investment climate can go hand in hand with clear frameworks of regulation and enforcement. The present time offers an opportunity for a wider understanding of the interaction between growth and the common good, and for establishing a system of governance that helps the world on its way up from deprivation and poverty to dignity and prosperity. He concludes that Europe has something precious to offer: the recognition of solidarity arrangements and consensus institutions as necessary preconditions for an inclusive and stable society.

Recognizing that we live in a different time and have to adjust to big changes in the world, Nancy Birdsall of the Center for Global Development (CGD) presented a global development agenda for the next US President, and elaborated on some key issues of CGD's Commitment to Development Index (CDI). She made it clear that the US must now adjust to a world in which it will be less dominant. The BRIC countries (i.e. Brazil, Russia, India and China) are growing in weight, and the largest part of the world population will be living in developing countries. There are increasing international risks that developing countries will not be able to contain within their borders.

The Center, therefore, chose four themes for its recommendations: the US should invest more in ways that would benefit people who are poor in developing countries; it should continue to press for open markets; and it should modernize its foreign assistance programmes and move towards a more cooperative approach to development issues.

The key issues included in the CDI are climate change, trade and migration. The US should invest more in solar/thermal and other renewable energy, provide duty free access to the US market to a selected group of developing countries, review its farm policy and issue more visas to both skilled and unskilled workers. While developing countries are expected to be deeply affected by the financial crisis, the poor in the emerging market economies where financial links are stronger will loose out even more.

The closing conference

The lecture series was concluded with a conference that looked more closely at the consequences of the financial crisis and the ways in which various countries in Africa, Asia and Latin America were dealing with those consequences. Though it became clear that economies that successfully emerged in the past two decades stand a better chance to endure the current crisis than do most of the Western countries, they do have serious financial problems related to their dwindling export earnings and levels of foreign direct investment.

In his opening lecture, Jan Kees de Jager focussed on the role of the financial sector. The financial sector in developing countries is small, and at first sight the damage seems limited. The small size in itself, however, poses a problem as it limits access to credit. This deprives potentially productive projects of necessary funds.

What are needed are inventive solutions that will not expose the economy to even greater volatility and stocks. Micro financing might be a good example, as might be the provision of new forms of insurance, including in the health area. There are also new initiatives in the area of small business finance. The Netherlands, for example, works with Small Enterprise Assistance Funds, a firm that takes equity interests in small businesses in developing countries and supports a global diversified currency fund modelled after the existing Currency Exchange Fund. These are two different ways to strengthen the financial sector in developing countries.

Panel I

The first panel focussed on diverse approaches to economic growth and development with specific attention on the need for social protection of the poor and vulnerable, and included views from Africa, Latin America and Asia.

Shenggen Fan of the International Food Policy and Research Institute drew attention to the recent food and financial crises and how they hurt the poor and the vulnerable. High and volatile food prices have severely undermined the food security and livelihoods of poor people, and slow growth and recession has added to their burden. Foreign direct investments have fallen significantly and the capital crunch resulted in higher debt burdens for farmers. The economic downturn has also led to reduced employment and lower wages for unskilled workers, for example in China.

Economic growth is necessary to fight hunger, and agriculture-led growth is particularly crucial for reducing poverty and hunger. In addition to growth, effective social safety nets are needed. They can promote economic growth at the same time and are particularly important during food and financial crises. China has been very active in implementing a stimulus package that includes spending on safety nets. Protective actions can be in the form of cash transfers and employment-based food security programmes. The tax base should be strengthened to provide funds for social protection.

In sum, strategies towards inclusive growth are needed to accelerate economic growth and increase its pro-poor qualities. Social spending and its effectiveness should also be accelerated so as to effectively target the poor and vulnerable.

Benno Ndulu, the Governor of the Bank of Tanzania, elaborated on three aspects of global interdependence against the backdrop of the financial crisis. First is that the division of labour has become part of the globalized process. Second is that economic and financial actors are now unconstrained by borders, weakening the role of the state. Third is that contagion has become a powerful tool for propagating booms and crises across borders. Africa is particularly vulnerable to this interdependence because of its reliance on primary commodities and on foreign savings and investments. Africa is also vulnerable because the various nations are, in general, small economies. On the other hand, interdependence has helped Asian, Latin American and African countries also to exploit globalization. Growth rates have gone up and inflation rates have gone down with a significant build-up of foreign exchange reserves.

The main concerns from the crisis are that it endangered the sustainability of the growth process and that it might undermine macro-stability and the progress achieved in creating social well-being. There is a danger that there will be a push back towards the achievements of the MDGs and a threat to social and political stability.

The main priorities are therefore protecting jobs, ensuring the availability of food, protecting life-saving programmes that combat HIV, malaria and tuberculosis, sustaining macro-stability and protecting the banking system. Finally, it is very important to protect investment in agriculture. At the international level it is important to avoid protectionism and to make sure that such crises do not return by initiating pre-emptive measures that focus on correcting regulatory failures. De-globalization, he concludes, is not an option for Africa because Africa's strong natural resource base makes it dependent on the world market, but it can change the terms of engagement. Secondly, Africa needs to build resilience to external shocks, via diversification of its economy, for example, and reduce reliance on primary commodities.

The Latin-American perspective, and in particular that of Brazil, is different from many other countries. Alfredo Valladão reminded the audience that, for the last fifteen years, the world has had the fastest growth in the history of mankind, lifting around 800 million people out of poverty. Also, inequality has been reduced. There were three reasons for this: increased trade, cheap credit and advances in information technology and transportation innovation.

The crisis may have given reason to doubt the sustainability of this process, and a lack of confidence leads to price increases for food, energy and raw materials. So what he recommends is not to slow down growth, but to have fast growth with less intensive use of natural resources, or what the G20 call the ecological economy, and to fight protection first. Secondly, there must be policies in place to soften the blow to the people who suffer from the increased interdependence and openness. According to Valladão, there should also be more regulation in the financial system, but we should not throw the baby out with the bathwater or kill the goose that lays the golden eggs. And we will have to find ways to make people consume more by the 'democratization of credit'; a problem that, in many countries like China, India and Brazil, is complicated. Finally, at the international level, it is important to give more of a voice to more players, which is difficult again because this means less of a voice for Europe. And the new players face a challenge of their own: what are they going to propose? Valladão reminded us that if you are not at the table, you are on the menu. But if you are at the table, you have to take responsibility to cook the meal and be criticized if the meal is not to the taste of a lot of people.

The Asian perspective was presented by Jan Willem Blankert of the EU mission in Indonesia. From his viewpoint, the news from Asia, as from parts of Latin America, is rather positive. He believes that there is less interdependence than we thought. China,

Singapore and even Indonesia are doing well, and productivity is improving. The Association of Southeast Asian Nations (ASEAN) is opening up, strengthening its regional integration and reaching free trade agreements with Australia, New Zealand, Japan, India and China.

Protectionism comes mostly from vested interests, and borders lead to costs. The EU in the 1980s discovered that it was wasting 5 percent every year by not having a single market. That set it on a path to create a single market. Still, Blankert insists we in the West have a long way to go to open our economy to other regions.

Panel II

The second panel dealt with innovative approaches to financing for development, taking into consideration that economic and political power has been shifting from the Western world to emerging economies and drawing lessons from the crisis at the macro, the meso and the micro level.

As Nanno Kleiterp, CEO of the Financing Company for Developing Countries FMO, remarked, we have learned one thing at the macro level, which is that markets are not perfect. The interests of society are no longer the sole responsibility of the government, but also of market participants. If financial participants only focus on shareholder value and ignore stakeholder values, they should lose their license to operate. At the meso level, the lesson is that confidence in the role of the banking sector has been undermined and must be restored quickly because finance is important to society, especially in developing economies and emerging markets where access to finance is still limited. At the micro level, the focus is on the role of entrepreneurs, who are the drivers of change. We can ask for all the regulations and government interventions we want, but without the drive and willingness to change we will get nowhere.

Trevor Manuel elaborated on the lessons at the macro level. He was the first to point out the risk of the pendulum swing: people may believe that those who are in the government have all the answers; they don't. He also pointed out that the economy is in the lives of the people. When we talk about development, then we talk about societies and their well-being. Manuel concluded that we need governments, even if only to place the issue of finance for development on the agenda, and that we have to address the issue of global governance, strengthen the capabilities of the state and eliminate policy contests that frequently impose a tax on the poor.

Peter Blom of Triodos Bank got at the heart of the financial crisis: namely, the practise of banking that has deteriorated in the last thirty to forty years. Banks must realign with the needs of society again. They need to realize that, in the end, we depend on what people produce, what services they provide, what is happening on the ground and what the real needs of the people are. That means that we have to change the governance model of banks and move from shareholder-based banking to a stakeholder-based banking system. We should also make a distinction between retail banking and investment banking. Investment banking is about taking risks, while basic or retail banking is about connecting depositors and lenders and providing them with good payment systems.

One of Blom's main conclusions is that we must make money a tool for change. Banks are there to help people make conscious decisions on how to spend their money. Once they realize that they can change their own situation with their money, then they will change the world.

Vineet Rai, a representative of Aavishkaar, an Indian Micro Venture Capital Fund, is a living example of effective and innovative approaches to financing for development. He was motivated to be active in this area when he realized that, in India, people live in two different worlds. About 30 percent are educated and are benefiting from the world economic boom. The other India, making up about 70 percent of the population, is struggling to create opportunities to survive. Sooner or later we will start getting pulled back if that 70 percent does not start to contribute to economic growth.

This challenge can only be dealt with through an approach that would differ by not giving out tools and alms, but by creating more inclusive, participatory growth. Micro finance has been successful in this respect as it reaches out to the poor while seeking out what they need. The real success of micro finance is creating choices that are needed at the bottom.

The second critical need, apart from finance, is talent. Dealing with social problems is far more complex than doing business. So, if you want to make a difference in solving complex social problems, promote economic growth and bring about development, you need to bring your best talent together, for example by creating non-commercial incentives that are far stronger than economic incentives.

Rai also shared some lessons learned through his experiences over the last ten years, including that business models need to address the needs of the people and not their wants, that the needs of business are very large and not likely to be addressed by multinationals and, thirdly, that the business approach should be used to effectively solve social challenges.

Allison Evans, summing up the conference, came to three main conclusions. The first is that, although the panic is over, we still have a long way to go in terms of shock proofing and building resilience into the economy. Secondly, we still have to sort out global governance issues. Lastly, development strategies at the national level are going to be different as a result of the financial crisis. Successful countries will have to be more pro-active in their response to crises. So, she concludes, diversify, integrate, sort out some of the institutional rules of the game, support stronger markets that connect people to regional supply chains, and crowd in private capital that is responsible and focused on values and long-term development outcomes.

Acknowledgements

Those were the kind of lessons that could have been hoped for when setting up the lecture series on economic growth and the common good, and that came to the forefront in both the lecture series and the closing conference. SID Netherlands again deserves credit for organizing this series together with its traditional partner organizations, in particular the Vrije Universiteit in Amsterdam, the Radboud University in Nijmegen, and Maastricht

University as well as the Institute of Social Studies (ISS), the Netherlands Institute of Foreign Relations Clingendael and the Netherlands Ministry of Foreign Affairs (MFA). They were closely involved in scheduling, choosing subjects and speakers and hosting meetings at their institutions.

The main focus of the lecture series was determined in a number of brainstorming sessions in which both partner organizations and board members of SID Netherlands participated. They benefited from written inputs of staff members of SID and Socires, in particular its director Cor van Beuningen and Margreet Mook, temporary staff member of SID. Other participants were Jacob Bouwman and Kees Kouwenaar (VU), Henny Helmich (NCDO), Paul Zwetsloot (MFA), Jos Walenkamp (Nuffic), Ruerd Ruben (Radboud University), Louise Anten (Clingendael), Rolf Wijnstra (MFA), and Veronica Santander (SID). The proceedings were chaired by Jos van Gennip, chairman of the board of SID Netherlands.

SID staff members responsible for and taking part in the implementation of the programme were Annette de Raad, Gordana Stankovics, Veronica Santander and Fenna Egberink, its director Iem Roos and Wilma Bakker, personal assistant to board chairman Jos van Gennip.

Particular mention also goes to Toon Bullens of Achmea, who showed a special interest in the subject of ways to promote social security in developing societies and the role of the state, markets and cooperatives and who chaired a discussion on the subject, as well as to Danielle Hirsch, director of Both Ends, who participated in the preparations for the jointly organized lecture devoted to the legacy of Joke Waller-Hunter by Vijay Paranjpye on the contribution of agriculture and rural development to inclusive growth.

The closing conference was jointly organized with and supported by the Finance Company for Developing Countries, FMO. Nanno Kleiterp, its CEO, and staff members Ruurd Brouwer and René de Sévaux were actively involved in the preparations and the selection of subjects and speakers, and also contributed to the debates in the conference itself. SID Netherlands is grateful for the hospitality offered by the first chamber of the Dutch parliament (Senate) and to Professor Hans Franken, vice-chair of the

Committee on Foreign Relations, as well as to Sylvia Borren and Herman Wijffels, co-chairs of the Worldconnectors, who operated as moderators in the two panel discussions of the conference.

As always, the staff of SID Netherlands has been supportive in the preparation of this publication, in particular Gordana Stankovics, Fenna Egberink, Iem Roos and Wilma Bakker. Margreet Mook and Cor van Beuningen had a great part in the conceptualization of the subject of this lecture series. Jos van Gennip was, as always, a great inspirer and driving force. Member of the Board of SID Netherlands and Chairman of the Board of the Royal Tropical Institute (KIT) Jan Donner also encouraged this publication throughout.

Lianne Damen of KIT Publishers, who also accompanied SID Netherland's earlier publications on *Democracy and Development* and *Emerging Global Scarcities and Power Shifts*, was again ready to assist in the publication of this third volume on *Economic Growth and the Common Good*. She never failed to show confidence and patience, even when deadlines became close. I am very grateful for her perseverance and ability to inspire confidence.

Of the speakers, only Ad Melkert and Jan Kees de Jager provided a written version of their lecture. The other speakers were provided with a written version of their lecture, prepared by the editor, and they were invited to give their comments for the preparation of a final version. As editor, I have opted for a certain amount of conformity in the format while at the same time preserving some of the flavour of the spoken word. To enhance their comprehensibility, I have included some illustrations that were used in their Microsoft PowerPoint presentations.

Last year it became clear that SID Netherlands would have no choice but to take the financial crisis into account in preparing for this lecture series on economic growth and the common good. The outcome of the lecture series and the closing conference, of which this publication bears witness, will hopefully contribute to a better understanding of its origins and point the way for a better contribution of economic growth to serve the common good.

PART I

Economic Growth and the
Common Good

Growth and Volatility in Developing Economies: A Political Economy Perspective

Rick van der Ploeg

What I am going to talk about is partially based on some work I have done together with a former PhD student, Steven Poelhekke, who is working now with De Nederlandse Bank (DNB), and partially also on some work I have done and am still doing at the African Development Bank (ADB).

Just this morning, I read a story in the Independent about Congo and the war going on over there, and about somebody who was gang raped and shot with a pistol while still in his pyjamas. Then you think, after all the horrible stories you hear of Congo: what is going on over there? Is it really just a war? And if it is a war, what is it all about? According to my colleague, Paul Collier, in Oxford the Congo is not embroiled in conflict because the people there are more violent and like to knock each other's heads in and gang rape each other. They are fighting about control of natural resources. In light of this, I believe there is also a responsibility for us as Western consumers.

For example, every mobile phone is produced with a material called coltan (columbite-tantalite). More than 80 percent of the world's reserves of coltan come from Africa, and 80 percent of that can be found in the part of Congo that is governed by rebel groups, militias and the corrupt and underfunded state army. Congo is also big in diamonds. There are accusations, though hard to confirm, that international mining companies have helped to fund rebel groups and armies to protect access to valuable natural resources. It is no wonder that empirical evidence finds that most wars are fought in poor sub-Sahara, since they are driven by greed about natural resources. Paul Collier and his co-authors give detailed empirical evidence that shows that conflicts and wars are more common in countries that are resource-rich, and which also are polarized by having many different ethnic factions. And, of course, Congo has a unique history of its resources being stolen by King Leopold of Belgium.

But the central idea is that there are rational reasons why there are wars, and that these wars are driven by greed, perhaps as much as or even more so than by grievance. Also, we should realize that, sometimes, Western companies pay various rebel groups to try to gain control of particular resources. As an academic and a former politician, I want to shed some light on this in a more systematic way. That is why I look at the way resource-rich countries write contracts with exploration and mining companies, and I study the economic policies of these countries.

What I would like to talk about today is the fact that most of the problems we are seeing, particularly in large parts of sub-Saharan Africa but also in many other resource-rich countries, are really due to the so-called curse of natural resources. In the Netherlands, of course, we are familiar with what we have dubbed the Dutch disease. But the problem goes much deeper and much further than that, as it is about economic and political distortions caused by having a wealth of natural resources.

Looking at the origin of the natural resource curse, most right-wing colleagues of mine, (and even I myself if I have had a bad night's sleep), would apply the same argument to foreign aid. It is not just William Easterly and others; in the Netherlands you have Sweder van Wijnbergen, and at the London School of Economics the eminent Lord Peter Bauer, who of course was sceptical about foreign aid many decades before everyone else came to be. But it is true: much of foreign aid, if you think about it, might have a similar kind of adverse effect on the economy and society of a given country as oil would have in Nigeria or sudden windfalls from gas exports would have in the Netherlands.

The resource curse in a historical context

Let us talk a bit more about the resource curse. I will give some historical and case study evidence on the natural resource curse, and I will end with saying that the quintessential feature of natural resources is that they hurt and harm many economies through conflict and through volatility. Now look at the price of oil: it went all the way up to 160 US dollars per gallon, and then went all the way down to forty US dollars per gallon. This same volatility can be witnessed for prices of many other commodities. This up and down of the price one can fetch on world markets for one of the main outputs of a developing economy really ruins the prospects of such an economy. Take Nigeria, which is a big, extremely wealthy country and one of the richest countries in the world in terms of oil. At the same time I guess it is one of the poorest countries of the world if you look at the wealth of individual people. It is strange that, in a country like Nigeria, the per-capita income has more or less stagnated since 1965.

At the same time, you see some countries in Asia, or even other countries in Africa (like Botswana), with a spectacularly fast growth path. In Nigeria, the percentage of people earning less than one dollar per day has increased from about a quarter of the population to now almost three-quarters. This figure indicates that poverty has increased enormously in Nigeria, despite the fact that the country is one of the biggest oil exporters in the world.

There is also a staggering amount of inequality for Nigerians. When I was in Paris visiting UNESCO, there were lots of super-wealthy Nigerians going on a shopping frenzy in Kenzo, which is an expensive place to buy clothes. That was just the top of Nigeria, however, as some people there are extraordinarily rich while the majority of people remain poor.

Take capacity utilization in Nigeria: two-thirds just lie idle. Nigeria is one of the few countries in the world that has seen its total factor productivity decline. Almost no other country in the world has had that experience. And this is not just during the last two or three years: we are looking over a forty-year period. So for forty years individual citizens of Nigeria have not seen any increase in their well-being or in their income per-capita, and have been producing less than is warranted by their inputs of labour and capital. This can only be explained by rampant rent seeking and possibly corruption.

We hoped at one point that the scholar, politician and World Bank expert Dr. Ngozi Okonjo-Iweala, Minister of Finance of Nigeria between 2003 and 2006, would try to improve transparency in regards to how much oil was pumped out of the ground, how much of the revenues went to the government and how much to the oil companies, how much was saved and invested and how much consumed, and so forth. This courageous minister really meant business, so she was promoted to become the Minister of Foreign Affairs, a position wherein she could do less harm to those who wanted to get their hands on oil revenues. Now she is out of politics altogether and back at the World Bank. Nigeria is back to the bad old days as it was before.

That is just one example. Look at some other countries such as Congo or Indonesia. What you see is that those countries that are doing badly, like Congo, Nigeria and Venezuela under Chavez, have very bad growth, are typically more corrupt, have many more conflicts and have a lot of inequality. Still, what I am trying to say is that the natural resource curse is not cast in stone. Botswana, for example, which is a fairly homogeneous country with not many different ethnic factions, is doing spectacularly well in economic terms and is one of the fastest growing economies in the world. It has been growing by about 8 percent per year for decades. As a consequence, it has seen its per-capita GDP double. Compare that with other countries like Nigeria where the GDP has stayed more or less stagnant, and you see that it is not necessary that natural resources work against you. They can work very well for you. But in the case of Congo, the per-capita GDP has gone down from 221 US dollars to eighty-five US dollars. That is what the war has done: it has ravished the economy.

Let us look at some historical figures. The Netherlands did not have many natural resources in the seventeenth century. Spain, on the other hand, got a lot of gold and silver from the New World. Yet the Netherlands enjoyed its Golden Age while Spain, with all of its natural resource wealth, was doing pretty poorly. Oil-rich countries like Venezuela, Iran, Libya, Kuwait and Qatar have experienced negative growth rates for decades. This negative growth did not only occur in the non-oil part of the economy. Even if you allow for all the oil money coming in, they were doing extremely badly. Oil income has not helped them, but has harmed them. Even if you look at the Organization of Petroleum Exporting Countries (OPEC) as a whole, the GDP has been declining.

Figure 1   Negative correlation between economic growth and resource dependence

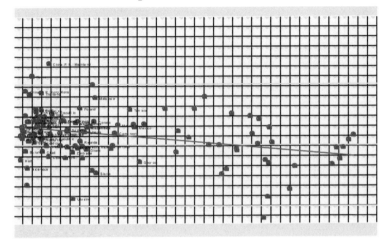

Figure 1 plots the ratio of dependence on natural resource exports for individual countries on the horizontal axis and economic growth on the vertical axis. All of these dots represent individual countries. What you see is a very strong negative correlation between natural resource export dependence and economic growth. Thus, natural resource dependent countries tend to be countries that do fairly poorly. Now this is just a partial correlation and, furthermore, I have said nothing yet about what is causing this. But it is definitively a negative correlation. Jeffrey Sachs was the first who noticed this and made a big deal about it.

Before I say a bit more about it, there are also countries that have had positive experiences. Take Botswana again: 40 percent of its GDP comes from diamonds, but Botswana puts all of its money in education and has enjoyed the highest average growth rates in the world since 1965. Its GDP per-capita, which started at roughly the same level as that of Nigeria, is now ten times as high. Of course, the United Arab Emirates have not done so badly either. They have at least used their oil money to build all of these islands in the sea, along with a lot of other infrastructure, and have managed to provide education for all.

But perhaps the best example is the United States. If you look at the old historical work of Paul David, who is also a colleague at Oxford University, on the course of the US economy, you will find that the US was originally a frontier economy where the marginal cost of land was zero. You grab a new piece of land, and that is how America became colonized and developed. Land was the first, prime driver of growth in America. Then there was a whole century when America was a mineral resource rich economy, not because it had a comparative advantage in mineral resources but because it had a government that said: 'We let you, the private sector, make profits on minerals, whether it is iron or bauxite or oil or whatever it is, but we as a government won't touch it'. Then, secondly, they invested enormously. If you now look at the great educational institutions such as the Massachusetts Institute of Technology and all these agricultural universities, the big universities of the States, they were founded in that time, together with the exploitation of mineral resources. The government did an enormous amount of investment in education and claimed no ultimate titles to mineral rights. According to the reading of historians like David, together with all of the learning by doing and the returns to scale this generated, the US enjoyed a mineral boom that sustained a period of rapid growth. Maybe Germany or Britain were much better off in natural resources, but they did not do so well in terms of resource-led growth of the economy: they did not have the right conditions.

So what I am trying to say is that natural resources can be bad for you, but under the right circumstances they can also be good for you. With many African governments, the challenge is to find out what can be done to make being resource-rich less harmful for them. Some lessons to draw from these experiences are not only based on academic evidence, but are also derived from detailed examination of the experiences of resource-rich economies.

Although it is easier said than done, a country must avoid corruption, diversify its industry, educate its people and particularly exploit the complementarities and the linkages between manufacturing and the resource sector.

Most of these economies really depend on one export sector, namely oil, gas, gold, silver, copper, bauxite or diamonds, and they are not very diversified. That makes them extremely vulnerable to volatility of their commodity prices. There is also a negative relationship between corruption and resource abundance. Resource rich countries are typically more bureaucratic, have bad rule of law, have more governance instability, have a less developed financial system, have more external conflict and have lower life expectancy.

Four arguments why resources may be bad

What are the reasons for this? Basically there are four reasons why resources may be bad for a country. One reason is the Dutch disease. You may have an enormous oil bonanza and have all of this foreign exchange coming into your country. Everybody wants to buy your currency, and wants to buy your oil. What this really does is drive up the value of your currency, just like that. Then what happens? On the one hand, this is very good in the sense that you can buy a lot of products. But it really screws up any export from any other sector in your economy. As a consequence of the Dutch disease, your export sector is going into decline and you'll get a boom in the non-tradable sectors such as construction, service, and so on. This means that those sectors that are considered the engines of growth – the manufacturing industry and other export sectors, for example – go into decline because of this highly appreciated currency. These sectors cannot export anymore.

Let us now make a little detour on the financial crisis of the moment. Many say that it really started with all of these greedy, overextended people. But the big thing of course was the US dollar, which was being propped up by Russia and China. China was propping it up because they have these big export markets, and they need the export revenues in order to buy up more American foreign debt and get a more powerful geopolitical position. Russia has also done a similar thing in order to avoid some of the appreciation of the Rouble. Russia has been trying to support the dollar by buying dollar assets in order to soften some of the adverse consequences of all of this gas from Siberia on the other export sectors of Russia.

So really, the traditional Dutch disease stories are also relevant for Africa. When people speak of the African disease, such as Sweder van Wijnbergen or Jan Willem Gunning of this university, who is perhaps the best development economist of the Netherlands, they would argue that a lot of foreign aid would have those adverse consequences and that it would lead to an appreciation of the currency, would worsen the country's competitive position and would lead to a decline of exports. Since it is the export sector where typically all of the learning by doing occurs, where all the growth factors are, where the engines of growth are, you are permanently worse off. Economists say it is very ungraceful to talk of a disease, but it really is a disease. While a decline of the export sector may be just an efficient response to the resource boom, the argument is, according to Paul Krugman (Nobel Prize winner for economics) and Sweder van Wijnbergen, that the export sector is the sector where most of the growth originates.

A second argument is that volatility is very harmful for the economy. If you look at commodity prices and the historical evidence over the last hundred years, you can say that commodity prices have been fluctuating very much. But that is not the longer trend. In the long-term, they have been fairly stable. There is not much evidence that commodity prices are on an upward spiral. There is, on the other hand, a lot of evidence that what commodity prices lack in trend they make up for in variance. And it is resource rich economies like those in Africa that are extremely vulnerable to the high volatility of resource prices, particularly, of course, when the supply is inelastic. It is particularly harmful for them because they are not diversified and have a small, sheltered sector. There is a danger that, due to this volatility, the whole economy shrinks and goes away. So that is very bad for growth.

A third reason why resources may be bad is that they encourage bad, unsustainable policies. In the Netherlands in the 1970s, we made a big Christmas tree of the welfare state and Ruud Lubbers, Wim Kok and now Jan Peter Balkenende have to take a lot of the balls out of the Christmas tree again in order to get a welfare state that is a bit more sustainable. It is because we became giddy-eyed because of all of the gas that would last forever that we were kind of making the Christmas tree bigger and bigger. It is the same thing, this erosion of the critical faculties of politicians, which you see in other countries as well. That people lose sight of growth oriented policies.

We older people particularly remember that in1970s and 1980s there was much state-led industrialization. With Chavez in Venezuela that is still the case. I remember in 1981 and 1983, I was in Mexico; they used all of the oil to give huge subsidies to domestic industries that were basically uncompetitive. This idea of state-led industrialization for import substitution and heavy subsidies for manufacturing is very bad for the economy, and in the end these things are unsustainable.

Another reason that resources can be bad is that resources lead to rent seeking and corruption. If you have some able people in the economy – and every country has some able people – you may hope that when they are smart they become academics. They might also actually set up a company, make some money and do something productive. But in resource-rich countries, like for example the island of São Tomé compared with, say, the island of Cape Verde, what is happening there? They have a lot of money coming from oil from offshore drilling. So what are all of the kids doing? They all come to MIT, Harvard, Oxford, to LSE and to other places. The idea is that they go back to their own country. What do they do there? They become civil servants. What do you do if you become a civil servant over there? Then you get all of the claw-backs from the oil industry. So you have got detailed micro-evidence that this is exactly what is happening. The people are choosing their careers not to be productive entrepreneurs, but to be rent seekers.

That is why we find corruption, political instability, bureaucratic inefficiency and, in the worst case, assassinations and conflicts in resource-rich countries. We have a lot of evidence that the resource curse operates via the worsening of institutions and the erosion of legal systems. Also, we have ample evidence from people like Paul Collier and Anke Hoefler that natural resources, as I said in the beginning, are really the main cause for most of the conflicts in the world, from civil strife to wars, particularly in Africa, and that this is due to the weakening of the state or because the natural resources just pay for the financing of rebels.

And it is particularly bad for what we call point-based resources rather than so-called diffuse resources. What do we mean by point-based resources? These are resources that are easily plundered. They are typically compact, whereas diffuse resources are, like rice or bananas, big lumpy products that you cannot loot so easily. Thus, the evidence indicates that these point-based resources like diamonds, gold and oil are the culprits.

Why do countries grow?

What makes countries really grow? The main reason why countries grow is that they are, normally speaking, very poor. When you are very poor, there are lots of opportunities to invest, and then you grow. That is what Bob Solow, who developed this theory, got his Nobel Prize for in 1987. He found that the lower the level of initial income, the faster you grow. But growth also happens if you are an open economy. Open economies typically grow much faster than closed economies. We also find that if you have strong rule of law or good institutions and if you invest a lot in education and productive capital, then typically such an economy is going to experience a lot of growth. But even if you allow for all of these important factors, there is strong evidence for a negative effect of natural resources on growth. If you allow for all the usual determinants of economic growth, there is a very big negative effect of natural resources. What is more, the negative effect of resources on growth is particularly high in countries that have bad institutions, while in countries with good institutions, such as Norway, natural resources might actually be a boon for growth.

What we find is that natural resources are particularly bad and have a negative effect on growth in countries with terrible institutions, as measured, for example, by the International Political Risk Guide, whereas countries with good institutions, like the

Netherlands and Norway, could possibly benefit from their natural resources. The resource curse is particularly bad for gold, silver and diamonds. The more point-based resources are, the bigger the resource curse.

Volatility and growth

If you measure volatility as the standard deviation of yearly GDP per-capita growth, and you relate this to the average growth rate per-capita, you find a fairly robust relationship between volatility and the growth performance of countries. The more volatile a country is, the lower its growth performance (See Figure 2). We also find that developing countries are much more volatile than, say, the Organisation for Economic Co-operation and Development (OECD) countries. Sub-Saharan Africa, for example, is three times more volatile than Western Europe. Also, the Middle East and North Africa are incredibly volatile if you compare them, for instance, to North America. Thus, the big problem with North Africa and the Middle East in particular is that they are incredibly volatile.

Figure 2 Volatility and growth

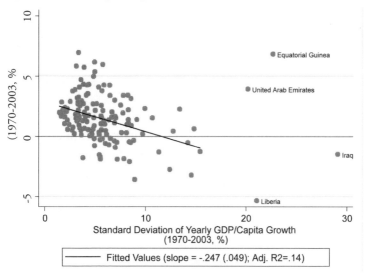

39

We also find that countries with poorly developed financial systems and bad banking systems are more volatile. And of course, countries that are land-locked, that is, that are not on the ocean and do not have big rivers, and that do not have good airports are also very volatile. Resource dependent countries are also extremely volatile. That is not so strange, as it follows from the relative volatility of commodity prices.

So we ask ourselves the following: is it volatility that affects growth negatively? The answer is 'yes', resource dependence explains volatility and we argue that the quintessential feature of the resource curse is this volatility argument. So I am going to show you that, if we allow for volatility, the more volatile a country is, the lower its growth.

One thing that people often forget is that Africa's poor growth can be at least partly attributed to very high population growth rates. One of the things we know is that countries with high population growth rates grow very badly: their growth per-capita is disastrous. Jeffrey Sachs goes a bit far in this respect: he wants to introduce a huge kind of birth control policy similar to that of China in Africa. The best thing to help Africa, I think, would be to have lower population growth and better quality children. So invest more per child, but also have far fewer children. Not six or seven per woman, but perhaps one or two.

The main thing is, though, that volatility is very important. As I said, volatility is particularly bad in countries that are not well developed financially, that are fairly closed off from international trade and that are land-locked. So what we are really arguing is that the higher the volatility of commodity prices, whatever way it is induced, the higher the volatility of the growth rate and the lower the growth prospects. Volatility of commodity prices, by the way, may be induced by being land locked, by not having a good financial system, by not being open to international trade, by having bad institutions and by being dependent on point-based resources like gold and diamonds.

That, we argue, is the main reason for low growth in Africa. And if that is the case, and the story may be a bit more complicated than that, then it also points to some helpers for Africa. One is to help them to get better financial systems, another is to get them some railroads and airports so that they become less geographically isolated and also, in relation to the WTO agreements, to try to make them more attractive and actually open their borders to international trade.

The variance of the volatility index is particularly high in Africa and much higher than in other parts of the world, which confirms that the big problem of Africa is its volatility problem. For countries that are financially highly developed, the effect of resources on growth is positive, while if they have very bad financial systems resources harm growth. So it is crucial to get good financial institutions in Africa, and then perhaps natural resources will have positive effects.

Countries that have a lot of governance instability are more volatile, which again is harmful for growth. And countries that have a lot of current account restrictions, which also means that they do not allow free trade and they impose restrictions on exports and imports, also will be much more volatile, which is again bad for growth.

Capital account restrictions, on the other hand, work the other way around. They stem these large flows in and out of the country and are usually very good for growth. That is what Korea and the other Asian Tigers did after the Asian crisis. Therefore, one should make a distinction between trade restrictions and capital restrictions. If you look at the IMF consensus, its basic message is to open all markets, but start with goods and services and then steadily open up on capital flows.

We also show that ethnic polarization is important, and ethnic restrictions in particular are important. Look at Botswana, which is a fairly homogeneous country compared to Congo and Nigeria where there is a lot of ethnic polarization. They will be much more volatile, and that will be bad for growth.

So the bottom line can be seen from what you may call a thought experiment. Imagine that resource-rich Africa would have the same characteristics as the Asian tigers. How would they have fared in terms of economic growth? For example, the Asian tigers grow by 4 percent per year. Resource-rich Africa grows one-quarter percent per year. If this goes on for many years, some countries growing by 4 percent and others by one-quarter percent, they really go like that: one remains poor, the other goes way up. And that is what has actually happened. The Asian tigers went up, while resource-rich Africa stayed poor.

The problem of the bottom billion, which also happened to be the title of the book by friend Paul Collier, is really an African issue. If we think of the poorest billion people in the world, we have to think of Africa. Many people there are impoverished, and we have to try to understand why this is the case. One could argue that it is because in resource rich Africa, population growth is much higher than in Asia (2.75 percent compared to 1.87 percent). If Africa had had the same population growth as the Asian tigers, they would have had a half percent extra growth per year, each year. That makes a huge amount over the whole period. That would have had much more of an impact than any development aid that we could possibly think of. If Africa would be able to only bring their population growth rate down to the Asian tigers' level, they would gain a growth bonus of a half percent per year.

The measure of the level of education is about four in Asia, and it is only about one-and-a-half or less in Africa. If Africa would only have the same education level as the Asian tigers, they would have had an extra half percent per year growth bonus. This goes on all the time, and the most interesting thing is that Africa does invest a lot even compared to the Asian tigers. After all, the aid money has to go somewhere, and there has been a lot of foreign aid. That also includes things like dams and other infrastructure. If you realize that the initial income per-capita in Africa is roughly the same as in the Asian tigers, you see they started off at the same level. And now the tigers are very high, they are middle-income countries, and Africa is still poor.

But the biggest thing I want to draw your attention to is the measure of volatility. In the comparison between Africa and the Asian Tigers it is seven times more important than human capital or getting population growth rates down. If it would be possible to take the volatility of resource-rich Africa down to the level of the Asian tigers, they would have three-and-a-half percentage points more growth per year than they have now. That is a huge, whacking amount.

What we are arguing for then, and increasingly so because volatility is so important, is that we try to find mechanisms to get financial experts and financial instruments to give those countries more financial stability, and therefore less volatility of unanticipated output growth, and better growth prospects. That would be the biggest thing. That is the story of what we really think is important.

Let us now look at the bottom line, which represents the variance equation and which shows the effect of making your countries more open, having better financial systems and making them less geographically isolated. That will have a huge effect. That is why we are working together with the World Bank on the Resource Charter and trying to get other people, such as the Bill Gates Foundation and Jeffrey Sachs, to join in. Another important initiative is the Earned Income Transparency Initiative. If you look, for example, at the national accounts of a country like Nigeria, there are hundreds of millions of dollars missing. This money may end up in Swiss Bank accounts, but we do not know. It is embarrassing to see how much money is just stolen away. What we are trying to work on is to get a revenue charter that would allow for increased transparency of resource revenues. So at least through naming and shaming we can try to get the countries to account for what they are doing with funds, to publish what they sell and to explain what they have done with the revenue. There is an enormous amount of work to be done there.

So my conclusion is that the volatility of unanticipated output growth is the quintessential reason why there is a natural resource curse. It is true that having a high level of natural resources with a lot of oil or gas or diamonds may actually be good for growth, but the problem is that having a lot of oil or diamonds typically makes a country much more volatile, and much more susceptible to the huge gyrations of commodity prices. This is the real source of harm. If that is the real reason why a lot of these countries are doing badly, the same thing can be said also for conflicts.

Some of you may know Angola better than I do, but in Angola there are diamonds and oil. So imagine if the price of oil rises, and one army gets a lot of money to buy weapons to knock the heads in of the other army that is financed by diamonds. Then, if the price of diamonds rises relative to oil, that army is going to kick the heads in of the army that is financed by oil. So what we find is that volatility is also a very important explanation of natural resource conflicts, and most conflicts are natural resource conflicts.

With high levels of investment (including in education), more open markets in goods and services and some capital restrictions that actually help, Africa should have grown spectacularly. It had all the preconditions there to do so, but it has not grown. And that is something that we should be worried about. Particularly the distance to waterways, ethnic polarization and current account restrictions, in addition to the volatility factor explain why Africa has failed so miserably in lifting its citizens out of poverty.

Genuine savings and exhaustible resource rents

Now let us think of the wealth of a nation and relate that to the concept of sustainability. What is sustainability? Sustainability is a very overused word, and most people do not know what they are talking about when they use it. But let us look at genuine savings, or real true savings: what is it? It is savings, minus investments. What I save is what I earn more than I consume. But there are also savings that consist of investments in productive capital, like machines, cars, roads, infrastructure or dams. There is also my spending on education, because if I spend on education I am building up my human capital. I will not bore you with all of the details of how to value that properly, but those are all savings.

Don't we need to be a bit cleverer than that? There is this ideal, as my mom always used to say: 'I leave the world to you the way I found it, and you leave the world to your children the way you found it'. That is something that you here at the Vrije Universiteit will understand. So, really, what we are saying is that if there is less of savings than we have more to deduct. For example if we put CO_2 in the air, which we can value now, then we have to deduct that. The same applies with particle matter, the particles of dirt that enters the air from the use of diesel. These particles are harmful, having a strong negative effect on health, life expectancy, productivity, and on everything. So value all of these things in the best possible way, and then deduct them to get to true savings.

Finally, if I dig oil out of the ground, I have to value it and have to use a true accounting price. I would not bore you with that either, but I have to deduct that from my savings. If I eat up all of my ore and all of my diamonds, they are not around anymore for my children. So I deduct that.

By doing all of that – and you will get very important people who do this, such as the World Bank, which is now quite far on that – you will get something called 'genuine saving'. And this genuine saving represents the change in the net wealth of a nation. So if genuine saving is zero, then my children will not be worse off than me. If genuine saving is positive, I have used up less or have invested more than the worth of that which I have taken out. So then the country is getting richer. If the genuine saving is negative, the country is becoming poorer all of the time.

Very bright people like Ken Arrow, another famous Nobel Price winner, or Partha Dasgupta, an eminent economic philosopher, developed these ideas. Now the bottom line is that we need to look at the relation between exhaustible resource rents and genuine savings. The sad thing is to see what those countries that are very resource-rich in terms of having mineral energy rents in the form of profits make of it after they pay for their costs. Genuine saving should be zero. That would be the social welfare optimum, if you will. But it is actually negative: the higher resource rents are, the lower are genuine savings.

Those countries that are full of diamonds or oil are actually borrowing like hell. They are becoming poorer! And the situation is worse still because, if you think about it, many of the countries that we are concerned about, that society is concerned about, have an extremely high population growth rate. Then it really is like a treadmill: if you have a high population growth rate, you want your actual genuine saving to be positive. If you want to maintain your wealth per person, you have to save more to provide for all of these extra souls being born in the country. Thus, genuine saving

Figure 3   Genuine saving rates and GDP growth

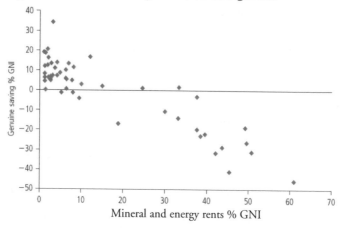

in resource-rich countries with high population growth rates should not be negative or zero; it should actually be positive.

In Figure 3 you see all of those countries that have positive genuine saving, with China, Botswana, and Ghana as the big growers. These are the darlings of the World Bank and the IMF. Mind you, don't think that democracies are fast growers. Dictatorships are fast growers. Whichever way you look at it, even if you look at all of the best evidence, the economies of autocrats and dictators typically perform much better than democracies. This is a very worrying thing, and I see here a very eminent list of speakers invited by SID, such as Ad Melkert from New York, who should be worried about this. So China is, of course, whatever way you call it, not a democracy, as is true for many other fast growing countries.

Applying the Hartwick Rule

Take Venezuela, a country that has become worse rather than better under Chavez, and is very bad in terms of performance. Now imagine that countries like Venezuela followed what is called the Hartwick Rule. The Hartwick Rule is a kind of form or optimum that says that all the money that you take out of the ground from oil or diamonds or gas should be reinvested again. So the Hartwick

Rule says: reinvest! I won't bother you with the arithmetic, but the rule says reinvest in infrastructure, productive capital or education in order to prevent yourself from eating up your exhaustible stock of capital. You must transform it into a productive stock of capital or in education, which lasts forever.

So imagine if Nigeria, for example, would have done that. It doesn't do it, but it is a useful counterfactual exercise. Imagine if Nigeria or Venezuela would have invested its resource rents. They would have had an enormous increase in productive capital, an increase of four times (see Figure 4, vertical axis).

Figure 4   Counterfactual Hartwick rule

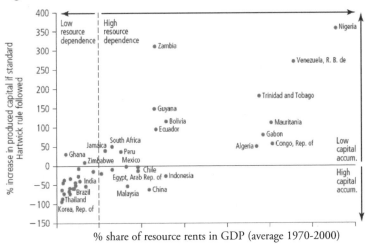

% share of resource rents in GDP (average 1970-2000)

This is really a way of showing the effect of all these resource-rich countries squandering their natural resources and not transforming their exhaustible stocks of natural resources into ever-lasting productive stocks of capital or productive stocks of human capital. In that sense they are truly not looking after the interests of future generations.

Now why do these resource-rich countries have negative genuine saving rates? People in those countries may say that, in the future, oil prices will still be high. Maybe if I am selling oil and Americans are buying my oil, then maybe they could argue that the Americans should be saving, not us! And they wouldn't be completely wrong. It is America that has to provide, that has to save in order to be able to afford the higher oil price that they will be charged in the future. I should be borrowing now, because Hotelling's rule says that I should borrow now if I know that all prices will go up.

Do people know Hotelling's rule? This is so beautiful in terms of virtual economics that it is, by way of explanation, nice to tell. At what rate should the price of oil increase each year? How would economists address this question? Ah, they would say, you could do two things with oil. You could keep it under the ground or you could take it out of the ground. If you take it out of the ground, you sell it and put the money in the bank. So what do you get? Yet get something called the market rate of interest, which is your return on it. Now what is your rate of return if you keep the oil under the ground? It may become higher in value, or it may not. Then your rate of return is the expected capital gain, or the expected increase in price. So economists predict that the rate of increase in oil prices should be exactly equal to the market rate of interest because otherwise you could make a profit leaving oil underground rather than taking it out of the ground.

Generally speaking, that is the argument. If people are expecting and if the OPEC countries always say, like they used to do, that oil prices are bound to go up, then they can always borrow against their possible future income. Thus, the American people should be ready to pay the higher prices in the future and should be saving now.

The problem with Hotelling's Rule is that in practise it is not as beautiful as it seems, because the production cost does not work like that. It is a good argument in theory, but if you look at the empirics of it, it doesn't work. It doesn't explain the reality.

So the real argument is this: suppose we are having a bowl of yoghurt or whatever, something nice to drink. And I sip it. You also have a straw and you sip it. Then I become worried that you sip it before I do. And then you get worried that I sip it before you and you start to sip even faster, etc. And before you know the oil is out of the ground.

This is called the voracity effect. The idea is that, because of dynamic common pull problems, e.g. because of the fact that property rights are not perfectly defined or because of the fact that you have often very badly enforceable legal systems, people tend to be voracious. Normally they want to slow down their rate of depletion of oil or the rate at which they take diamonds out of the ground, in order to do it more slowly. But for fear of other rebels doing it before you get the chance, you do it first and sell it off very quickly, much quicker than at a social optimum rate. So that could possibly be an explanation of negative genuine saving. It is still an open area for research, so I shouldn't say much more on that.

Harvesting windfall revenues

To close off, I will present to you some policy proposals, apart from the ones I have spoken of before, on how to reduce volatility. These policy proposals are to be presented in a paper that, together with Paul Collier and others, I am doing for the IMF. This is on harvesting windfall revenues.

If something is bad, we call it the IMF or the Washington consensus. If you are left wing, the Washington consensus basically means you leave everything to the free market, you liberalize everything, you go away and you leave the country in ruins and come back when things are getting better. Dani Rodrik is sceptical about it, and I think that the current financial crisis gives us some backing for that.

The argument is that if a country has oil, it should be used to build a sovereign wealth fund, not unlike Norway does. Now is that a good policy? It is what the IMF is recommending all of the African states to do. Do you think that is a good idea? It means that if you put the money in a foreign fund that invests in shares in America, Europe and China, the interest rate on that will go into some form of citizen dividends for the people of Africa.

Paul Collier, Peter Venables, Michael Spence and I are very much against that because we think that, in Africa, the money could be better spent, and we show and prove this via academic arguments that I won't waste my time by going into now. But we say, maybe a lot of these African countries have very high-risk premiums. The interest rates spreads in many countries in Africa are very high. They have to pay so much that many of these governments in Africa are stifling their economy. Their economy is held back because they have very high rates of interest. Under these conditions, nobody is investing, there is little capital accumulation and growth is low.

Why are they paying high interest rates? It is because they have high levels of foreign debt and not much foreign reserves. So, working on this Resource Charter, we argue that it may be better for some of these countries to use the oil to pay off their debt and to have lower rates of interest, rather than put the money in a sovereign wealth fund and actually earn a lower rate of return. It may even be better to give it to the people that at least are not corrupt, rather than putting it in a sovereign wealth fund. Or at least give it back to the people in terms of education or in terms of citizens' dividends. But do not put it in a fund that would be more easily raided by corrupt politicians.

So what we are trying to do is to set up a matrix where you look at what kind of conditions there are in a particular country and then see what you should do with the windfall revenue. Don't forget that a lot of this windfall is temporary. These countries get it for fifteen to twenty years, and then it is finished. What could you do to give them everlasting use of it, even for generations after the windfall has ceased? That is one of the big questions we need to solve.

You could distribute that citizens' dividend, for example, but for the most corrupt countries we actually argue for them to try not to take the resources out of the ground. Leave them there until they have sorted out their business, rather than wasting it for corrupt things, and then it will be all gone and will have harmed the economy. It may actually be better to close the mines and wait until the country normalizes. How that is implemented, we do not know but at least it is something worth thinking about.

We also need to think about Shell and other mining companies, and about how to put pressure on them. I am not so keen on corporate ethics, but they should, for example, employ former rebels, soldiers, child soldiers and whatever they are in order to get them on the peace table and get them in an alternative job. There is, in terms of social responsibility, and I dare say this in this university, a role for Western companies, including many Dutch companies. We have many mineral companies in the Netherlands and we should put political pressure on them.

I may be a little rude, but people my age like sex but they are not getting it. So what do they do? They go to Bangkok and they have sex with young, underage people. That is a criminal offence in the Netherlands, and we have this law nowadays that allows us to arrest them in Holland.

So, if our companies, I mean some of the French companies are much worse, Exxon for example, but if some of our companies are not behaving as they should in those countries, maybe we should have some legislation in this country, and preferably at the European level, to make sure there is no unfair competition and to actually enforce that some of these things get done. So, as an analogy to the prevention of child abuse in places like Thailand – and we have now some good laws on that – you can also think of something similar for our companies.

I already said something on transparency. It is very difficult to do something about it. The World Bank has tried it. It made debt relief contingent on transparency, free press and anti-corruption efforts. Maybe also Western banks should be punished for allowing money of doubtful origin to be deposited. According to the best information we have, money is laundered by British and Dutch banks. We should have much more information on that, and that should be discussed in the public domain. Do we, as a country, want to make money out of that? Do we want our pension funds to invest in those companies? I think not.

Long Term Growth and Short Term Headwinds for the Developing World

Michael Spence

In this lecture, I would like to pick up what I thought were the highlights of the Growth Report. Then I would like to focus on the longer-term challenges to developing country and global growth and finally, I would like talk about the financial and economic crisis and what it means for the developing world.

By way of summary: I get often asked whether, after everything I have written about growth, it makes any difference now that we are in this economic crisis. My answer is: yes! We will get out of this crisis. We don't know how soon or how well or with how much damage, but I believe that the kind of growth dynamics that are associated with the post World War II growth that we have seen in parts of the developing world are still valid, even if there remain evolving challenges in the global economy that Rick van der Ploeg talked about in his lecture, and that I will talk about today.

In the short run there are real issues: the developing world was dealing with price volatility, particularly in commodity prices which caused several kinds of problems, and then the financial crisis struck. While it looked as though the crisis might sail asides of a good chunk of the developing world, that perception changed completely in the fall of 2009.

I will try to show you what happened, but essentially it was capital vacuum or, to put it differently, the damaged balance sheets in the advanced countries that caused a reduction of capital inflows and actual capital outflows in the developing world. This is because of exchange rate depreciations and the immediate and severe credit shortage that we are now wrestling with.

I think in the longer term there is going to be a complete rethink of the way in which we approach economic management both at the level of the country, especially in developing countries, and the global economy. This crisis has shaken people a great deal, and what has happened is not consistent with the image of what should have happened, given the confident advice that developing countries were given for many years.

To set the scene, Figure 1 shows us, and most of us know this already, that if developing countries, in particular countries like China and India, run ahead of the US and the EU growth by about 6 percent in real terms, then this is what will happen:

Figure 1 China, India and the USA-EU GDP

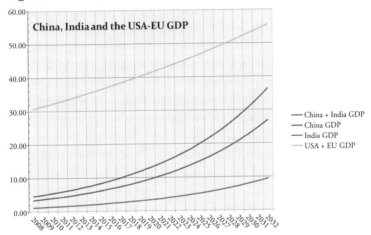

China and India will be a set of pretty big players in the global economy. It has a very high probability of happening in the next little while, and it is going to be a different kind of running a world like that.

The growth report

I want to emphasize that the members of the Growth Commission volunteered for this commission because they thought the exercise was useful. They were dominantly political and policy leaders from a wide range of developing countries, and they wanted to do this in order to address the exercise to their peers as well as to the next generation of young people coming up in those countries who are going to meet the very difficult challenge of accelerating and sustaining growth and poverty reduction in the developing world.

Rather than be abstract about what the dynamics are at the micro-economic level when countries are growing at a high rate, we wanted to put some numbers around it. So we looked for countries that had grown at 7 percent per year for twenty-five years or more. Those were very high standards, both in terms of persistence and rate. That is why there are only thirteen of them: Botswana, Brazil, China, Hong Kong (China), Indonesia, Japan, Korea, Malaysia, Malta, Oman, Singapore, Taiwan (China) and Thailand.

India and Vietnam are about to join this group, I suspect, because their underlying characteristics and accelerations of their growth look very similar to the other cases. Something can always go wrong, but the hope is that the general pattern of accelerating growth in the developing world, now interrupted for what I imagine to be at least two to three years as a consequence of what amounts to be a global recession as conventionally defined, will be resumed and that there will be others to join the party. But there remain issues that have to do with whether the fundamental characteristics are there.

Common characteristics

So how did growth happen in these thirteen countries? First and foremost, these are economies that show that *they are engaged with the global economy* and find a way to take advantage of their resources. One of their most important resources is a big market, so that once they find an area where they have what economists call comparative advantage, they can basically grow and not at the same time become a significant player in the global economy, which means that, in technical terms, the terms of trade will turn against them. The only exception is probably China, because of its size. But even that wasn't true at the time. People tend to forget that when China started growing in 1979-80, it was a miniscule economy.

The second, and probably more important resource is knowledge, which is sometimes called technology, learning or a lot of other things. The overall process is called catch-up growth. Without this, you cannot grow at these high rates. Advanced countries never grow for an extended period of time at more than 3 percent per year in real terms, because – and this is the benefit of insight we got out of modern growth theory focussed on advanced economies – in the end, growth comes only from moving the productive potential from innovation and technological progress. You just cannot do enough of that for an extended period in an advanced economy to make growth go higher. In a developing economy, they don't have to invent that stuff and, furthermore, they have a deficit in terms of capital investment, which is something that advanced economies do not have. In short, that which moves the productive potential forward, such as investments in human capital and infrastructure, private sector investments and inbound knowledge transfer, is basically what is going on. Anything that supports it will help accelerate growth, and things that get in the way will hold it back.

Now let me just say that we do not know anywhere near enough in detail yet about the knowledge transfer process. We just know it occurs. We know some channels. Foreign investment is an important channel. Foreign aid is an important channel. Foreign education is important. There are a lot of ways it happens. But this is the softer side of an economy, this information/network cycle, and it may be changing.

A second characteristic of high growth countries is *an environment of high levels of savings*. To be precise: high means 25 percent of GDP or above. We are serious about savings: if you don't save enough to cover most of your investment, both public and private, then you are borrowing and you are vulnerable in a variety of ways that lead to trouble. Now I cannot prove that. In fact, we can probably imagine that there will be counterexamples some time in the future, but we have not found one yet. So, it is not a piece of theory that everybody agrees on, but, practically speaking, it is true. And the public sector investment is important. We said it should amount to 5 to 7 percent of GDP, and that probably does not include all of the education.

These are big numbers in a poor country. If the per-capita income is 400 US dollars, and you are saving and investing a minimum of 25 percent of GDP, you are consuming only 300 US dollars per year. Now that is a big difference, and puts you under a dollar per day measured in consumption terms. All I am really trying to say is that we listen to numbers all the time, but we do not always translate them into something that has anything to do with somebody's life. These numbers imply huge choices and early short term sacrifices. These choices and sacrifices get this growth done.

The third characteristic of these high growth economies is they are *market economies*. There are two sides to that. One is decentralization, price signals, incentives and enough definition of private property so that you can actually have investment. The other, more interesting side is the dynamics that you find in economies that not only allow, but also encourage the Schumpeterian process of creative destruction. Companies, sectors and jobs are being created all the time, and they are being destroyed all the time. It feels chaotic, but it is the engine by which productivity growth occurs. For growth to occur, resources must be mobile. Capital has to go where it needs to go, labour leaves the countryside, goes into cities, moves into new sectors that eventually get destroyed, and so on.

You can go and see this in the data. If you look at a developing country in high-speed growth mode, every time you look at it, after ten years you will still recognize what the economy was, it will be close, but in twenty years you will not recognize it at all. That is how fast it is changing. So if you have an image of what this economy is, what the people in this economy make in terms of goods and services, then come back fifteen years later and it won't look that way.

The fourth characteristic is implied in John Williamson's original version of the Washington Consensus. I think it is important to say – and I want to be clear about this – that there are a lot of sensible things in it. One of them, for sure, is *macro-economic and financial stability and predictability*, both domestically and in the global economy. The reason for this is simple: a failure on that front deters investment by introducing risk or raising the cost of capital, and that slows things down.

Politics and leadership

When I went into this exercise of the Growth Report, if I am being honest, I probably thought that this was a subject that was mostly about economics and economic policy. Well, I was wrong. It is just as much about politics, political economy, leadership and the things that go into the consensus – or the absence of it – that does or doesn't sustain the policies and investments that drive the growth.

There is a very important body of research going on in this area by younger people in both economics and political science and political economy. I don't want this to sound like a summary of something that is at a very early stage. These are just some observations. It appeared to us that political leadership is extremely important. The things that an advanced economy relies on, especially at the early stages, i.e., a whole set of institutions that involve people and bring experts together in a way that makes sensible decisions usually come out, are all missing!

A developing economy is developing precisely in part because the institutions are in the process of being created: markets, regulatory arrangements, governance and others. So it does not do any good whatsoever to say: 'You need the institutions to do this', because the institutions are being created in parallel and at the same time.

Likewise, anything that has to do with growth and development involves things going on at the same time in parallel. We train ourselves, when we learn to think logically, to think in terms of first you do a, b and c and then that enables you to do d, e and f. That is not useful thinking. If you have a problem in institutions or human capital that you are interested in fixing, meaning investing in increasing your capabilities in these areas, you can also grow. It is just different in a dynamic growth process.

Long time horizons

Growth strategies have long time horizons. I apologize for doing arithmetic for you, but at the highest known growth rates, roughly 10 percent per year, it takes a minimum of over half a century to go from poor to advanced. Those are breathtakingly high growth rates. And anything below that puts you up in the multiple decades over that. And if you really slow down, you are talking about centuries.

Figure 2   Growth dynamics: transitions in years as a function of the growth rate

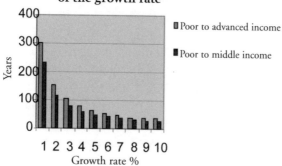

This means that persistence, i.e., understanding what you try to accomplish, having a social consensus or political consensus around that and staying at it, pays very high dividends, as does consistency. A crisis every decade or fifteen years, on the other hand, will halve the growth rate just by knocking it off for a period of time, and then you will have to struggle back again. If you halve the growth rate from 7 to 3.5 percent, Figure 2 shows what the consequence is.

Key ingredients

Key ingredients or dimensions of growth strategies are, according to the Growth Commission, inclusiveness and equity, structural transformation and competition, mobility and flexibility in labour markets, enablers in the capital markets like save savings channels and credit, and urbanization. These ingredients are extremely important. A major failure in any one of these dimensions will mean that the growth process that I am talking about will not work. And the Growth Commission would say that, among the key ingredients, *inclusiveness* is an incredibly important part of the growth strategy.

We do not have complete models of what an economy will do, so we do not have a good way to predict what the responses to policy choices will be. Therefore, there is a very high premium on being experimental and pragmatic, while not ignoring theory. This isn't an either/or situation.

Sometimes you just go and try stuff out, and then throw out the things that don't work and get on with it. It is that style that was a bit missing in the application of the Washington Consensus. Not the content itself.

Of the other key ingredients, I would say that mobility and flexibility in the labour markets are the most complicated for political economy reasons. The normal pattern is that there is a formal and an informal labour market. A solution that consists of allowing people in the informal labour market to all become competitors for the jobs of the people in the formal labour market who are paid more is probably not a politically or economically viable kind of policy choice to make, even though it is Pope-efficient. So the challenge in this area – Dani Rodrick has been very clear about it – is that you really make second best choices, meaning politically realistic choices. Instead of doing things in the natural order, you do them in the order that seems to make sense from the point of view of getting them passed through the democratic process. So it is this kind of opportunism and manner of operating so as not to threaten too many people that may result in a messy looking structure, if only temporarily.

So you end up in complex and controversial areas with benefits and risks, like special export processing zones. You know, most policy makers in a developing economy do not want to open the whole economy overnight because of the risks associated with that. So they create these entities that are favoured from a tax point of view, i.e., a tariff point of view, and they conduct an experiment to see if a sector will develop in that kind of environment and not open the whole economy at the same time.

Nobody knows whether this will work. Sometimes it is very badly done, but at the level of making sensible choices under uncertainty, in such a way as to manage the kind of benefit/risk calculation, it makes pretty good sense.

But there are additional issues. I would say that it is now pretty clear that the strategy 'grow first and deal with the environment later' is a very bad strategy. It is extremely expensive, even though it has been the norm: the environment until recently was viewed as a luxury. They say: 'that is something that people in Europe talk about, and it is fine for them because their per-capita income is 30,000 Euros or so. But we don't have time for that'. Well, that is a mistake because if you don't pay attention to the environment, you pay an awesome price for fixing it up later on, and not too much later on. As with so many other things, a bad environment adversely affects the poor more than the rich. I am talking about air and water quality, and not only climate change (which is what pops up in many people's minds).

The other thing that the report is very clear on, whether you agree with it or not, is that, while we are not against all subsidies or against fiddling with the price system, we are very much against what we see in the developing world in the form of subsidizing energy, particularly oil and gas. That is not great strategy. It is very expensive, and the costs are going up rapidly because it is an important instance of very poorly dealing with climate change. Because of that, this position with respect to energy efficiency and climate change is beginning to disappear. Not overnight, but in the developing world I think it is understood now that these were very bad ideas.

The section of the report I was proudest of was called 'Bad Ideas'. We wrote down some twenty-three really bad ideas in order to draw attention to them, sort of covering the rest of the report. Wow, people loved this! Journalists from whatever country 'x' on the borders of the former Soviet Union would write an article and they would say: "Well, there are these twenty-three bad ideas and our government does eighteen of them! Isn't that something?"

Complex and controversial areas, benefits and risks

There are areas that are complex right now and being debated, and the Growth Commission choose them because they thought they might have better answers to them. They were chosen also because they affect the key components of the growth strategy, and it is not obvious what the right answer is. There are benefits and risks of making various choices in these areas. The financial and economic crisis will, moreover, cause people to think that different choices are more sensible because they have different implications for how much risk you are exposed to and so on.

To a first approximation, the successful countries have been more interventionist than the prevailing orthodoxy at the time would allow them to be, meaning they managed their exchange rates more aggressively, they tended not to get rid of their capital controls overnight, and they were to varying degrees open on the capital account.

It is a very important function (and judgement) of policy to open by pace and sequencing the economy on the current account, i.e., trading goods and services in such a way as to not allow job destruction on job creation, because that slows growth and takes away the public support. It varies from economy to economy, but lots of economies have a rather fragmented, highly inefficient retail sector that employs a lot of people. If you expose that overnight to foreign competition, you could easily violate this rule of thumb that I use, which is: do not allow job destruction to open on job creation.

These are some of those areas that are fun to argue about. By the way, when we came to those areas, not only did the world out there – our academic colleagues and people that do research and write articles in newspapers – not agree, but also the commission didn't always agree with each other. Our strategy for dealing with that situation was to say explicitly that we didn't always agree with each other on these things either, and then approach them by trying to deal with the benefits and costs.

I draw your attention to the fact that these are areas in which you don't get *not* to decide. You do if you are an academic and you say: 'We are not going to cover this because we actually don't know yet'. But policy makers are either going to have the exchange rate set by the market, or they are going to manage it one way or another, and there aren't any other choices.

Long term challenges

There are a number of things we need to contend with. One is a very wide spread of rising inequality and perceived instability and, I would add, resistance to globalization in advanced and developing economies. The last Pew Survey of attitudes, which is done every five years and most recently in the fall of 2007, indicated that pretty much everywhere except in Asia, people had serious reservations about globalization. The evidence of this sentiment were bigger than in the last survey, meaning the trend is clear. On balance, people are losing interest. The Commission thinks, and I agree with this, that it has a lot to do with insufficient attention to distributional issues. Is it really true that enough people are benefiting from globalization and are being protected both in advanced and in developing countries?

Second, if you go into the developing world, particularly in places like Africa, and you say: 'Well, this is how you do this, and this is how you grow', they say: 'That is nice, but we are late starters, we can't do that'. So you ask: 'Why?' and they will say: 'Because we can't compete with China'. Very distinguished people who know what they are talking about, like Paul Collier, think that is probably right. It should not be dismissed as an argument. So the question is: is that a permanent problem?

This is in a class of problems that is called 'adding-up problems' that, as you know, Bill Cline originally analysed. The question at that time was, if everybody in the 1980s had done what the Asian Tigers did, would the global economy have been able to absorb this? Will the world prices fall to the point where it chokes off the return on investments, or will the markets that are consuming all of this choke and become protectionist? Those are the two channels by which adding up problems get to be a problem. I have views on this: I actually don't think so. Nobody would have bet against Bill Cline that you could add China and a bit of India to the Asian Tigers, but we did, and the dynamics are such that China is going to be taken out of this and India is coming in. The most important argument is that the late starters are now not big enough to cause an adding up problem. As part of global demand in a known sector, they just can't become big enough for that. So that is why I am cautiously optimistic.

Figure 3, however, shows China's effect on the relative prices of manufactured commodities. There is no question that it has become big enough to put downward pressure on it. Thus, the social return to strategies for non resource-rich countries, aiming for labour intensive products, may be lower than it was before.

Figure 3   Relative price of manufacturing declined, the China effect

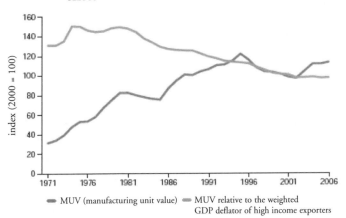

MUV (manufacturing unit value)   MUV relative to the weighted
                                  GDP deflator of high income exporters

Source: Development Economics Prospects Group, World Bank.

Volatility of commodity prices was the single most important thing that the developing countries were facing in the year, while we were essentially busy getting on with the financial crisis. It caused two problems. One is the food emergency problem among the poor who consume in the order of 50 percent plus of their incomes on basic food, so grains, rice etc. When the price of those doubles, it implies a huge cut in income and the result is starvation and malnutrition, which, I must say, were admirably taken up by the development agencies in many countries and by the World Bank. This is now subsided a little bit because of the economic turmoil in the global economy.

The other problem is the cost of inflation, for exactly the same reason. If a big chunk of your GDP is commodities, food, energy, and so on, and you get a spike in those things pretty much at the same time, then in Europe and the US you would get a 2 to 3 percent inflation problem. In developing countries, you would get a 10 percent inflation problem. So they were faced with something we don't normally think about, which is a trade-off between cutting off the second and third round of tax on inflation on the one hand and sustaining growth on the other.

The age problem

As you know, most of the developed world is aging, and the poor parts are doing the opposite. This is a kind of short version of the age problem. In some sense it looks like a nice match, but in fact it is not. The concern on aging is that it actually will slow growth. So we poked around and we asked some of the best demographers and economists around the world who pay attention to this: 'Is this really true? Is the growth going to slow because people like me, between 65 and 80-years-old, are dithering about?' The answer is no! For the most part, it may slow growth down, but it will be a slow process because our institutions are going to adapt.

I live in Italy, and the Italians are very much used to work and retire at about fifty-eight. Recently the policy reforms consisted of raising the retirement age to sixty, and then putting it back again to fifty-eight. Now that was fine when the Italians lived until the age of about sixty-nine, but it isn't so fine when they live until the age of ninety-five. And that is repeated over and over again in many other, similar countries. You can't do this because you are breaking down governments' finances and a lot of other things. So you can predict, however messy and ugly, that we are going to adapt these institutions over time to this changing age structure.

There is a more serious problem in the other place. The poor countries have high fertility, and in some cases reduced longevity, and a low growth environment on average. So huge numbers of young people come on the job market while it is not clear whether they will be able to find jobs. This is a kind of economic time bomb, and it is very common in the poor parts of the world and is understood. People work on this to find a solution, but, from my point of view, you cannot solve this problem unless the surplus labour environments can ship labour to the labour deficit or excess demand environments. That means that we are going to have migration for work, and I am not sure that we can get that properly supervised. And if we cannot, some of these countries and regions cannot grow fast enough to create enough jobs to absorb the young people remaining. It is just not going to happen.

You can see it in unemployment rates. The unemployment rate in South Africa is 25 percent. It is not much lower in Egypt. These are huge pools of young people whose future needs to be addressed as part of global and ethical policy.

Climate change

The Growth Report spends a little time on climate change, but we are slowly and rightly reaching the conclusion that this problem is interesting and very challenging, largely because of the growth of CO_2 emissions in the developing world. This is not meant to be negative, but the next figure is showing the current per-capita emissions in the world.

On the far left you see that in 2006-07 CO_2 emissions were, on average, 4.8 tons per person. Next you see what the ICC says is the

Figure 4 CO_2 emissions per capita

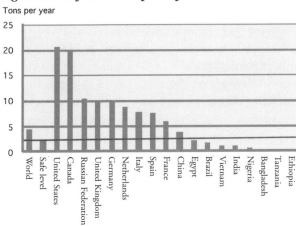

safe level, which is 2.3 tons per person per year. Then you have the US and Canada, and Australia is not far behind, at about 20 tons per person per year. Most of Europe is in the range of 10 tons running down to 6 tons in France because of its nuclear energy. China is at the global average of 5 tons per person, but their emissions are huge because of the number of people, about the same as emissions by the US in total. Finally, per-capita emissions of the entire developing world are under the safe level.

If you looked at that and if you thought that the world is not changing that much, you might conclude that the developing world doesn't need to do very much and that everything would be alright if we in the developed world would be able to reduce the overall emissions by a factor of two.

The problem, however, is that the very big countries in there, China and India, and others as well, are growing very rapidly. If you just do the mathematics, and if we did not do anything about climate change in terms of reducing CO_2 emissions and just let it grow, and wanted to know what the problem looked like in 2050, the answer would be that emissions per-capita would be about four times the safe level. That would be the case even if all the developing countries would hit the current European standards for carbon emissions and would not go near the rates of the United States and Canada. So that is a huge problem, and probably the hardest problem on the economic and environmental front in the world. That is because you don't want to choke off economic growth. Some people may, but most of us don't.

So the question is, can we get to safe levels of CO_2 emissions and still have 10 percent growth or 7 or 8 percent in a good chunk of the developing countries on the right side of that graph? And what does it look like over time? And who pays for the mitigation, meaning the reduction in carbon emissions? We try to make some progress on that, and I think we are getting there, but I have to tell you that we in the international discussions are still quite far away from grappling with the issues in a practical way. We are not even committed yet to the idea of equal per-capita emissions. Imagine a world in which we would all have the same incomes and somebody went out and said: 'Well, you are a big country that is annoying to us, so maybe you should have a per-capita allocation that is a quarter of everybody else's'. I mean, that is not going to fly! So some basic thinking on values still has to be done.

The financial crisis

Let me just give a quick summary of what the financial crisis means for the developing world. By way of summary, I would say that we are in for a deep and probably pretty long recession in America and Europe and maybe more broadly, and that growth will be slow in the developing world. We did not have to get there, but we did. We will have a complete transformation of the financial structure in the advanced countries. Major financial institutions, including banks, are just gone, taken over by the government or completely transformed. The total loss in value in global equity markets is 25 trillion US dollars so far, and that may be about as high as it gets. This depends on what happens in the markets, which were at the starting point admittedly inflated, meaning that 65 trillion US dollars of total share values were probably overvalued.

These are big balance sheet effects: this is a balance sheet induced economic crisis and recession, and not the normal 'we got too much inventory and a bit of excess capacity' kind of crisis. Excess capacity is part of the dynamics here, but it is not the fundamental starting point. It is not the only component in the dynamics. The emerging markets are down over 50 percent now and the deleveraging dynamics, which is the reducing of asset values out of the system because there is too much, is the fundamental characteristic of the present crisis.

From the point of view of the developing countries, it looked, up until September 2008, like they were going to be all right. They did not own a whole lot of toxic assets, they had an inflation issue and they pretty much knew that in some form or another we were going to have a recession in the advanced countries, and that that would reduce exports demand. So they would have to compensate for that, to the extent they variably could, with domestic economic fiscal stimuli. So you could say they were faced with tough but manageable headwinds.

But this changed dramatically when, in mid-September, there was a change in expectations. This occurred at probably the same time as the very rapid failure of two major regional banks, Fanny May and Freddie Mack, which were just seized overnight, the letting go of Lehman Brothers, the sale of Merrill Lynch to Bank of America, and the failure of AIG, which was bailed out but held some very large fraction of the credit default swaps (these are credit insurance products that were designed so that they wouldn't be regulated in the American market). And all of a sudden we had a credit lock-up. A credit lock-up is when short-term credit is not available, and it is the depression nightmare scenario, because it destroys businesses.

This crisis has been dealt with pretty effectively by extraordinary actions on the part of the Central Banks, including by buying commercial paper directly and lending money to banking institutions in return for collateral you never thought you had seen them take. The Federal Reserve's balance sheet, as a consequence, has gone from under a trillion dollars to close to three trillion already. What we missed was that that spread very quickly to the developing countries, because these damaged balance sheets required capital, increasing amounts of capital, that tried to come back and shore them up for solvency and capital adequacy reasons. So capital started rushing out of the developing world causing the exchange rates to fall and credit to tighten up and any dollar or euro denominated asset to become very expensive quickly. This is what the IMF is supposed to reverse, this externally induced shock.

This is described sometimes in the press as the flight to safety, referring to the euro and the dollar. There is an element of truth in that, but this isn't really a flight to safety, because that would imply that there is a lack of safety in the developing economy so you are flying back to a safe America or Europe. This was, in reality, a flight to a capital vacuum in America and Europe, with the state of affairs there. It caused the state of affairs in the developing countries to change very quickly as we will see the next series of figures.

These figures show the units of the currency per dollar, so when it rises, the currency is depreciated. What you see is that virtually

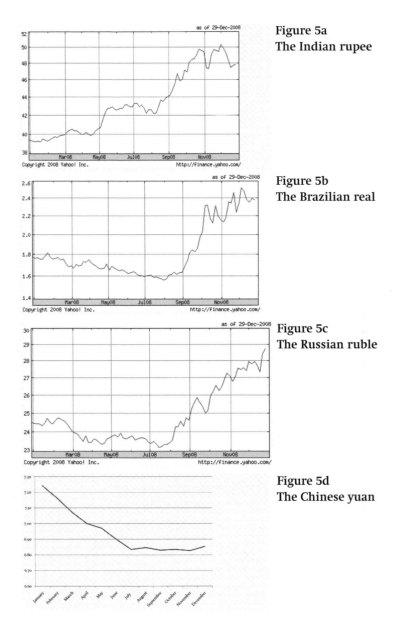

Figure 5a
The Indian rupee

Figure 5b
The Brazilian real

Figure 5c
The Russian ruble

Figure 5d
The Chinese yuan

every major currency, with one exception, started depreciating in the summer and fall of 2008, and this was accompanied by credit tightening of a fairly severe kind, requiring quick policy responses and shifts in asset values.

Figure 5e The South African rand

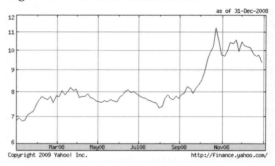

There are slight differences in pattern, but it is basically the same thing: capital that had been flowing into these economies in the past just rushed out. It will reverse eventually, but it causes big problems and this kind of volatility is very difficult to deal with.

There is one exception, however. The Chinese currency was actually first appreciating before the Chinese prevented any further appreciation. It is not depreciating either. Like in 1997-98, at the time of the Asian crisis, the Chinese are losing their competitive position relative to the other developed countries and the global economy. All the others depreciate. Only the Asian currencies shot down in 1997-98. Now we don't know how this happened as this goes along, but China, for the most part, understands that it can't use their currency to redress things. They may prevent its upside movement but they understand that they have to drive the economy's growth fundamentally with productivity. And that is what the developing world is wrestling with.

Discussion

The next crisis

If you ask me what will be the shape and nature of the next crisis and when it will occur, my guess is *not* in the financial area, because we will do everything to solve the problem of the last crisis completely and prevent a new one. Our next crisis will be more in the resources area, in energy or something like that, and it will be an environmental issue that will really be significant. Our capacity to respond quickly will depend on a level of economic and other kinds of cooperation that we, as you know, have not achieved.

Inclusiveness as a condition for growth?

In the countries that I singled out for high and sustained economic growth like Brazil, China, Indonesia, Japan and Korea, there are big differences with respect to inclusiveness and equity dimensions. I still feel safe in saying that if there is massive exclusion in the long run, that is if large groups are excluded from participating in playing the game, that this will show up in something that goes wrong in the political economy or worse. That will result in conflict some time later. But there are big differences across these countries, and there are big differences in the extent to which they managed actual inequality, which is a relative concept as opposed to inclusiveness, which is supposed to be more absolute.

I think that China probably has paid the least attention to that and has the most dramatic rising of inequality as a result of the growth dynamics. There is a lot of income inequality in Brazil and in much of Latin America, but that was there before. It is there basically because they redistributed the assets, including land. You see the same thing in Africa. So you will find high Gini coefficients both in Latin America and in Africa. But we really were not counting that, because that is not inherently related to the growth process. They probably need to get rid of it.

Brazil is an interesting case in this respect. It grew from 1950 to 1975 at pretty high rates. Then, for reasons that you would have to be an insider or a very knowledgeable observer to understand, (which I am not), the policies changed and Brazil adopted a kind of inward-looking, import substitution strategy that was much more reflective of domestic interest, and then had to battle with hyper inflation and so on. So they kind of lost it, which is a little bit surprising.

But the bottom line of what we wanted to say on inclusiveness is that, if you let inequality or exclusion get out of hand, you at least risk a response that will derail the growth process.

Protectionism as a defensive weapon

I think there is a risk that protection will be used as a defensive weapon in the context of a major financial crisis, but the G7 explicitly said that they would not do that and the G20 repeated it, and I hope they are serious. There will be violations, but it would be very destructive if we actually backtracked instead of made additional progress in the WTO for this reason. That would really be a major casualty of the financial crisis and global downturn.

I started to think about the WTO relatively recently. The negotiations are known to be long and complex, and the issues are nowadays even more complex compared to the early ones when they said: 'Let us lower everything by 20 percent and declare victory in nine months and go home'. Now the negotiations are about intellectual property and what kinds of flexibility you will be allowed, important issues for developing countries, and it runs straight into the clear rule based system in the WTO. It is a major challenge to rescue both the substance and the process at this stage because it looks pretty complicated. So my instinct would be: let us simplify. Let us take a few issues that we think we can agree on, instead of trying to do everything at once, and set ourselves a reasonable time limit and try and get it done.

Implications for aid policies

In the Commission we said: this is not about aid or what I call 'investment with a social return orientation'. Having said that, if you set aside the emergency response facility, which clearly is very important, and the IMF needs more money and it needs the governance structure that gives it the credibility to deploy this, the crisis as we described it could not be dealt with only with a 250 billion US dollar access to our reserves to be used to reverse those capital flows.

In the longer-term agenda, bilateral agencies and institutions will benefit from focussing on governance broadly, and by that I do not mean the form of government. There is a very striking lack of correlation among both the successes and failures between the form of government and whether anything good is going on in the economy. Let me be just specific and blunt. There are high performing autocracies and high performing democracies, there are appalling autocracies both in human and economic terms and there are a ton of democracies that are not producing any economic performance at all. So I think that should point people in the direction of thinking carefully about what they mean by effective governance, good institutions and what really matters, and not get lost over simple things like the form.

That would be my first bit of advice when you ask me about recommendations for development cooperation policies. My second would be to focus on investment in infrastructure and other basic conditions like education. Some contribution could be expected from thinking carefully and helping people with governance, including outsourcing. The chances are negligible that all of the countries that are resource-rich but poor now can master the art of mining, contracting, running public sector investments and the management of the currency in such a way as to transfer that natural resource into growth. Some of them will, but I don't see why a collection of European countries, including resource-rich ones like Norway, couldn't actually perform some of those functions for some of these countries. They would have to do that voluntarily. There would have to be a deal, and citizens and the government on their behalf would have to agree with it. You don't just go in and take it over!

My third recommendation would be to focus on learning. I mentioned it before, but I think there is a special capacity in the advanced countries to contribute more than we actually do in this area. It is partly the accumulation of human capital, including the upper end, tertiary-level of education. It is partly also broader than that, as it has to do with processes that help people learn more rapidly the kinds of things that, over the centuries, we have learned how to do. If you go to a major city in a developing country, their capacity to control the traffic in such a city will be noticeably different than in any major city in Europe or North America or even Latin America. I mention this and you may think it is silly, but there are literally millions of those things called capacities or capabilities that affect the productivity of an economy. You either have people sitting in traffic jams because you don't have the capacity to run the traffic lights for two hours every morning, or you don't. The government delivers services effectively through the Internet or it doesn't, etc. So I think we can make a big difference if we are ready to focus on these three areas, and there may be others.

The role of technology in the context of the financial crisis

Technology is certainly the platform on which the global economy and financial system is becoming increasingly integrated. The speed with which the crisis spread around is just different as a result of the integration in the global capital markets and the fact that those are heavily technology-based. And with integration and interdependence you get risk, or an expanded portfolio risk, and this crisis is an example of that.

This does not mean that you necessarily want to reverse that, but you want to manage it better. That is probably the attitude most of us would have. I guess some of us would think that it is not worth it to run that risk and would like to undo all of it. But it cannot be undone by policy. You can cut off the capital, it is hard, but you can do it. Capital markets and capital controls are known to be leaky, and some people believe that they are so leaky that you actually cannot do it. For the most part, technology is viewed as a very powerful force for transaction cost reduction for the benefit of the global economy, and you cannot cut it off just like that.

Which countries will weather the financial crisis best?

Open economies who have been successful in the past will probably also be better able to manage the financial crisis than closed economies, but we still need to sort this out. So far, I would have said that China is most likely to weather the storm. Now this is a relative concept. The starting point in 2007 was 11 percent growth, in 2009 the question is whether they can hold it at 8 percent. That is what they would like to hold it at. The betting odds are more like 7 percent. There are doomsayers who say that it is going to be much slower than that.

China went into this crisis with savings way over investments, which is frankly not a good strategy in a pretty stable world. It is just a waste of money. If you save more money than you invest, that surplus is equivalent to your current account surplus. Ten percent is a huge percentage of GDP, and it was actually 12 percent in 2007, which is an unheard of figure. The difference between what they needed to invest and what they actually saved was lent mostly to the US government at very low interest rates. Now that is not good growth strategy, but if there is going to be a growth slow down and you ask yourself which country has the capacity to have a fiscal stimulus without blowing the trade deficit or the budget, it is China! In fact what should have happened before was a gradual unwinding of the global imbalances in which they, and others, were saving less and the US were saving considerably more. Without that, we are going to exit from the crisis in a much more ugly way.

The other thing is that China has next to no domestic and foreign debt, and a pretty balanced budget situation: they have almost two trillion US dollars in reserves and they have complete control of their currency. They can make it go up or down or just hold it where it is and nobody is going to bet against them with reserves like that. You get killed if you tried.

So on the whole, I am not recommending these as policies because they have costs associated with them, but I have just talked about the benefits now that we are in a crisis.

If you look at India and their budget situation: up to now their revenues have been rising. This will reverse, but they are in good shape. India is different compared to China: it has a modest trade deficit, i.e., they are modestly dependent on foreign investment and foreign capital for their investment programme. But the government situation is worse. They have a big budget deficit, which limits the capacity for fiscal stimulus. They have a reasonable amount of foreign reserves, however, and a very competent reserve bank, the Central Bank, so they can probably handle the credit crisis situation. But the government, in addition to having a big budget deficit, and partly for that reason, is relying on foreign capital to fund the infrastructure investment in the public/private partnerships. Without that, the growth will slow down.

So the answer to your question, pending a more careful layout of the bits and pieces, is that if you wanted to be ideally situated for a crisis, you would go in with a balanced budget, a modest trade deficit, a mild surplus and lots of foreign reserves. In an ideal world the balanced budget is probably a good idea, because you could probably borrow a little more and you could accelerate investment if it wasn't unsafe, and you wouldn't need the reserves because the IMF would do it for you. Now you might have the reserves anyway because of your current account management process, but this is very complicated stuff where there are lots of opportunities to misstep and there is no agreement on the optimal way to go about this.

Economic growth and poverty alleviation

For countries that are poor, growth and poverty alleviation are approximately the same thing. Poverty alleviation is arithmetically impossible without growth. In a country with a per-capita income of 400 US dollars, it doesn't matter how you redistribute income. For countries that are further up in the income distribution, global poverty reduction can imply income distribution, sometimes with growth, sometimes with less growth. But that is a different issue. What I am trying to say is that there are two kinds of poverty: one is poverty in the context of where everybody is poor, and to solve that you have to grow; the other kind of poverty is where you have a group of people in a society that, for whatever reason, is not benefiting from social services, etc. That is a subgroup problem. Both kinds of poverty exist, but the lions share of large-scale poverty is in a context where everybody is poor, which is why we are so much focussed on growth, and therefore on GDP per-capita.

On measuring growth

The work that is going on with a broad array of people among the academic community, including psychologists, has to do with expanding the array of measures at our disposal for economic growth, including ways to measure it dynamically. One thing that the Growth Commission Report says is that we do not even think that growth is an objective. When I am describing this to people I say that I don't know anybody, including myself, who gets up in the morning and thinks about growth! I am thinking about my kids and our grand kids, about opportunity and creativity, or a chance to be employed or have a family and have them be healthy. Almost the only thing you don't think about is growth.

We did that on purpose, because we wanted to explain why we focussed on growth and therefore on GDP or per-capita income. It is not because we think it pre-empts this other work to get better measures of things that are more fundamental to people, but because it seems that economic growth in terms of GDP per-capita is an awfully important instrument for getting there. I don't believe that most of the MDGs can be achieved without additional growth, and I don't think they can be sustained only on the basis of a constant flow of external contributions.

So we focussed on it because it is hard to do, it is relatively easy to measure and it seems to enable an awful lot of stuff and, overall, there is a lot of leverage in figuring out how to do that. But it really was not meant to be a substitute for these other attempts at measuring.

On the Washington Consensus

In a world of policy, particularly as practised by economists, the concept of strategy is often completely missing. A strategy is a set of policies and they don't seem to have a whole lot to do with what is going on in practise. Otherwise, you wouldn't get a set of policies that look like it doesn't matter what country they are meant for.

So the way we went about this is to remind ourselves that there is a difference between strategy, and how it is constructed, and policy. And there is a difference between strategy and a framework that helps you to do a strategy effectively.

By way of example: a very good friend of me, Michael Porter, wrote a book called "Competitive Strategy", and what it is not about is a strategy for all companies in all industries that works wherever you are. So you might say: "What is it"? And the answer is: "It is a framework!" It is a set of things that you really ought to think about if you are formulating a strategy for a particular company in a particular industry with a particular history.

That is what we in the Growth Commission have been trying to do as well, and that is different even though the words sometimes sound similar to the Washington Consensus. I don't want to distance myself from John Williamson, because I think most of what he had to say was right, but what it missed, apart from the politics and the political economy in the contributions that were made, was that, in the long run, development is a learning, experimental process and not just a set of policies that you ought to implement.

I am sounding more critical than I intend to be, so let me try again. The Washington Consensus is a list that probably looks like a set of necessary conditions for growth, with the benefit of hindsight. These conditions are not sufficient, and the sufficient ones are much harder to get your hands on. The Growth Report says that explicitly. I believe the current state of knowledge is that we know, or suspect we know, a lot of necessary conditions and I am almost sure we don't know the sufficient ones. And the Washington Consensus came off as necessary and sufficient, and when practised it felt like this. This is the last thing I leave you with.

Making Globalization Work

Martin Wolf, with panellists Sylvester Eijffinger and Hans Schlaghecke

I am first going to deal with what I think were the failures of the international financial system that created at least part of the backdrop to the present economic crisis. Secondly I am going to explain what this crisis means for the developing countries and third what this implies for at least some aspects of the future of the global financial and monetary systems in the way of having a more stable world order.

If you look at the globalization process from the point of view of economic relations rather than of external factors, such as the issues of the global environment, climate change or geo-politics that clearly have economic aspects, the failure of the financial system is by far and away the biggest single problem we are confronted with.

Since we started liberalizing the global financial system in the late 1970s and early 1980s, there have been about 120 financial crises. Most, but by no means all, of these were in emerging economies. The most important of those, in terms of influence on the way the global financial system subsequently emerged and evolved, was in the late 1990s: the Asian financial crisis, which actually occurred at the same time as the Russian and the Brazilian crises. But I think the Asian financial crisis was the core of this, because it happened to the most successful developing countries in the world.

This crisis was preceded by a period when capital flowed into Asian countries that found it very easy to borrow. They expanded in many cases the current account deficits. They had huge property booms domestically, which is very much the story of Thailand, as the most obvious example, though its story was a bit different from

South Korea's. In 1997 and 1998, people became worried about the stability of their financial system. Capital flowed out, exchange rates collapsed and – because they had borrowed very heavily in foreign currency, above all the dollar because that was the key currency of the system – most of the financial system and their corporate sectors were immediately bankrupted. Their currency collapsed and fell by between 50 and 85 percent in terms of external value.

The lesson the Asians drew from this, both the ones directly affected just as those who saw what happened, in particular China, was twofold: that it was much safer to go back to export-led growth, and that they needed to insure themselves against events of this kind if they wanted to remain part of the international system. And in the subsequent period, up to today, they did indeed do this. The foreign currency reserves of developing countries, predominantly in Asia, rose by about 5 trillion US dollars between 1999 and today, because they ran very large current account surpluses for a long period. Most of Latin America proceeded to do the same. Oil exporters also emerged as significant exporters of capital.

So somebody in the world system had to run deficits. That is true by definition. And it turned out, and not surprisingly, that those countries were predominantly the developed countries. They, in particular the US, had the key currency and imported about 70 percent of the surplus capital that the world generated, largely as a result of these crises.

Now, the first point about that obviously is that it is insane: it is completely ridiculous to have a world system which generates incredibly large capital flows, enormous relative to GDP, from relatively poor countries to the richest country in the world. The second thing about this is that it is unsustainable, both externally and internally. It turned out that the internal side was more important. That was the theme of my second, most recent book on 'Fixing Global Finance', that the external accumulations turned out not to be as big a problem as one expected. The internal accumulations, which I also discuss in the book, namely the domestic counterpart of these huge external deficits of the US and the UK, became the biggest problem. Huge borrowing by household sectors were basically driven and facilitated by housing bubbles.

I do not want to argue for a moment that this was the only or even the main reason for the present financial crisis, but it was in my view a crucial part of the background: the failure of the global financial system to transfer resources smoothly to developing countries led to this ultimate result.

Now what has this crisis done to developing countries? It is pretty obvious that we now have a major financial crisis, a flight from risk worldwide. As in any flight from risk worldwide, there is a flight from emerging countries, because they are always perceived as more risky than the triple-A-rated borrowers. The countries that are worst hit are those with large current account deficits, booming property sectors and large inflows of net capital financed by banks. It is the capital flows from banks that are always the most unstable, not foreign direct investment.

The region of the world that happens to meet those criteria perfectly is, of course, Central and Eastern Europe, which is the only region of the emerging world to behave exactly as Latin Americans, even more than East Asians, did prior to the Asian financial crisis. So this is the region that is now being demolished by these capital outflows. This is an absolutely classic emerging market countries financial crisis, associated with the panic stage of a global crisis. It is the most severe for this region because their deficits were so large, as was their exposure to foreign currency borrowing.

Of course, Central and Eastern Europe is not the only region to be adversely affected. All of the developing countries have been adversely affected to some degree. But, by and large, the countries that have been least affected have been those that had build up these large foreign currency reserves. They will be reinforced in the view that this is a sensible thing to do. And a lot more developing countries will do that in the future.

That leads me to my final and third point in this short introduction. What does this tell us about the future? In my view, it is very likely that emerging countries will want to run a balanced account, to run a surplus and to accumulate even more reserves than in the past. The only exception will be those countries in Central and Eastern Europe that are allowed relatively soon into the euro zone, in which case they won't need to build up reserves.

But those that are not allowed in will need to build up reserves. That means also that when the oil price gets up again, and we have a recovery, we are going to have a large accumulation of current account surpluses around the world, and somebody is going to have the deficits. It is pretty clear to me that it will again be the US, and the counterpart this time will be fiscal deficits in the US, not household or corporate deficits. Running these deficits will simply prove to be unsustainable: there is going to be a blow-up.

So that leads me to my very last point, which is where we should go from here. There is only one way out of this, which is that we have to have a global financial and monetary system that does not make it impossible for emerging countries, which naturally are most in need of money to run current account deficits, to import capital. And we have to make this system at the same time more stable than before.

In my book, I recommend two things and here I will stress a third. Although this is clearly not sufficient, one lesson is that if you are going to borrow substantially abroad in a multi-currency world with floating exchange rates, *you will have to borrow in your own currency*. You cannot borrow in foreign currency because the risk of currency mismatch is too great. So a big part of the story is: develop your currency as an internationally tradable currency. We have moved some way in that direction: there are a lot of countries that can now borrow in their own currency, but by no means all.

The second thing we can do is immensely *increase the insurance arrangement* that the International Monetary Fund (IMF) now represents. The IMF is essentially an insurance system. It allows countries that do not issue key currencies to finance their way through a crisis. At the beginning of this crisis, the IMF's lendable resources were 250 billion US dollars in a world where there were seven trillion US dollars of reserves. Obviously it was irrelevant. So it has to be enormously expanded and, I think, increased about tenfold from that 250 billion US dollars to something like 2.5 trillion US dollars, with much more automatic lending to countries that are running their policies well. So there has to be an insurance system.

The third thing we can think about is the *issuance of the SDR* on a sustainable basis to emerging countries, which is actually what the Governor of the People's Bank of China has been recommending as a way of diversifying out of the single currency, the key currency dominated system.

The big point I want to leave you with is this. Though this crisis was certainly not caused only by the history of financial crises, the truth is we have not created a stable financial system to facilitate the transfer of private sector resources to emerging countries. Every time we have had a large transfer of resources, we have ended up in a financial crisis. This is one of the reasons for the present crisis. If we don't fix that problem – and I have suggested some ways of trying to do it – we are not going to have a reasonably stable world financial order that allows the financial system to operate on a liberal basis, and we will all have to go back to more autarkic financial systems. And if you have autarkic financial systems, it may be very difficult to sustain open trade. So this is a very big issue for our future about which I am delighted to be able to debate here with my distinguished colleagues and with you tonight.

Sylvester Eijffinger:
I had wanted to start with a remark by Governor Zhu of the People's Bank of China that struck me in the last couple of weeks. As Martin Wolf mentioned, he proposed to replace the dollar by the Special Drawing Right, which is the reserve currency of the IMF, a kind of monetary equivalent of Esperanto. He wanted to revive it from the death. Coming to think about that, you wonder how could it come so far, that, after more than half a century, the US in economic, financial and monetary terms is questioned like that? My explanation is the following.

If you are the dominant economic, financial and monetary power in the world, as part of the deal you have to deliver three things: economic, financial and monetary stability. So I will take you along this brief journey to tell you what my vision is. That vision is clear: the US did not provide *economic stability* according to the analysis of the emerging economies, in particular China. American academics, we know them all very well, for example Ben Bernanke, have explained this by pointing at the savings glut. They say that the rest of the world is saving too much: those poor guys in the rest of the world are saving so much that the US will help them and at least find a productive way of using all these additional savings! That has been to some extent the approach of the US: 'We will help you. Therefore it is good that we create a shortage in the current account, that we have expansionary fiscal policies and that we have a government budget deficit. In this way we are helping the rest of the world'. However, and this is the point, it did not help to create economic stability.

Now, did the US provide *financial stability*? We know that the shadow banking system, the 'originate-to-distribute' model, which distributes fear rather than risks, has delivered a lot of financial instability in the world. Normally every 10 to 12 years there is a financial crisis in the US. I have studied many of these crises. The last one was the Savings and Loans crisis in 1989-90, which was a small one. Maybe it was too small, but it created already the moral hazard and the root for the next crisis. Anyhow, these crises were always limited to the US itself. However, the present crisis has become a problem to the rest of the world as well, following from the 'originate-to-distribute' model that was introduced by the shadow banking system, where mortgages were securitized as bundles. So also financial stability was not really created.

What about *monetary stability*? Having the nominal key currency in the world gives you advantages. One of them is that you can finance your current account deficit in your own currency. That is fantastic, but in return you have to deliver monetary stability. Another advantage is that you can have a liquidity premium in the international financial markets. Portis and Rey estimate an amount of 25 to 50 basis points, which is quite a lot! And, of course, the last but not the least of advantages is inflation tax or seignoirage. The question is how much is the inflation tax or has it been for the US? Is that 0.1 percent of GDP or 2 percent? It is always very difficult to make those estimates, but at least you know that there are considerable benefits from having the key currency, the international key currency in the world. But you still have to provide monetary stability!

Now you know that the usual way various US administrations went along with this was to say that this was their currency and that instability was not their problem. They said to have no problem with a weak dollar because that gives also the opportunity that a lot of their debt in real terms to the world is depreciated, whether as foreign direct investment, or investments in stocks or as debt in dollar terms.

So actually you see that, to put it mildly, the US did not deliver stability to the system in economic, financial and monetary terms. While I am not a US basher, and have been visiting the US every year and have many friends over there, I still say: they did not deliver. And if you do not deliver, your dominance is questioned.

The question is: which currency could replace the US dollar? There is no alternative at the moment. The SDR is not a real alternative because there was the old idea of the SDR substitution account, and you don't want to create 3 trillion SDRs while there is so much excess liquidity in the world. The euro might be a competitor as international key currency in due course, but at this moment it is unclear what amount of euros are kept as reserves in the international economy. For example, China does not want to reveal the composition of its international reserves. It is suggested that one third of its reserves are held in euros and two third in dollars, more or less. That distribution will change. It may change to fifty/fifty, but there is no way that only one currency can replace the dollar.

So we have a problem. But the problem is more what will be the design of a new financial architecture. That new financial architecture can only be designed in an international setting with a more balanced approach between the developed world and the emerging economies. Even if it may take a long time, I believe that the G20 might be a new forum for that. But that does not mean that we have a replacement for the dollar or that we have solved the question of how to provide stability to the system.

Martin Wolf:
I have been put into a position that, as a non-US citizen, I should not be in, i.e., defending the US. But I think that the problem with this analysis to me is that it seems to ignore what was discussed in particular by Triffin in the years leading up to the collapse of

the First Bretton Woods agreement. The system we have had, and I describe that in my book, targeted exchange rates to the dollar at what I think was an undervalued level. That was referred to by some at Bretton Woods II when they said: go back to Bretton Woods I.

The problem, Triffin basically argued, is that if you use a national currency as the principle reserve asset in the system, even if it is the currency of a very big country, then this country has to issue large amounts of internationally tradable short-term securities, which will be the reserves for everybody else in the system. This is rather different from the gold standard where in principle everything is pinned to an internationally traded commodity. But we have not been on a gold standard for nearly a century. One could say that the proper gold standard really did die sometime between the first and the second world war, which is pretty close to a century ago.

You could imagine a situation where the long-term capital inflow more than offsets this effect, which is in essence excess demand for the country's short term liquid liabilities, such that the balance of payments, the overall current account, remains in balance. It is logically possible but in fact, as Mr Triffin pointed out, this is not very likely to happen. There is no reason why it should happen. It happened, by the way, to some extent to the US in two periods when it did lend long and borrowed short, but not fully so: a large part of the inflow took the form of a current account deficit.

That is linked to the point that Sylvester Eijffinger did not seem to agree with, but which seems to me demonstrably obvious: there was a savings glut as you see in these colossal current account surpluses that countries like China are running. They are not purely monetary phenomena, they are results of policies that affect savings and investments and are, therefore, perfectly understandable. As a consequence you end up in a situation with a large number of countries that want to run these current account surpluses in order to accumulate net foreign assets. They did not just substitute long for short or short for long: in fact it is worth thinking about how much the long-term capital inflow into China should have been in order to offset the short-term accumulations they were interested in.

This resulted in the sort of deficits we saw in the US, financed by relatively short-term assets that were accumulated by foreigners. The problem, Triffin pointed out, is that, as these liabilities of the key currency country, particularly short-term liabilities, accumulate, they have monetary characteristics. The confidence in that currency will fall and sooner or later there will be a crisis. Because people will say: "We do not want anymore of this stuff, we want you to start pursuing what we would think of as a much more prudent policy". That basically means: "We want you to deflate". Obviously, the key-currency country does not want to do that, and that was the reason for the crisis we had in 1969 to 1971, and you know how that ended. And that is how the crisis will end this time as well.

You could say that the US should be prepared to go through the process Spain is now going through. But it is not going to do so, and the whole system will remain unstable. So this is not a good way of supplying reserves to the system, because it depends on the issuance of one single central bank and on associated current account deficits. I think that Sylvester Eijffinger raised exactly the right question, but I am less convinced that it is impossible to create international reserves based on an agreement on the global issuance of reserve money that is convertible in all major currencies. Certainly I think that would be a better system.

If we are going to stick with the dollar as he suggests, then we must expect a series of major crises associated with the dollar. It is absolutely inevitable, and the next one we can already see coming down the road, because what we have seen thus far is only a small taste of a new crisis a few years from now. Because a few years from now, when the gross debt of the US relative to GDP is at 120 to 130 percent, and God knows what the total outstanding liabilities of the US Federal Reserve will be, there will be a dollar panic. There will be a crash, the dollar relative to the euro will go through the roof, and I will be very interested to see how European politicians and the European Central Bank will respond to this. It will be an unbelievable shock.

So it is a fundamentally unstable system that we have, and it is by no means good enough to say it is a rotten system and not do anything about it.

Hans Schlaghecke:

I would like to ask some questions rather than make a statement. But, in a way, what I am going to say is a sort of statement. It is about the essence of your book on global finance, where you say that an international financial system has to be liberal and market-based and that you need to have a global economy that is not relying for its overall macroeconomic balance on the US, as it does at the moment. But seeing this economic crisis now developing, I wonder if it is still possible to have such a system. I think that globalization requires one dominant political power, as was the case in the late nineteenth and early twentieth century with the UK as dominant power until the first World War, and with the US as dominant power after World War II.

As in the past, after 1918, the US surpassed the UK, so now China is doing the same with the US. In 1918, the US developed surpluses while the UK was in much more trouble than the US is now. So perhaps we are at the moment experiencing the end of the second globalization, and are heading towards a world divided into five regional blocks consisting of the US and the EU, an Asian block maybe including Australia, South America and the Middle East, and may be, after some time, Africa. As you can see, Asia is already planning on these regional blocks. In Bali, they said that they want to create a new financial and economic space by upgrading the Asian Development Bank, referring to the European Union and driven by a mistrust of the IMF and the World Bank, and disappointed by the failure of the WTO to bring the Doha round to a successful conclusion.

This is another sign that we are moving in the direction of a sort of regionalization, a new phenomenon that comes in the place of globalization that we have now and that is built on the US as a super power. I think that this will have major implications for the international financial architecture. It may become impossible to upgrade the IMF in the world as it is now, because it will clash with the blocks I have described above, and which is a completely different situation compared to the kind of globalization that you describe in your book.

Martin Wolf:
Those are very important and interesting questions that I certainly thought about a great deal. As is pretty clear already from our discussion on the global monetary system, we have, and this is quite shocking really, no sense of what a global monetary system should look like. Without that, it is really very difficult to talk about a global financial system because it is bound to be crisis-prone. I have discussed some moderate ways out of this dilemma. Some of those really amount to going back to some ideas in Bretton Woods. The SDR, for example, fits very well into the Bancor idea that Keynes put forward at that time, and which was rejected, of course, by the Americans and was essentially an international settlement currency.

First of all, you say that globalization requires a dominant power or hegemony. Well, if you think of the modern era, by which I mean since the industrial revolution and the era of rapid economic growth, this has been true. But the problem is that the sample is really only a sample of two, and so it is difficult to draw a scientific conclusion from such a sample. You may ask whether this is necessarily the case. I don't want to push this parallel too far, but let us call the European Union, which is a functioning international system, in aid. Although it has heavy trans-national elements, it is still, I think, fundamentally an international system. And though there is a single country within the system that is more important than any other country, I don't think that it is easy to argue that Germany is a hegemony in the same way as we think of the US as a hegemony. If a system like the European Union works at all, and it seems to work quite well, it is because of some sense of shared common interest.

So I would argue in response to your first point that, and this is very important in comparison to what happened in the 1920s and 1930s, all of the major governments in the world, with the possible exception of Russia, recognize a profound interest in international commerce and in the growth and development that international commerce could give them. There are no important governments in the world, again with the possible exception of Russia, that have ideologies that are even close to the sort of extreme nationalistic and autarkic ideologies of the 1920s and 1930s. So the development of a world system based on a sense of shared interest and, of course, some sort of sense of mutual responsibility doesn't seem to me impossible, though I don't deny for a moment that it would be difficult.

The second point I want to make is that I think we should be very careful when making parallels between the US and the UK, China and the US, etc. It is worth mentioning that the US had a bigger economy already by the 1890s than the UK. So the UK was a relatively small hegemonic power already thirty or forty years before the system collapsed. The First World War destroyed the principal resource base of the UK, which was an incredible acquisition of foreign assets. The ratio of foreign assets to GDP in 1913 was three times, and that was all lost and was never recovered. Its economy was also fundamentally non innovative. By the 1920s, it was already the third largest economy in the world after the US and Germany, and so it was in a hopeless position to be a dominant power. It wasn't even able to manage its own security.

The Chinese economy at market prices – I think that is what is relevant – is at present still only about the size of Germany's. It is only about one third of the size of the US economy, and it might actually be even less than that, and in every technological dimension, every dimension of innovation, every dimension of cultural influence, there is simply no competition. There is none.

Do we look to the Chinese president to lead the world in a crisis like this, or do we expect the American president to do so? Where do we expect the next range of fundamental innovations in technology and science to come from? Which country has the most advanced university system? Which country has the largest military system? I am not trying to say that that is the most important thing. It was ludicrous how exaggerated that was under the previous US administration. But I don't think that there is any comparison. So I don't think that China is close to being a hegemony. I like to say, as I told the Chinese at length in lectures I gave: there is no great superiority in accumulating by agony and pain two trillion dollars of reserves that the Fed could and would print in a night!

The final point I would like to make is that I really think that stable regional blocks are an illusion. There are many reasons why this is the case. I will give two main reasons, and then I will stop. The first main reason is that all the major players depend on global trade: China's trade is not with Asia, China's trade is with the world. Have you looked at its balance of trade with the EU recently? It has a huge surplus both with the EU and the US. Without that it would be in considerable trouble.

All big economies have global trade: Europe couldn't function as a self sufficient system, nor could the US. And that links with the second reason why we are going to need a global solution. For now, and at least for the foreseeable future (at least the next twenty or thirty years), we all depend on fossil fuels, the largest reservoir of which can be found in the Middle East. We can't be self enclosed without getting hold of this region, and therefore the implication of a closed block system is a war to end all wars for the Middle East. I don't think that is a rational way to go.

So I come back to where I started: we have to make the global system work. We just have to make it work cooperatively, and I don't see why that should be impossible. But a good starting point would be for Europeans to recognize that they cannot have eight out of twenty seats in the IMF Board and they can't have a third of the votes in the IMF. So *they* are the problem, not the Americans!

Sylvester Eijffinger:
I think that this is the key question: we have to create a system that provides stability. That was also the key to my earlier remarks. Now the question is: which group of countries or which institution can provide that? Let us take the IMF. It is a nice example. Did the IMF say something about the global imbalances to the US, its biggest shareholder? Did the IMF say something about the 'originate-to-distribute' model or about the leaks in financial supervision regulation?

You know, of course, that in the US financial supervision is a kind of patchwork, developed since the civil war. I cannot keep track of the number of financial supervisors in the US, I always forget, but there are a lot! And the problem is that there has been no remark by the IMF supervisory department about this. Take the Asian crisis: the IMF, but also the US, said to all countries: you are naughty boys, you shouldn't do this, do like us, open up your markets! But there was no balance in the sense that the US was also supervised by the IMF's regulatory supervisory system. Of course I know the remarks about the brothers Wright, who never got a flying license to take off with their little airplane. But it makes sense that there is some sort of supervisory system to deal with the supervisors. And last but not least, if you see what the US is doing in terms of quantitative easing, but even in intervention in the credits market, you wonder. Bernanke is a great academic; there is no doubt about that. I have known him for a long time, but being a good monetary economist doesn't mean that you are necessarily also a good policymaker. What I see in quantitative easing, but also in direct intervention in credit markets, as if credit markets are segmented markets, makes me very scary about the future. So if you look at that, you may ask, which organization or group of countries, the G20 or the IMF, could provide stability to the system? Because we need stability after all.

Hans Schlaghecke:
After you have killed my two birds – of China becoming a dominant power and the other one on stable regional blocks – let me try a third one. You made a very interesting observation in your latest book on the international financial system. You said that the international financial elite doesn't have a clue of what is happening in the countries they are investing in, and that they should better look at what resident lenders do, because they know their system best and they know what action to take if there is a political or other crisis coming up. On the other hand, the international banks didn't have a clue and had to gallop away in twenty-four hours or so when a crisis came up. So what you say is that you have, on the one hand, an international global financial system and, on the

other hand, you have sovereign states who are more or less closed entities with their own rules and their own moral systems and God knows what else. There is a mismatch between the two.

The observation I want to make in this connection has to do with democracy. In Great Britain, in the late nineteenth century, the political elite who voted for parliament was only a small minority of the people who believed in a global system where Britain was ruling the waves. But after World War I, you saw the British working class coming up. They worked very hard during the war and they got their voting rights and they said that they didn't want to pay for a second UK-dominated globalization. So it is democracy in a country that is making globalization more diffi-cult. You saw it also in the US senate, which was always opposed to the IMF and blocked the establishment of the WTO in 1949 because they didn't want it to interfere with their sovereignty. That is another point supported by Geoffry Freedman, who I think wrote an article called 'Will Global Capitalism Fail Again?'

Martin Wolf:
It is interesting to note that you two, one very much the economist, the other the political scientist, are actually raising the same ques-tion, which is: how do you combine some form of global order, which includes an integrated economy and provides opportunities to trade, particularly for developing countries (which I think is very important), with the reality of national sovereignty, particu-larly in a democratic age?

I wouldn't quite go along with your description of the expan-sion of suffrage, as the suffrage in the UK in the late nineteenth century was wider than you imply, but it is still basically true that we, by which I mean the developed countries today in Europe and the US, moved toward universal-suffrage democracy in the early part of the twentieth century, and that made the gold standard inoperable. You couldn't deflate the whole economy for twenty years in order to satisfy the rules of an international system, as I think, talking about today, you are going to find with Spain or Ireland. But leave that aside because it may not be the question you want to raise here.

But universal-suffrage democracy changes the calculation in the most profound way. So how do we do this? That is essentially Sylvester's question. Because, of course, the reason Ben Bernanke does what you regard as all these unreasonable things is that his charter is that of the Federal Reserve, and the responsibilities of the Federal Reserve do not include stabilizing the global financial system. I promise you, if you look at the law that established the Federal Reserve, this is not one of the objectives. The objectives are to deal with growth and employment in the US.

Now you could argue that he is doing this in the wrong way, and that if he understood as much as Jean Claude Trichet does, and if the Americans understood as much as the Europeans do, they would run a more sensible monetary policy. But it is not clear that they would, not least because, again, as you rightly set out, so much of the cost of their 'mistakes' would be borne by others. If you are a large debtor and you choose to inflate, then much of the costs will be borne by foreigners. And there is nothing to fix this.

That was the deep problem Keynes was aware of. It was for this reason that he wanted countries to be able to pursue policies that would stabilize the domestic economy. He saw that this is often incompatible with their international monetary obligations, i.e., to provide a stable monetary system. He assumed that the consequence would be that we would not allow free capital movement. That was clear in the original IMF. And he wanted an international settlement currency, so that we would not get to where we now are. But we did get where we now are, and we have no way to provide a stable international currency that is also a national currency. And I would not suggest for a moment that we have a solution.

So everything I am suggesting is a palliative, because, unlike some of my friends, I don't think we can go back to the gold standard. I don't think it would be credible for a minute. In any situation in which the rules of the gold standard clashed with the requirements of the domestic policy, everybody would go off gold again. That is why we did go off gold in the 1930s.

So all that I would leave you with is this big point: making a system that resolves this problem is a very huge problem. You could envisage a global euro – a nice concept – but that would take, of course, a much higher level of global cooperation than anything we can now imagine. But, maybe one hundred years from now, it is imaginable, provided we don't blow ourselves up in the meantime.

May be we can envisage moving to more of a block-type world, but not closed blocks, rather "semi-open" blocks. We could imagine, and this is conceivable, moving to a world of probably three key currencies: the euro, the dollar and the renminbi (it wouldn't be the yen). As soon as the renminbi becomes an international convertible currency, the other Asians will certainly go on to the renminbi and shift from the dollar. The Chinese will manage that as a hegemonic system.

Now it is possible to imagine that these three currencies float, and each of the core countries provides reserves to peripheral countries in a crisis (which the ECB in the present crisis has done poorly). That would stabilize smaller neighbours. They wouldn't need reserves so much, because the dominant power would provide them in a crisis. And you could still trade between the regions, but of course you would still have the currency instability to cope with. That doesn't seem to me to be a terrible outcome of this crisis, and it seems to me quite a likely one over the next twenty years.

That is why I don't expect the dollar hegemony to disappear tomorrow. We might well be seeing that happen, evolving over the next twenty years, depending on how well the euro zone is managed. I am not incredibly impressed by the way the management of the euro system has gone in this crisis, particularly vis-à-vis Central and Eastern Europe. I don't think they have realized how significant the effect of the crisis on these countries is.

The future of the international financial system depends even more fundamentally on how the Chinese choose to internationalize their currency, which is a huge issue for them because it means getting rid of exchange controls and therefore losing control over the domestic financial system. Combined with some SDR issuance for poor developing countries in Africa and so forth, we might be beginning to get somewhere through the relatively pragmatic course I have just outlined.

Is there a glimmer of hope?

I think that Jean Claude Trichet got it right when he mentioned that there is an inflection, by which he meant a deceleration in the rate of decline. There is some evidence of a turn around in the short run in consumer confidence, with purchase managers' indices indicating a turn around in the desire to purchase by corporations. This is particularly the case in manufacturing, which of course has experienced a tremendous slump.

Nonetheless, I would agree very much that there are several reasons for being worried about the stability of any recovery. One mentioned was those emerging economies that ran large current account deficits, spent a lot, imported capital and are now in terrible trouble and are going through very serious slumps. I discussed this in my introduction, and that is likely to be long-lasting. The consequences of such crises in emerging economies historically lasted many, many years. I don't see why that should be different now. I think we in Europe have made a profound mistake in not helping Central and Eastern Europe more in this crisis.

But what is even more significant is that we haven't found a replacement to balance the whole global supply and demand, which does not include this much lower US excess consumption, except that now the counterpart is fiscal deficits. We are racking up an incredible amount of fiscal debt across the whole developed world, and sustainability will at some point become an issue. It is clearly not a sustainable course. We are a long way from what we really want, which is a sustained, global, private-sector recovery. We will see a bounce in the inventory cycle in the manufacturing sector, and it will probably be quite strong. Plus, the end of the collapse of conventional housing investment in a number of countries will come about, but that is not a sustainable recovery, it is just the end of agony.

There is the issue of non-linearity. I think that is right, everybody who studied the economics of bank runs knows that these are non-linear: you get information cascades and suddenly everything goes crazy. What we have witnessed, in essence, is probably the biggest bank run in the history of the world, namely a comprehensive run on all banks and financial markets simultaneously at the end of last year in which almost nobody could raise money for anything. I am not persuaded that greater transparency would have helped much, unless transparency allowed you to discriminate perfectly between long-term solvent institutions and insolvent ones, and you were sure that everybody else would act on the same information in the same way. It is rational to run from a bank you believed to be solvent if you think everybody else is going to run from that bank. So what you are concerned about is not merely the underlying condition of the bank, but the intentions and motivations of everybody else in the world. The problem with systems that involve human beings is that they deal with people.

Related to the question on China as 'consumer of last resort', let me tell you that I am a very simple human being and my proposition is simple and Keynesian, because I happen to think he was a great economist. I know this is a minority view around the world, but it happens to be my view on macroeconomics. It says that at the aggregate level, potential world supply and demand may not be equal. This is the great controversy between Keynes and the classics, and I happen to think that he was right. Now I am not saying that in the very long run they would not be equal, but the problem is that the long run could be half a century. And it is not good enough to tell people that they are going to live in a slump for half a century, and that all will be fine in the end.

So the question is how supply and demand are going to be balanced in the world by the private sector without the government playing a big role, which is clearly desirable. It seems to be obvious that if you want the US, the UK and other high-spending, low-saving countries to save more, and you don't expect their investments suddenly to take off – and there is no reason why it should, because investment wasn't capital constrained – somewhere else in the system spending must rise. It could be either investment or consumption.

But if you are looking at China, which already invests 50 percent of its GDP – they save 60 percent so there is a surplus of 10 percent – it doesn't seem to me to be very obvious that a poor country like China should invest 60 percent of its GDP. Don't you

97

think 50 percent is enough? Consumption is 40 percent, which is ludicrously low. As a result, Chinese consumption standards are not much higher than India's, even though GDP per head is well over double. So it seems to me quite reasonable to suggest that China should raise its consumption.

This is a very complicated thing to do in China, which would take too long to explain. I fully accept that. Let us imagine the following world: they invest 50 percent of GDP, they consume 50 percent of GDP and the current account surplus disappears. So world trade will diminish by the extent of the Chinese trade surplus. But the trade will still be at the level of twice the Chinese imports. That is an incredibly large number. In other words, you don't need huge current account surpluses and deficits, net transfers of capital in other words, across the world to have very buoyant trade. You can see that historically: we did have very buoyant trade before this happened. In fact, I think it has made it less stable, not more so.

So I wouldn't consider it impossible for China to stimulate consumption. As a matter of fact, for anyone who studied China at all closely, it is very difficult to believe that China's investment need to be more than 40 percent of GDP to sustain present rates of growth. They could raise consumption to 60 percent of GDP and that would increase it by 50 percent without any significant growth rate decline. This is an incredible waste of resources. And let us remember, all they have done is pile up dollar reserves with that surplus of which the US is quite certainly going to default. So what then on earth is the point of this all?

Climbing out of the Ditch, Shared Growth, the Asian Experience and its Relevance

J. Edgardo Campos

About a decade ago, I got fascinated with the rapid growth phase of East Asia from the 1960s to the 1990s and started to write quite extensively on it. Today, I look at this story in a different way and give it a different interpretation on the basis of my experience in the field since then. It was because I got tired of what I had been doing, having been in the World Bank for too long, that I decided in 1998 to take a leave of absence. I then joined the Ministry of Budget and Management in the Philippines because I wanted to know what it was like to be in the engine room, as opposed to looking from outside and trying to figure what people were doing on the inside. I spent four years there as an advisor on public sector reforms, and then went on to Bangladesh to have a taste of the real challenge of moving reforms forward.

Revisiting the East Asian experience

This combination of experiences in the field has led me to think about the East Asian experience somewhat differently. For me in a way this lecture is a new journey through a similar forest, but perhaps trying to chart a slightly different path through that forest. Allow me to start with the contrast between two extremes. One is what we used to call an underdeveloped country with its basic characteristics. Take your typical fragile state in Africa, and you see all of these characteristics: political instability, poor governance, inept government, weak capacity, wide rural-urban disparities, high unemployment, low per-capita income, high illiteracy, crushing poverty and high mortality rates.

Contrast that with what we call a developed country, the other extreme, where things are working reasonably well. If you think about these two states, you begin to think that the real challenge of development has to do with this status quo and people thinking: we are poor, we need to get richer, we need to go forward, we need to develop. And on the other, hand you have the desired state, that is where they want to be, where people think: in twenty years time we want our per-capita income to be maybe three or four times higher.

But the challenge, of course, is that whole gap in between the status quo and the desired state; that itinerary does not proceed linearly. There was a point in time when we thought that develop-ment over time proceeded linearly, and that an economy moved from the agricultural space to the manufacturing phase and then to the service phase. That has, of course, changed over time. The reality is that the movement from a poor or underdeveloped state to a developed state or a better state is really fraught with a lot of uncertainty. There is no magic bullet; there are no formulas for these things. You have to deal with them almost on a daily basis, and on a learning-by-doing basis.

When you are faced with this challenge, it jumps at you. If you want to move from the status quo to the desired state you have to address so many interests, different parties and different groups. So the main challenge is not so much what are the right policies but it is more like: how are we, given the right policies or semi-right policies or the policies that we agreed upon, going to manage the politics of change? Because those policies will require us to move, to change over time!

Managing the politics of change

Being in the field is probably the most challenging demand that I have faced. It is fairly easy to understand what needs to be done and to understand what is wrong. The biggest challenge is, if you know both, also to know how to move forward. That is where the big challenge is, and one way to think about East Asia's experience, at least its rapid growth stage from the early 1960s until the late 1990s, is by looking at the leadership in those countries.

I must have thought: whatever policies we are going to pursue, we are going to have to consider the fact that this is going to be a political game. We are going to have to get people on board, and therefore we are going to have to manage the politics of change that occurs with the development process.

I wanted to be able to get a better handle on this, and I asked myself: 'How do we conceptually try to get a handle on this, what we call, managing the politics of change?' At that time I wished I had more time to read, so I tried to read in between all the work that I had been tasked to do in the field. But while reading the development literature and elsewhere, I realized there wasn't a body of systematic thought around this issue. There are a lot of articles written on this, but one has really to try and pull these different articles together.

Then I found something attractive in a completely unrelated field, which is the management field in business. The reason I got attracted to it is that, when one thinks of change or change management, almost always the knee-jerk response is to look at the corporate sector, because that is where a lot of change management actually has occurred.

From the literature, I picked up what I would consider as probably the best book on change management, at least according to what people say. It is a book by John Kotter, a leader in change management, and he basically lays out eight requisites or eight phases of managing change:

- Establishing a sense of urgency
- Creating a guiding coalition
- Developing a vision and strategy
- Communicating the change vision
- Empowering broad based action
- Generating short term wins
- Consolidating gains and producing more change
- Embedding change in the future

I thought that perhaps on this basis one could reinterpret the East Asian experience, at least during the rapid growth phase. And that is what I am going to try to do now.

Requisites or phases of managing change

The first phase is establishing *a sense of urgency*. In East Asia, the thing that actually drove a lot of governments to pursue growth was the threat of a communist take-over. It was very real in that part of the world. That is not surprising, because you had China and Russia at the doorstep. The two biggest surrogate wars between the East and the West were actually fought in East Asia, in Vietnam and South Korea.

I grew up around this time in the 1950s and 1960s, and I could clearly remember that this was constantly in the newspapers: that if there were a communist take-over, things would change radically and that there may be some real difficulties that would emerge as a consequence. This was the equivalent of establishing a sense of urgency, in this case an urgency to develop rapidly. This was the only way to actually deal with the communist threat and provide an alternative to the communist view of the world.

Having done that, the ruling parties and their leadership all had some sort of a vision for where they wanted to take their country, and a strategy for getting there. That is where this whole concept of shared growth actually emerged. I did close to 200 interviews across eight countries, and what was very striking was that, although they would mention things in different ways, what it all boiled down to was some sense that it is important to somehow promote and sustain a shared growth process.

Let me try and explain what is meant by shared growth. There was a lot of confusion at that time about this concept. It was the Deputy Prime Minister of Malaysia at that time who best explained this to me. He said: 'The idea is fairly simple, it is this. You have this wealth pie and the idea of shared growth is basically as follows. Unless necessary, we will not touch this distribution, this pie, we just leave it like it is. But then we are going to try and share all increases and increments to the pie with different groups in society'.

In the extreme, you can start the process with the existing pie. In some countries in East Asia, this is taken to a much further extreme than in others. In Japan, Korea and Taiwan, the existing pie was somewhat divided through land reform. It is politically easier to launch the process by leaving the existing pie as it is, but then to put mechanisms in place to make sure that any increase in income will be shared among the population.

Let me now provide some data on the shared growth phenomena. As we like to do at the World Bank, we grapple with data and try to support what we argue. So we did a correlation between GDP per-capita growth rates and Gini coefficients between 1970-90.

Figure 1   Gini coefficient and GDP per-capita growth rate, annual average, 1970-90

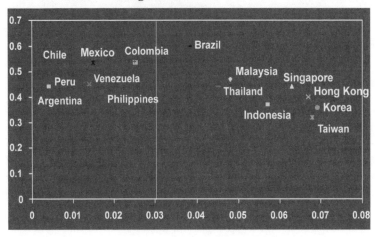

What you find is what you would like to observe, which is that countries that are farther to the right are also lower in the diagram, so in the southeast corner. Countries with lower inequality in terms of their Gini coefficients have higher growth rates per-capita. That is, in some sense, the direction in which you find the East Asian countries, whereas you find the other countries in the world in the different quarters. In fact, it was this set of data that led us to the concept of shared growth, which led everyone on the team to agree that we should adopt this concept as the anchor for a report that we were preparing at that time.

In another set of data (see Figure 2), we were looking at the ratio of the top 20 percent to the bottom 20 percent. East Asia, with the exception of the southern region, excels in this as well. The performance of the southern region is no surprise given that, first of all, South Asia has a huge population and, secondly, there never was a problem of land distribution.

Figure 2   Ratio (un-weighted average) of top to bottom quintile and per-capita growth rate (selected years: 1976-88)

Region	GNP per capita growth (per year) 1965- 1990	Income share of bottom 20 percent of households	Income of highest 20 percent of households	Ratio of top 20 percent to bottom 20 percent
East Asia, Fast Growers	6.1	6.7	43.3	7.0
East Asia Slow Growers	3.6	6.1	47.5	8.3
Latin America	1.4	3.6	55.1	16.4
Africa	0.3	4.3	54.0	15.0
South Asia	2.2	8.0	43.5	5.5

It is on the poverty angle where the fast growing countries in East Asia – even Indonesia – have finally excelled. The financial crisis set them back somewhat, but they have gotten back on their feet and poverty is not anywhere near to what it was in the 1960s. In some countries like Singapore, there is no poverty, at least not the way we define it in the World Bank. Neither is there in Taiwan or South Korea and even, I might say, in Malaysia. So they really have gone past this discussion of serious levels of poverty.

Communicating a change vision

It is one thing to develop a vision, but it is another thing to communicate it. You need to be able to communicate this constantly because that is how you build support. There are many examples of this in East Asia, but I am just going to mention two of my favourites.

One is this vision 2020 in Malaysia. I remember flying into Kuala Lumpur and one of the first things I saw was something on a sign at the airport: 'Vision 2020'. So indeed, anywhere you went in the country at that point in time there was some reference to Vision 2020. The Prime Minister, Mahathir, who was Prime Minister for twenty years, made a point of emphasizing this every time he spoke on economic development, at least at major events.

When you spoke to the Malaysian bureaucracy, they would also mention this to you. It was very much immersed throughout the government and society, this notion of Vision 2020: that Malaysia was going to be an upper-middle-income country by 2020. I think that they are certainly well underway to doing that.

The other example is the annual awards for export performance in South Korea. That was a very big thing because it was attended by the president, who handed out the awards. This was done every year, and it emphasized that 'growth is what we want to promote and we are going to do this through exports'. In fact, there were quarterly export briefings that involved the business community and the government and which were also covered by the media.

The role of institutions

You can't really talk about shared growth without talking about the role of institutions. You may have a vision, you may have a strategy, but one way or another you need to implement the vision and the strategy, and this is where institutions matter a lot.

Let me just again emphasize that the challenge is how you manage the politics of change. The rest of the world is blessed by the fact that there are democratic institutions. These are democratic institutions that are designed to manage and resolve conflicts among different groups in society and enable a country to move forward, even if there are some serious changes that need to be made. So in that part of the world these institutions have been mature.

Now think about East Asia right after World War II. Put yourself into the position of someone like Lee Kuan Yew of Singapore in 1959, when they all of a sudden were booted out of the Malaysian

Federation. They had nothing, they had no resources: what would they do? You had a multicultural population of Chinese, Malays and Indians. That was certainly a potential recipe for ethnic strife. When you think about it, this isn't really something simple to get a handle on.

The same thing was true for Suharto in Indonesia in 1965, when essentially there was no government to speak of. Without any capacity in government, how would you begin to move the country forward? It is a completely different world that these countries faced back in the 1950s, 1960s and 1970s. They had to fashion institutions that somehow would help them manage the change process.

The paradox of autocracy

Now let me emphasize one thing. The predicament of many of these leaders, which is the predicament of most leaders anyway, is twofold: one is what the scholars call the paradox of autocracy, and the other is the time inconsistency of economic policy. Let me explain each briefly.

The paradox of autocracy is really a story of property rights. If a government is the only power or authority, as in an autocracy, it can easily grab property rights. So it can move things quickly, *but* this is a double-edged sword. By the same token it can as easily withdraw those rights. In that context it is very hard to encourage investment of any sort, because investments are going to be very short-term due to this uncertainty. So this problem needed to be addressed, and the governments were aware of this issue in one way or another.

Time inconsistency of economic policy

The other predicament is time inconsistency, which is the fact that, for any policy, the population bears the costs today, at the present, and the benefits generally come later on, in the future. They may come six months down the line, one year later or even after five years. They come at some later point in time, and anything can happen between today and tomorrow. As far as a typical citizen is concerned, well, how can he be sure that tomorrow will in fact happen? And if not, why should he support this government? That is a very real political concern. If you were in the prime minister's shoes, this was something that you would have to deal with if you wanted to implement policies that would promote investment and growth.

Credible commitment mechanisms

To address this issue, economists had this concept of credible commitment mechanisms. The whole idea is that you can address these two somewhat related problems through mechanisms that credibly commit the government to deliver what it has promised. Democratic institutions do this for government because they provide checks and balances. When there are no checks and balances, then how do you get commitment? It becomes a struggle of how to develop institutions that somehow can achieve part of what democratic institutions can do.

I have identified three categories of institutions in East Asia that can do this. One is what we call *deliberation councils*. This has to do with the relation between the government and the private sector. There are also *welfare sharing institutions*, which has to do again with the relations or the implicit contract between the government and the larger population, particularly the poorer segments where collective action problems are serious. Finally, there is *the bureaucracy*; there has to be at least part of the bureaucracy that is functional and competent enough to be able to implement or manage these mechanisms.

Creating a guiding coalition

Having very briefly dealt with the role of institutions, let me relate it back now to the change management process. This has to do first of all with creating a guiding coalition. Deliberation councils were essentially part of the coalition that was needed to move the growth process forward.

This is very well developed in the literature. Many people, myself included, have written quite extensively on networks in

Japan and South Korea. There are similar networks, though less developed, in Taiwan, Singapore and Malaysia, where they had an equivalent of this. The function of these councils is twofold. One function was the coordination and levelling of information so that all firms that were engaged in a particular sector got the same information. There was no sort of favouritism. You could say that there was a level playing field as far as that was concerned.

Secondly, they were a mechanism through which rents were allocated in a somewhat systematic way. In Japan for instance, when one firm in a particular sector was not able to meet its part of the bargain, there would be negotiations to move that operation to another conglomerate. It was a pretty complex system, but it worked because there was a presumption that, if in another sector a similar thing happened, the one firm that was not able to deliver in the first sector and that was the strongest in the other sector would be asked to tackle the problem so that the portion of the program then would be moved on to that firm.

This is a fairly transparent way of allocating rents, and given their situation I think that it is probably the best that they could have done. In the end it is a commitment mechanism that government could not just walk away from. Government could not penalize a whole sector for fear of stunting economic growth, but it could penalize a particular firm and allow the rest of the sector to continue to function and perform.

On the other hand, firms themselves could not walk away from this because a lot of their support actually came from government. The laws, subsidies and policies that were needed and helped the firms grow depended very much on government. So in a way you can think of a deliberative council as a crude form of a credible commitment mechanism.

Wealth sharing mechanisms

Wealth sharing mechanisms came in many different forms: land reform, developing rural infrastructure, investing in basic education, promoting small and medium enterprises and labour intensive manufacturing, allocating corporate equity, worker cooperatives and public housing programs. The whole thrust of this was to signal to the community: 'you are all going to partake in this pie, this increase to the pie'. There were conscious efforts to make sure that people in fact did get a share of the goodies. Land reform was certainly big in Taiwan, South Korea and Japan.

Figure 3   Distribution of land and owner-cultivated households in Taiwan, by size of holding, 1939 vs. 1960

	Percent Distribution of owner-cultivated households	
Size of Holding (chia)	1939	1960
Less than 0.5	43.2	20.7
Between 0.5 and 1	20.9	45.9
Between 1 and 3	24.6	30.1
Greater than 3	11.3	3.3
Total	100.0	100.0

You can see that there was a massive redistribution of land in Taiwan, and it was this move that helped to push the small and medium enterprise industries (starting with agricultural processing). There was also a lot of effort put into infrastructure in the rural areas, as opposed to just keeping it in the urban areas. I remember the first time I visited Indonesia; the first thing that struck me going to the provinces was that the roads were very well built. I come from a nearby country, the Philippines, where if you move away from the major cities the roads become rather decrepit.

Basic education is one of the pillars of East Asia, and it is not just enrolment rates that matter. School performance in these countries is significantly better than in much of the rest of the developing world. It is not surprising that back in the 1960s, Thailand was sending a lot of its top scholars to other countries, including the Philippines. Today they don't do that anymore. Now they have Thammasat University and Chulalongkorn University, which have really achieved quite a bit, and in fact are now taking scholars from other parts of the world! So there has been a big thrust in education in these countries, which probably explains why they have been quite successful in the information and communication technology race.

Labour intensive small and medium-sized enterprises got a lot of attention in Taiwan, and to a lesser extent in the other countries of East Asia. In Korea, many of the Chaebols were linked to small and medium-sized enterprises. The Malaysian New Economic Policy was very interesting because this is where this whole idea of shared growth was most vivid. The starting point of the growth process in Malaysia was probably 1969, when they had terrible riots. It really scared the hell out of government then, and was largely driven by the fact that the majority of the population, which was 60 percent Malay, was very poor and did not have any opportunities. It was the smaller Chinese and Indian minorities that were getting all the benefits of growth and investment.

So this New Economic Policy, which was meant to give the Bumiputras, the native Malaysians, opportunities to own and share capital, was put in place. Drastic programs were put into place and, although the targets were much higher than what eventually emerged, today there is a burgeoning Bumiputra entrepreneurial industrial class.

The role of the bureaucracy

In this last part, I wanted to tie this change management process to the role of the bureaucracy, at least part of the bureaucracy that could function. In East Asia there are three aspects to this. There is formal merit-based recruitment and career advancement, which is most developed in Japan and in Singapore and least developed in Indonesia. You will find that in the whole region there is some sense of merit being used to recruit key people into the more important parts of the bureaucracy. There was also consideration given to compensation. With the exception of Singapore, salaries in the public sector never match salaries in the private sector, but the discrepancies have been much smaller in the East Asian countries than elsewhere.

Figure 4   Estimates of per-capita GDP and ratio of public to private sector salaries, developing countries

Country/Region	GDP/Capita	Senior Level (%)	
		A	B
Singapore	14,920	114	114
South Korea	7,190	69.3	69.3
Taiwan, China	7,954	65.2	65.2
Malaysia	5,900	40	40
Thailand	4,610	47.1	47.1
Philippines	2,320	27.7	27.7
Chile	6,190	70.36	70.36
Trinidad and Tobago	8,510	63.53	63.53
Venezuela	6,740	29.54	29.54
Uruguay	6,000	n.a.	n.a.
Argentina	4,680	24.11	24.11

The data were not good, but nevertheless they did illustrate the gap between public and private salaries in East Asian countries, and that they were significantly smaller than in other parts of the developing world. Singapore in this respect was most astonishing. There, the government makes it a point to have the public sector salaries track one-on-one private sector salaries. To do this they undertake massive detailed surveys of private sector salaries every year, and then they adjust their salaries. If you think about this, as I remember one minister explaining to me, it was Lee Kuan Lee's view that the task that a minister of any agency faces is much more difficult than the task of any chief executive officer of any corporation anywhere in the world. Therefore you need to pay a minister just as much as you would pay a CEO. That was essentially the philosophy, and they did actually deliver on it. Back in the late 1990s the salary of a minister was something like 750,000 US dollars, and you could work out that even at entry level government officials got fairly good pay. That is why they have been able to attract the best and the brightest in the Singaporean bureaucracy.

Protection against arbitrary political interference

One of the features of East Asia is that, for at least those agencies that were very much involved with the growth process, there was some protection from arbitrary political interference. You need that sort of insulation in order to have those agencies perform their tasks. When you have a lot of changes in the political sphere, then that translates into changes in appointments into the bureaucracy that run very deep. This can create very serious problems. Let me contrast my own country, the Philippines, with South Korea. The Philippines is very much a US model, so every time there is a change in administration, there is a *massive* change in the bureaucracy, whereas in Korea a change in administration would at most go down to the deputy minister level and oftentimes it just stayed at the ministerial level. If you combine that with the ratio of public to private sector salaries, and it is really much lower in the Philippines, then you end up with this result that the Korean bureaucracy is far more effective and more capable than the Philippines in terms of delivering what it has been tasked with. This is not surprising given the contrasting incentives between the two countries.

Accountability

The third pillar of the bureaucracy is some form of accountability. When you have been given some form of autonomy, which is what many of these economic agencies in East Asia were given, then there has to be some balance of accountability. They need to be made aware that they are accountable for what they are being tasked to do and they are taken to task for it. This was certainly very true in the North East Asian countries, such as Japan and

Korea. It is a different kind of accountability, but it was in the deliberation council that part of this accountability was enforced because the bureaucracy was asked whether it was able to implement what the government had promised in the previous year. If any of them failed, heads did roll and this was in the context where the private sector was present. It was a very open and transparent sort of venue.

Growth and institutions

Two of my colleagues in the World Bank, Stephen Akin and Phil Randis, have done an extensive study on growth and institutions. We took one of their empirical studies and their econometric equations and decided to just look at the variance, or the portion of the growth that could not be explained by any of their variables. We then correlated that with an index of bureaucratic effectiveness, and this is what we got.

Figure 5   Unexplained growth rate and bureaucratic effectiveness

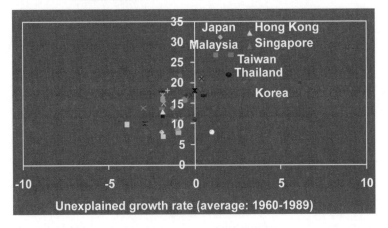

This implies that a lot of the unexplained growth can perhaps be explained by the sort of informal institutions that the East Asian countries have developed over time. Most revealing to me, in Singapore it was explained to me that the annual increases of a proportion of the salaries of the Civil Service was tied to the growth rate. You had the whole civil service being concerned about the growth rate. So this became a big thing every year. This was an example of what is called generating short term wins: every year you see that things are actually happening.

The role of culture

The one big difference between Latin America and East Asia is that, although both had started with a protectionist, import substitution kind of model, East Asia managed to move away from that model over a thirty to forty year period. In some sense, the notion of exporting and competing in the world market became embedded in the culture of the private sector, the government and even in society over this period. Of course it takes a long time to do this. Today, if you go to any of these countries, the thought of protectionism is something that they don't even entertain anymore. That is when you know that the old culture and habits are dying.

But again, it takes a lot of effort to do this. In fact, even within change management processes in organizations, culture is probably the most difficult to change. A lot of times what happens is that the change management team leaves before, or management decides to declare victory before this change actually has been achieved, and that leads to problems down the line.

To conclude

In the context of East Asia, I don't think it will ever go back to a world where countries will fall back on protectionism, protecting their infant industries or their industries in general. They are now able to compete with the best of the world. They know they can do it and are even getting into areas that the developed world is only now beginning to get into, like biotechnology. The South Koreans are quite aggressively getting into this, much more so than many other countries in the developed world.

Discussion

If you realize that the communist threat is no longer there, the question is whether the change model as presented is time contingent. Will elites that are no longer challenged by a communist threat out of rational insight opt for the same strategies? Is such a threat replicable in another time or at another place, say in Africa or Latin America? And is there a risk of Asia falling back? Will there be a regression of the growth process and a fall back to the situation of thirty to forty years ago?

Today the world is much different compared to thirty to forty years ago. Change is occurring much more rapidly than in the 1950s and 1960s. That, in itself, makes things more challenging. With regard to how replicable the motivation to adopt this shared growth perspective is, certainly it is true that you cannot manufacture a communist threat or something like that. And it certainly is not something that will emerge anytime soon in Africa or in Latin America. You can't engineer it.

But having read Paul Colliers latest book on Africa, 'War, Guns and Boats', he points out one thing that struck a chord with me. One thing that fragile states need, because there are no institutions in these countries and because they are starting from scratch, is fairly progressive leadership. This was one of his main points. So what he was saying is that you need someone, or a group of people, with the same sense of common cause, to be able to move this country forward.

Now what would induce them to do that? Unfortunately I do not have the answer. But assuming that there is that incentive that comes from somewhere, then certainly what it is that the East Asians have been able to do could be quite instructive. Deborah Brautigam has done some work on Mauritius, a country that is very different than other countries in Africa. It is closer to East Asia than it is to Africa, but it is on the African continent. What she found is that the strategies of the Mauritians came much closer in nature to what the East Asians have done, as opposed to the rest of Africa. They in a way have adopted the East Asian growth model.

So I think there is something to learn from East Asia. There is something that can be adopted, perhaps applied in a different way, because there is now a much more challenging environment. But the incentive for leaders in these countries to do that is probably path dependent or historical.

Is the Asian crisis of 1997 a case in point? I remember in 1997, I was having this debate with some colleagues from the IMF. They were saying that all of this was happening because of these public private councils, and that corporate malgovernance had led to this crisis. I told them, look, I think you need to study this much more closely. I told them that these countries would bounce back fairly quickly, and I wasn't wrong. Within a year Korea bounced back, and Malaysia wasn't even touched by it. Malaysia in fact challenged the IMF prescription! The only country that has not recovered to the level or the trajectory of pre 1997 is Indonesia, and there is a reason for that. Indonesia, of all these countries, was largest in size, had the least developed institutions and was the most impoverished. Today it has 200 million people, has democratic institutions and is starting to mature a little. So I am really not too worried about Indonesia. I think they will continue to manage to move forward.

On the risk of East Asia falling back: there are always risks in any strategy. Take the export push in Japan or South Korea, where there were certainly quite a bit of failures. Although people say that the whole idea of industrial policy was about picking winners and losers, there was a conscious recognition that we may pick successful industry winners today, but there is always the possibility that we will not be able to make it in that sector. So I think risk is now part of the way people do things in East Asia. I find businessmen there much more willing to take risks than in other parts in the world, including Africa.

But I think that the institutions in these countries have evolved sufficiently so that you are not going to find them back in the 1960s ditch very soon, whether it is South Korea or even Indonesia. The democratic institutions have developed to a point that they are now functioning reasonably well. This is certainly the case in South Korea. There are now much more effective checks and balances in the country than before. Even in Malaysia, where Mahathir was a virtual dictator, mechanisms have now been put in place to check the power of the prime minister.

On the question of the difference between Africa and East Asia in their perception of risk, where in East Asia risk is identified as a central element in the political culture whereas in Africa there is very little reasoning in terms of risks, but rather a feeling of a treasure being stole from them: if you had spoken to East Asian businessmen thirty years ago you would probably have gotten the same response that you are getting today from the Africans. Rapid growth has a way of gradually changing the way people think about the world. When a country is growing 7 or 8 percent per year for fifteen or twenty years, the landscape changes dramatically.

Even in the Philippines, which was probably the laggard in all of East Asia, I remember there was a spurt in growth during the Ramos administration during six years when there was a sense that it was becoming a baby tiger. You could feel the discussions in the business community were about what investments one could go and get into: these are the risks and these are the potentials.

That has been the whole culture that was in a sense eventually implanted in the business community, and in the population in general, through many decades of just pushing the same model, manifesting itself in different ways and demonstrating that it worked. The important thing is that they were able to show that if you pursue this model, that you would get this result. And because they got the results that they had promised, that became the culture!

Today there is so much dynamism in the business communities in East Asia that you will not find either in Latin America or in Africa, largely because of this thirty to forty year growth phase where things really changed so dramatically.

On the role of the ASEAN and the other supranational organizations in Asia, one can say that they weren't important players in growth from the 1960s to the late 1990s. Growth strategies were developed at the country level. Japan and South Korea, for example, proceeded on their own, and their battlefield was the global market. It was possible for these countries to compete with each other in a rather large field because the markets both in Europe and the US were opened up. But, having said that, given the challenges that most countries face today, particularly in Asia, there is a need to develop much more effectively these supranational entities. For instance, there are serious political issues surrounding certain islands in East Asia. Four countries are competing for them because of the oil revenues that probably could be generated from there. That is certainly something that could not be solved by the four countries amongst themselves, and could probably best be solved at a supranational level.

I think ASEAN is evolving into such an entity because it has been able to address some smaller tasks. For instance, it was very easy for ASEAN countries to agree to have citizens from other member countries entering without visas. This was early on, ten or fifteen years ago. There are now some agreements on trade. Over time, as they are beginning to realize that they have to get together to resolve certain regional public goods, ASEAN will evolve into a fairly much more influential organization.

Did Japan in the past play a similar role in East Asia as China at present in Africa? Certainly, Japan played a very important role in Asia, and the various East Asian countries were a very hospitable environment for Japanese direct investment. Besides, I must say that there were also considerable investments from Europe and the US that went to East Asia, mainly because they saw that these countries could get things done.

With regard to Africa, China is certainly flexing its muscles. There is a program at the World Bank called the South-South Exchange Programme. It is about an exchange of ideas and experiences between Africa and China. So we have African leaders, both big and small, coming to China, and Chinese officials and scholars going to Africa. There is movement now. There are now a number of African countries seriously looking to East Asia to see what it is that they can take from East Asia.

A very good example, and I would not have expected this five or ten years ago, is Rwanda. Not too long ago, Rwanda was a real basket case with genocide and all sorts of nefarious events. But today Rwanda is probably one of the most promising countries in

Africa. If you look deeper into what is happening in Rwanda, you have this leadership, largely driven by the fear that they don't want what happened ten years ago to happen again. They have officially teamed up with Singapore to help them move forward on a number of things. They have an official Memorandum of Understanding, and there are a surprising number of Singaporean experts in different areas in Rwanda. Just about two months ago, I found out that they have experts in ports and water systems who are now based in Rwanda.

So a number of countries are seeing the relevance of the East Asia experience. Of course China is helping out on this because it is now awash with money. They are always accused of using money in somewhat political ways. In reality the Chinese firms are looking for places where they can invest, much like the Japanese were doing back in the 1950s, 1960s and 1970s in South Asia.

During my two years in Bangladesh, one of the things that astonished me was the increasing number of Chinese that were moving into Bangladesh, a place where you would not expect China to go easily. Many of their firms had moved in because they were looking for low labour costs. So now you are seeing the flying geese phenomenon being replicated in somewhat similar ways in other countries, and in Africa in particular.

Gender Equality and Economic Growth: A Rights Based Perspective

Diane Elson, with comments by Geske Dijkstra

Let me recognize the allure of economic growth: it appears to be very desirable because it looks as if it will provide more resources to be used to meet development objectives, such as the MDGs. Economic progress is widely judged in terms of economic growth, as measured by an increase in Gross Domestic Product per-capita, and falls in the rate of growth or no growth at all are widely viewed as a cause for concern. So today, as the financial crisis turns into a recession with global ramifications, one of the indicators we are often told about is the slow down in economic growth in fast-growing developing countries like China and India, and the falls in economic growth that some countries in Europe are experiencing. These are seen, quite rightly, as cause for concern.

But I also want to place on the agenda some doubts about economic growth, not all of which I am going to pursue but that I want to at least acknowledge. There are people who raise the question of whether what we think is economic growth is actually illusory and unsustainable. Does the growth process as we see it today really increase resources, or does it deplete resources and simply make them more visible by transferring them to the market? This is obviously a question that many people concerned with the environment have raised about sustainability and resource depletion. Many people concerned with social sustainability have raised questions about how equitable the kind of growth that we see today, the kind of growth that has been experienced in the last twenty to thirty years, actually is. Is it equitable or does it require and create inequality? Perhaps that is something that Michael Spence touched on earlier today in his presentation, but there is growing concern that the kinds of growth that we have seen, even in the fastest-growing countries, have been accompanied by substantial and indeed widening inequality, and China is a case in point.

Does it exclude many groups of people? That is also a question that is often raised. Does it leave some people behind, rural people, people in remoter areas of the country? Does it leave people who are not participating in labour markets behind and exclude them? I would also like to put on the agenda the question of whether it entails deprivations that violate human rights, recognizing that human rights include not just civil and political rights but also economic, social and cultural rights. And I will be particularly concerned with economic and social rights, and recognize that there may be people that certainly include it in the growth process, but not in ways that are fully consistent with human rights.

I want to focus particularly on the issue of gender equality and economic growth, and to signal that there are a variety of viewpoints on this. As I have only a short time to speak and cannot give a detailed overview of the whole field, I decided to pick out three contributions in particular. First, an early contribution made in the 1950s by Nobel Laureate Arthur Lewis, a Jamaican economist working also in the UK. He was a founding father of development economics. Secondly, mainstream economists such as Stephan Klasen from Germany, who has done a lot of detailed work recently on gender equality and economic growth. And thirdly, a feminist economist, Stephanie Seguino from the University of Vermont in the USA, who has also done a lot of work about gender and economic growth and came to somewhat different conclusions than Stephan Klasen. So I want to talk about the variety of views and the policy conclusions that might be derived from the evidence we have today.

Arthur Lewis on gender and economic growth

Let me start with Arthur Lewis, who was concerned with the implications of economic growth for people and for poverty. He argues that economic growth benefits women even more than men. In his book on the theory of economic growth, he had no doubt about this. He said: 'Women benefit from growth even more than men. Women gain freedom from drudgery, she is emancipated from the seclusion of the household and gains at last the chance to be a full human being exercising her mind and her talents in the same way as men'.

If economic growth could always be relied upon to bring those things about, then I would be inclined to agree with him. But I want to raise the question of whether the freedom from drudgery may sometimes be an exchange of one kind of drudgery for another kind of drudgery. Maybe the relinquishing of the drudgery of grinding and milling rice, grinding grains of various kinds and fetching fuel and water (through investments in an infrastructure that would do that for them) means assuming another kind of drudgery, like working very long hours for low pay in factories that produce exports for the world market, but which do not always pay a lot of attention to the health and safety of their workers.

Did women 'emancipate from the seclusion of the household'? Well, yes, that can be the case. But there is also the possibility that they can be part of the growth process. They can be getting paid for what they do, but while working at home where they are still in the seclusion of the household doing home-based work on contracts for factories that are producing toys or garments or fire-works to be sold in the international market. So the emancipation from the seclusion of the household is not guaranteed, and indeed there is evidence that home-based, paid work on sub-contracts of this kind is in fact growing, not withering away.

Then women 'gain at last the chance to be a full human being...'; well the problem is that the kind of growth that we have seen today goes along with a lot of segregation in the labour market. Women and men are typically segregated all over the world into different segments of the labour market, and women tend be much more segregated into the lower tiers of the labour market than are men. So again, that is a limited gain.

So if these things did take place, I think it would be a benefit. But we cannot assume that they do take place only because countries are fast growing. Therefore, we need to look at the quality of the growth, not just whether growth is taking place.

A particular reason why Arthur Lewis thought that growth reduces women's drudgery is, as he said, that most of the things that women otherwise do in the household can in fact be done much better or more cheaply outside. That is because of large economies of scale, specialization, and the use of capital. I can give you examples: grinding grain, fetching water from the river, making cloth, cooking midday meals, teaching children, nursing the sick, and so on.

I would agree with that assertion, if indeed economic growth does invest resources in applying capital to the production of these kinds of services, either in the private sector or the public sector. But we also need to have a caution here: we don't want a growth process that tries to get rid altogether of all unpaid work that people do in families and communities, particularly the unpaid work of caring for their loved ones. This is work that is very often a social obligation of women and girls to carry out (much more so than for men and boys), but work that does have social value and rewards as well as, potentially, being a source of drudgery.

We need to think not only of reducing the drudgery, but also that we have a growth process that enables people to combine unpaid work in their families and community with paid work outside the home. And is it a growth process that enables men and women to do this on an equal basis? Or are women still expected to specialize in the unpaid work that goes on in homes and communities to the detriment of their equal opportunities in the market-place?

Stephan Klasen's research on gender equality and economic growth

Now I want to talk about some more recent research looking at a different aspect of the relationship between gender equality and economic growth. And this doesn't look at whether economic growth reduces gender inequality or does or does not benefit women more than men. It looks at the relationship from the other angle: does gender equality promote economic growth? If a government pursues the policy of fostering equality, is it also a policy that will help foster faster economic growth? The research of Stephan Klasen has very much tended to give an answer of this being the case. He has done quite a lot of work on gender equality in education, arguing that this indeed promotes economic growth.

In an early and influential piece of work in 2002, he compared Sub Saharan Africa and East Asia. Sub Saharan Africa is a slow-growing region, if there was any growth at all in the period of 1960 to 2002, while East Asia was a fast growing region at that time (Klasen, 2002). He also looked at the gender gap in education in both cases. He found, of course, that in East Asia the gender gap in education has been eliminated. Girls and boys all go to school. But in Sub Saharan Africa, the gap has not yet been eliminated. The gap is such that far fewer girls than boys are in school, although that gap has been narrowing. So he looked at the implications of this, comparing growth in Sub Saharan Africa with East Asia.

He argued that the higher gender gaps in education in Sub Saharan Africa, and the slower reduction in the gender gaps, was one of the factors that accounted for why Sub Saharan Africa grew more slowly than East Asia. It is not the only reason of course, but it is a significant one. He argued that it accounted for 0.6 percentage points out of the 3.5 percentage-points-difference in the growth rates between the two regions in this period between 1960 and 1992.

More recently, he has done work with a colleague focussing in particular on the gender gap and growth in the context of the Millennium Development Goals (MDGs). As you know, closing the gender gap in enrolment in primary school by raising the enrolment of girls is a priority of the MDGs, and was supposed to be done by 2005. I am afraid it was the first MDG that was missed. But what Abu-Ghaida and Klasen (Abu-Ghaida & Klasen, 2004) examined was which countries were on track to meet this target. Many countries in regions like East Asia have already met it, but in the areas where they weren't, they investigated which ones were on track and which were not, and what was the impact on economic growth. They found that the impact on economic growth of countries that were not on track to meet this target was negative, and that these countries would have grown faster by 0.1 to 0.3 percentage points if they had been on track to close the gender gap. This is not an insignificant percentage point. These kinds of things make a difference to the kind of growth trajectory that countries of Sub Saharan Africa achieved compared to East Asia.

What is the underlying economic intuition? I think there are two kinds. One is that more educated workers are more productive and will therefore generate more output when they are employed, and that girls who are not as well educated as boys will have lower productivity when they engage in production.

The second is a somewhat more complex point about the demographic dividend. This is the point that more educated women, other things being equal, will have fewer children than less educated women. When women have fewer children, there is less need for government to invest in services for children. This frees up resources that can be used to invest in other things that can promote faster economic growth. For instance, they might switch from a lot of services in education and health for the children to more investment in infrastructural business services. For a couple of generations, this gives you what is known as the demographic dividend.

This is also an argument that underpins the quantitative econometric results achieved by Curfin, but as often in econometric analysis some other economists will come along and say: isn't the causation the other way around? Which means, as we say it in English: which comes first, the chicken or the egg? Another economist, Robbins, has argued that the causation is actually the other way around, in that the causation goes from increases in growth to increases in education of girls rather than vice versa. He found in a study of six Latin American countries that economic growth leads to rising educational attainment by drawing more women into the labour force. There are more jobs to be had, it increases the opportunity costs of women's time, it reduces fertility and it leads families to invest more in the education of their children, girls as well as boys. If you think that your daughters are going to be able to get jobs and bring money into the family, you will be more likely to send them to school. So he argues that the causation is the other way around, and that growth comes first and educational attainment comes after.

Paul Collier (Collier, 1994) and others also looked at gender equality in participation in the labour market as a promoter of economic growth. A study by Klasen and his colleagues for the Middle East and North Africa (Klasen & Lamanna, 2003), and also a study by another economist, Berta Esteve-Volart on India (Esteve-Volart, 2009), suggested that in both these regions economic growth would be higher if the gender gap in labour market participation were reduced through more women entering the labour market. Here again, the idea is that there are barriers to women entering the labour market and that if the government can have public policy that reduces the barriers, there will be more labour available and this will increase the rate of economic growth. But again, we could ask the question about causation: is it higher growth that pulls more women into the labour market rather than women entering the labour market pushing up economic growth?

I think this is a particularly pertinent question at the moment in the context of the global economic slowdown, because higher female participation rates might lead to higher female unemployment rather than higher economic growth.

Stephanie Seguino on economic development and gender equality

But I promised I would also look at the work of Stephanie Seguino, who is a feminist economist very concerned about economic development and gender equality. She looked at a different dimension of the labour market. She looks at gender inequality in wages, and she came up with a somewhat more disconcerting answer. She found that gender inequality in wages *promotes* economic growth. She reached this conclusion on the basis of looking at data for excessive export-oriented semi-industrialized countries from East Asia and Latin America, largely in the period between 1975 and 1995. She found that a 0.1 percentage increase in the gender wage gap leads to a 0.5 percentage point increase in GDP growth (Seguino, 2000b) (Seguino, 2000a). What is her economic theory underlying that?

Her theory was that in order to get economic growth, one of the important things is a stimulus to investment. You have to get

126

businesses deciding that it is worthwhile to invest. Because it is risky to invest, they need to be assured that they will get a good return on their investment. If there is a gender wage gap, which means that you can pay women lower rates than men, a substantial one, then this will give a particular incentive to companies to employ women in those export oriented industries, which is part of the first stage of fast export-oriented growth; industries in garments, in electronics assembly, and so on.

And indeed, this is what happened in East Asia: it gave a stimulus to companies to invest in those sectors that employ a lot of women so that they will make a good return on their investment, and, in addition (because they produce for exports) the country will reap foreign exchange. This foreign exchange can then be used to import technology from abroad that would spread the benefits of growth throughout the different sectors in the economy. The technology might not actually be used in the sectors that employ these women, but the fruits of their work will generate the foreign exchange that can pay for imports of new technology for other sectors in the economy.

She illustrated this important theory with a comparison between Korea and Chile in the period she was looking at. She found that GDP growth in Korea was 8 percent per year, and in Chile it was 5.3 percent per year. She argued that the wage differential in Korea was higher than in Chile, and that the wage differential accounted for 1.2 percentage points of that difference between the 8 and the 5.3 percent growth rates of Korea and Chile.

She also took on board the objection that could be made that this gender wage gap reflects the lower productivity of women workers because they have less education. So she did her analysis again, correcting the gender wage gap for gender differences in education and she found that it lowered the impact slightly but not substantially. There was still a 0.1 percentage increase in the gender wage gap that led to a 0.1 percentage point increase in GDP growth.

Again, with the point I made about Stephanen Klasen's work, one could raise the same issue about Stephanie Seguino's work: which way around is the causation? It could be argued that it is the faster economic growth in, for example South Korea, which kept the gender wage gap high. Faster economic growth has brought less educated, less skilled women into employment and this would have depressed the average level of women's earnings and tended to widen the gender wage gap when compared with countries that employed few women and only the more highly educated sector of women.

So it is fair to say that there are questions one could raise about both the work of Stephan Klasen and Stephanie Seguino in terms of the direction of causation. I have signalled that, but I also for a minute want to put that aside and look at the policy conclusions stemming from their different research. What we might conclude from their work is that to promote faster economic growth, a government should do three things: it should make sure it educates girls to the same level as boys by raising the education of both and it should reduce barriers to women's participation in the labour market, but it should not act to reduce the gender wage gap. So: 'Educate your girls but continue to discriminate against them in the labour market', might be the slogan we are getting at.

The gender wage gap and human rights

If we came to that conclusion and gave governments that advise, would it be in compliance with the human rights obligation of that government? I turn now to the Convention on the Elimination of all forms of Discrimination against Women (CEDAW), which has been signed and ratified by most countries in the world, albeit with some get-out clauses on family law by some countries. But it has been ratified by most countries in the world, and this places the obligation on governments to eliminate all forms of discrimination against women.

In so far as the gender wage gap reflects discrimination against women, advice to educate girls but to do nothing to diminish the gender wage gap would not be compliant with CEDAW. I use this just as an example of a tension there might be for governments about acting in compliance with their human rights obligations, and acting so as to try to maximize economic growth.

There are, of course, a number of other obligations on economic and social rights that governments should have regard to. Governments have obligations to protect workers' rights and their right to social security. I think this is spelled out in detail in the International Covenant on Economic, Social and Cultural Rights and the ILO Convention. Again, this is an instrument to which most governments in the world have committed themselves.

In this context you might note the growth of informal employment. Even in countries with fast economic growth, there has been a growth in informal employment that lacks those rights, does not have social protection and does not have strong rights to work. Informal employment has been growing, in fact, as a share in total employment and women workers in developing countries are more concentrated in it than men, that is they work more often in informal employment in the more precarious types of work with the lowest income. I refer here to some of the literature on this, for example a recent study published by UNIFEM, which brings together a lot of the evidence on this subject.

So I would like to emphasize that rapid employment creation might be necessary and that growth should be inclusive, but we need to go beyond that, because inclusion alone is not enough. It depends on the quality of employment, the quality of the labour market and on whether the labour market is regulated in a way that is in compliance with a government's human rights obligation.

Human rights and economic growth

Let me come to my final point. You might say: 'that is all very well, but is it possible to have human rights-compliant growth? It is difficult enough to have growth, why are you raising questions about whether growth is compliant with human rights?' Well, I am raising this because all of you here are concerned not only with growth but also with development. You are concerned with what the implications are of this growth on human well-being, not just how much output a country can produce.

So I want you to leave with the thought that human rights are compliant with growth, but that this requires well regulated markets, monetary and fiscal policies that focus on the provision of decent work, industrial policies that promote high productivity jobs, respect for the rights of workers to organize themselves and at least the taxation and public expenditure to provide public services and redistribute income.

This is perhaps a viewpoint that those of us in Northern Europe are somewhat familiar with. Today, some countries, particular in Northern Europe, have managed to combine rapid economic growth with similar policies and have the world's best outcome for gender equality.

But what about developing countries? Is it possible for them? Well, Stephanie Seguino, together with another economist, Caren Grown, have discussed this and have argued that a similar policy package for developing countries that emphasizes growth through enabling labour to be more productive and the return to be more fairly distributed, rather than growth fuelled by cheap labour, is possible (Grown & Seguino, 2006).

Obstacles to human rights policies compliant with economic growth

Is it possible for countries to perceive such a policy? I think there are obstacles to human rights-compliant policies, but there are also new opportunities. One internal obstacle in countries includes elites acting to safeguard their own privileges, and there is quite a good analysis of this in the World Development Report on Equity and Development which points to this problem.

There are also external obstacles, especially in poorly regulated international markets, that put pressure upon governments to compete by keeping labour cheap, by failing to protect workers rights and that punish more progressive policies with capital flight. Just recall what happened when the current Indian government was elected. It came to power having promised a policy of an employment guarantee scheme that would guarantee every rural household in India the right to one hundred days of work. If they could not get enough work from the other things that they were doing, the state would guarantee to provide them with one hundred days of work. The government recognized the right to work was part of their economic policy, but the news of their election was greeted with falls on the Mumbai stock exchange and a degree of capital flight. So here is a situation, and this is not the only example that I could give, where a government that did have some commitment to try and ensure that their policy for growth also addressed the issue of human rights (economic and social rights in particular) was punished with capital flight and falls on their stock exchange.

New opportunities

I think that the global economic crisis that we are now in has destroyed the case for the kind of regulation and organization of international financial markets that punish progressive governments that try to combine growth and human rights. So there are new opportunities for new thinking here. Particularly today, when I see what has been announced in the UK, where the government has now been forced to take over 70 percent ownership of one of the largest banks in the UK and opposition members in parliament say: 'Well, why don't we go for outright nationalization? Then it would be a lot easier to know for sure how many bad assets this bank actually owns!'

There is a lot of ferment for new thinking: we have got the thinking about a new Bretton Woods Agreement and new thinking about how to regulate international finance. Actually, we might say that it is more of a *rediscovery* of what the principles and objectives that the original Bretton Woods Agreement were, but which got displaced and lost over time. And within that I see some possibilities for new thinking about the Bretton Woods agenda, which the Group of Twenty (G20) is now going to have some meetings about: to push on the agenda the idea of broadening out the objectives and the framework, and to focus more explicitly on people's rights and, within that, on gender equality as a right.

What has given me cause for optimism? I have been invited to attend the Rights and Humanity meeting in London, which is being organized by the South African High Commission in London, the South African Human Rights Commission and the UK Rights and Development Organisation. The purpose is to bring together expertise from various fields to produce a document that tries to give some kind of rights-based moral compass for the G20 and their deliberations. This has the backing of both the Government of South Africa and of the UK.

So I do not think it is totally starry-eyed to start raising these questions. Yes, economic growth is very important, but it needs to be the kind of economic growth that helps the realization of human rights rather than undermines it, and within them then recognizes governments' obligation towards the elimination of all kinds of discrimination against women.

Comments by Geske Dijkstra

I don't disagree much with what has been said by Diane Elson, who really is a great name in the field of feminist development studies. What I will present is more of an extension of what she has said.

The efficiency argument

Let me therefore turn to my own argument for gender equality. This is not based on econometric research. This is partly based on observations, partly on empirical studies by others and partly on a kind of assumption. Of course you might question me on these assumptions. If you do not agree with me, I would like to hear it.

When I look at the efficiency curve for the whole economy, there is maximum allocative efficiency if we cannot move one productive factor to another use without reducing the benefits. So all production factors, capital and labour, are allocated in such a way that the net benefits for the whole economy are maximized. So this holds also for the production factor labour, for men *and* women. This means that if all talents are used to the maximum, and all persons do what they are best at for the economy, output will be raised to the maximum.

But this is a static form of efficiency. If I can prove that gender equality is good for allocative efficiency, it is static because moving for example women from unpaid work to paid work may lead to a simple once-and-for-all increase in output. But after that you don't get additional increases.

There is also a dynamic efficiency argument, and this will be about increasing the growth rates to permanently higher levels. So not only, for example, 3 percent growth in one year but permanently a 3 percentage points higher growth.

To prove this I need Diane Elson's book, which takes account of the male bias of the economy, 'The male bias in the development process' (Elson, 1995). Diane Elson argues that if you want to analyse macroeconomic issues, you have to take this male bias into account at three levels. First, the sexual division of labour, in terms of the different jobs that men and women have in the economy, then you must take into account the division of paid and unpaid work and care, and then finally the inequalities within the household.

To analyse gender inequality in the macro-economy, we have to look at these three levels. Combining these perspectives, I first try to show that gender equality increases the allocative efficiency. Well, men and women have different positions in the labour market. We call this segregation and this means that men tend to get higher positions in the labour market but also that men and women have different occupations at similar levels. If we could say that this is biological, that this is something inherent in how men and women are, and that this would explain fully the segregation, then economists cannot do anything anymore.

I argue, however, that this is not fully biological, and you can prove this by looking at different cultures. In the Netherlands, for example, for a long time you hardly saw any female medical doctors. In Russia there were *only* female medical doctors. So this proves there is nothing inherent, there is nothing automatic that men should be doctors, because in different cultures you see different things. So you can assume that less segregation probably means better allocative efficiency, that people use their talents better if they will move from one job or occupation to another.

As to the second level, as Diane Elson said, in all cultures it is mostly women that do most of the unpaid work and care. Also here we could say that this is not according to talent, but is mostly according to culture, power relations, stereotyping and the social-ization of boys and girls. Therefore, allocative efficiency in the economy could improve by having men doing more of the unpaid work.

Then, within the households, the third level, there is an unequal distribution, although this has been neglected by econo-mists for a long time. Many feminist authors, however, have written about this and found that the household is often a place of violence, neglect and discrimination. Also, here we could say that the advantages that men have in households, and boys as opposed to girls, especially in developing countries, are not due to any biological difference. This is not good for the economy. Of course, I am not saying that girls should get more food and boys should get less, but there is no inherent reason why boys should always get more than girls. And there are also other things aside from food – although many studies show that in developing countries girls get less food than boys – such as access to sleep, leisure, health care, education and so forth.

On the basis of this you can say that allocative efficiency in the economy, and thus economic growth, can increase as a conse-quence of more equality between men and women at all these three levels. That more gender equality also improves dynamic effi-ciency is a little bit harder to demonstrate but it is possible.

With respect to allocation of labour by gender, there are more and more studies that show that mixed teams perform better. If you have in a Board or in a company or a public body men and women working together, these companies have higher profits. This means you have a permanently higher growth rate if you have mixed teams.

With respect to unpaid work, we can assume that if men are more involved in the care of children, that children also benefit from that. It raises the quality of care. It is also possible to assume that if there is a more equal distribution of assets within house-holds among, especially, boys and girls, human capital improves. Human capital is an important factor in raising the growth rate in an economy. That is why, in all economic regressions, the level of education is so important. So, more equality in access to assets within households may also improve dynamic efficiency.

In this sense I would say that we don't need the human rights approach. We could use this efficiency argument, but I very much agree that we do need gender equality as a separate objective *along with* economic growth. Public policies are important for all of them, to foster economic growth itself, to secure growth with equity, including gender equity and also to promote gender equality separately. I think this is much more than to secure socio-economic rights. I do not think Diane Elson meant something else, but I just want to stress that. It is not just about these economic levels in society. Gender equality, as I said when I explained my argument, is about culture and power relations.

Dimensions of gender equality

Let me finally present the full picture of gender equality in all its dimensions as I see it, and I think that public policies have a role to play in all of them. *Gender identity* is one dimension that is about the socialization of boys and girls, the stereotyping of jobs for example, this cultural aspect. *The autonomy of the body* is another dimension that is about the sexual and reproductive rights of women and the absence of violence. *Autonomy within the household*, which is about the decision-making power of women as opposed to men in the household, and also the freedom to marry and to divorce. *Political power*, which is about decision-making powers above the household level: municipal, provincial, national, etc. *Access to social resources* like health and education, *access to material resources* and here we can speak of land and credit, labour and income; this is the whole area of wage policies, social security policies, also the division between paid and unpaid labour. And finally an important dimension, you would perhaps say this is all but there is another one which I particularly like, and that is *time*, time use of men and women, because this means access to leisure and sleep. In all societies on average men have more access to leisure and sleep than women. I think that this is even the case in the Netherlands, but it is especially true in developing countries.

I think this is a very important dimension. And, as I said, public policies in all of these areas are important to bring about gender equality in all its dimensions.

Comments by the Mayor of Dar es Salaam, Tanzania

I agree with the suggestion that there are strong links between gender equality and economic growth. Or in other words: gender based inequality limits economic growth, and it diminishes the effectiveness of poverty reduction efforts. I am also convinced that closing the gender gap in schooling will boost economic growth.

In Tanzania, there are three different regions where the education gap was closed during the colonial time, brought about by the missionaries who came to those areas. These are the areas around Kilimanjaro, where there are mainly coffee and banana growers. The standard of education of both boys and girls even before independence was very high. And today you see that the standard of living of both men and women in that particular area under the foot of Mount Kilimanjaro is very high compared to the rest of the country. Then there is the region of Bukoba around lake Victoria, which is also inhabited by coffee growers and fish eaters, where the standard of education has been very high all along. Therefore, in comparative terms, compared with the rest of the country, there is a big difference: its economy is doing very well.

Likewise, the missionaries came to Southern Tanzania. Let me compare the level of education of that place to the place where I come from, where 95 percent of the population is Muslim. I can assure you, we did not have education: the level of education of boys there is minimal, that of girls is negligible.

Now the growth pattern in our culture makes different demands on men's and on women's labour, with different implications for the distribution of labour and the distribution of income. In our case, women are engaged in heavy workloads on many shores: you find women fetching water and fire wood, caring for children, the elderly and the sick (including those suffering from HIV) and looking after the cattle and, of course, milking them. And if you question a typical African man about this, he would say: 'But what is wrong with this? It is just a division of labour and specialization!' If an African man would listen to the lecture today, he would say there is something wrong with the lecturer.

Given the economic potential that women possess, we just condemn them in those activities. We are not tapping their economic potential. Besides, they are not rewarded justly for this kind of work, because they are not selling anything or receiving pay or rewards. Their employment becomes a tool of oppression. They get oppressed or, to be ruder, they get condemned in their areas.

What needs to be done? They need to be liberated from these heavy workloads, they need to be enabled to provide their labour as economic producers and be rewarded justly. They need to benefit from the budget of the ministry of national resources by reallocation of land, and to be provided with other assets such as bank loans so that they can also enjoy the fruits of economic growth and contribute more effectively to their economic well-being and that of the nation.

Public policies need to recognize women's contribution to national economic growth. For example, their contribution in taking care of future labour is very important. Because: who provides for the future labour of the country? We all know the answer. With this recognition, public policies and budgets need to be redirected to meeting and benefiting the needs of women.

There are also issues of maternal health services and water services. There are still women in Africa who live under a lot of stress because they have to go 10 miles to fetch water. She typically cares for the family with a bunch of firewood on her head, a baby on her back and buckets of water in her hand. This is a typical situation that still exists in some parts of Africa. Women are typically persecuted in wartime because there is gender violence. And there are still some tribes that do not only marry between five to ten wives, but they also beat them. When they are very happy they beat them, and when they are very angry they beat them.

References

Abu-Ghaida, D., & Klasen, S. (2004). The costs of missing the millennium development goals on gender equity. *World Development*, 32(7), 1075-1107.

Collier, P. (1994). Gender aspects of labour allocation during structural adjustment; A theoretical framework and the African experience. In: S. Horton, R. Kanbur & D. Mazumdar (Eds.), *Labour markets in an era of adjustment*. Washington: The World Bank.

Elson, D. (Ed.). (1995). *Male bias in the development process* (2d ed.). Manchester/New York: Manchester University Press.

Esteve-Volart, B. (2009). *Gender discrimination and growth: Theory and evidence from India*. York: York University.

Grown, C., & Seguino, S. (2006). Gender equity and globalization: Macroeconomic policy for developing countries. *Journal of International Development*, 18(8), 1091-1104.

Klasen, S. (2002). Low schooling for girls, slower growth for all? cross-country evidence on the effect of gender inequality in education on economic development. *World Bank Economic Review*, 16(3), 345-373.

Klasen, S., & Lamanna, F. (2003). *The impact of gender inequality in education and employment on economic growth in the middle east and north Africa*. Munich: University of Munich.

Seguino, S. (2000a). Accounting for gender in Asian economic growth. *Feminist Economics*, 6(3), 22-58.

Seguino, S. (2000b). Gender inequality and economic growth: A cross-country analysis. *World Development*, 28(7), 1211-1230.

The Technological Divide

Luc Soete

In this lecture, I will focus on the issue of technology and look at three different topics. First, I will discuss how the technological divide as we know it has changed over time, and what it represents today in view also of some of the shifts that have taken place with respect to the way we look at science and technology. In particular, I will focus on the debate on how technology has shifted to innovation. I will try to be pretty short on this, and will come back later to some of the aspects of information and communication technologies and the nature of technological change.

I will then enter into a topic which is at the centre of current concerns: the notion of 'research on the move' and the way in which research has changed within companies, public organizations and universities, and how we should go back to the idea of 'recherche sans frontières'[1] as an idea of research that unites us globally and that is also globally seen as a common good. And, of course, I cannot escape talking a little bit about the challenges of the financial crisis with respect to this particular topic.

The technological divide

It is really surprising to see how development took place from the beginning of the nineteenth century up to 1973 with a continuous increasing divide in welfare between the West, the advanced OECD countries, and the rest of the world.[2] Behind that increasing divide is primarily the development of China and India. It is remarkable to see that in the period from 1820 until 1973, the population share of these two countries increased continuously while their share in GDP diminished. Nineteen seventy-three was probably the year with the highest imbalance in the world's concentration in GDP as compared to the world's concentration in population. It is not surprising that many of the people of my generation were probably mostly influenced by that period, in which they also did their economic studies while witnessing a continuously growing divide between rich and poor. It is also remarkable to see how strongly that translated into social science research. Ulrich Beck[3] made reference to that in his recent book, referring to the fact that most social scientists focussed on aspects of national competitiveness, and that domestic competitiveness, and in particular technological competitiveness, is an essential feature of a country's future economic growth.

The consequences of globalization for sociology have been spelled out most clearly in the English speaking countries, but above all in England itself, where it has been forcefully argued that conventional social and political science remains caught up in a national-territorial concept of society. Critics of 'methodological nationalism' have attacked this explicit or implicit premise that the national state is the 'container' of social processes and that the national framework is still the one best-suited to measure and analyse major social, economic and political change. The social sciences are thus found guilty of 'embedded statism' and thought is given to a reorganization of the interdisciplinary field.

This search for explanations for growth is furthermore based on this continuous divide between rich and poor countries, as is shown in the following tables.

Table 1 shows that the percentage of China's population in the world was declining, to some extent contrary to India's population, between 1950 and 1973, while their GDP as a share of world income dropped to 4.6 and 3.1 percent in 1973. These two countries, together, represent something like 39 percent of world population, against only 7.7 percent of world GDP. You see also what happened with the figures of 2001 compared to those of 1973: while the share in world population more or less remained the same, their joint GDP increased from 7.7 percent in 1973 to 17.7 percent in 2001.

Table 1   China, India, Brazil and South Africa in the world economy

Year	China	India	Brazil	South Africa
Percentage share of world population				
1820	36.6	19.9	0.4	0.1
1870	28.1	17.0	0.8	0.2
1913	24.4	14.2	1.3	0.3
1950	21.7	14.8	2.1	0.5
1973	22.5	14.8	2.6	0.6
2001	20.7	16.5	2.9	0.7
Percentage share of world income				
1820	32.9	16.0	0.4	0.1
1870	17.1	12.1	0.6	0.2
1913	8.8	7.5	0.7	0.4
1950	4.5	4.2	1.7	0.6
1973	4.6	3.1	2.5	0.6
2001	12.3	5.4	2.7	0.5

Source: Maddison (2003).

If you look at long-term industrialization or the late industrialization of China and India, recent studies and calculations show that the current industrialization path over the last decades from a global perspective appears to be totally unsustainable. I refer here to a study of Alex Izurieta and Ajit Singh that was done in a very neat way in their work on the Cambridge World Economic Model.[4.]

As long as advanced countries grow at 3 percent per annum, aiming to respond to the needs of their aging societies, their social security needs and other promises with respect to public funding, and as long as China and India continue to grow at current growth rates of 7 or 8 percent, that would lead very quickly to supply shocks or supply limits with respect to both agricultural production, raw materials, access to water and climate impacts. Yet, at the same time, fast economic growth in China and India is really a social necessity because they are confronted with the need to shift hundreds of millions of people from farms to industry. Therefore, they need economic growth that results from these efficiency gains. Furthermore, in the Indian case they still have very significant population growth.

I wrote a paper last year as part of a European forecasting exercise. It is surprising to read again these forecasting exercises, which were all written before last year's quarter. The name of that report was: 'Malthus' Revenge'.[5] It took as its starting point the idea of the famous Malthus quote: 'The power of population is so superior to the power of the earth to produce subsistence for men, that premature death must in one way or another visit the human race'. If you take the different rates of growth, the arithmetic and the geometric rate of growth of agricultural production and population growth, and if you took out the word population, which of course has been to some extent the element by which Malthus has been disproven, and exchange it for consumption, and not just the real consumption but the aspiration to consume, linked to the diffusion of information and communication technology, which has made the differences in levels of consumption between different parts of the world transparent, than very clearly this Malthus quote becomes suddenly very relevant. This is because, to some extent, as you are dealing with information and communication technology a new level playing field has emerged: a level playing field in aspirations in consumption, income, quality of life, work and in that which everyone expects of this life in terms of achievements for himself or for his children.

The technological divide that I am talking about here is expressed in the usual way in Figure 1, which shows almost physically the countries in terms of their R&D expenditures. Of course you observe immediately the very dramatic dominance of the US, Europe, Japan, and, increasingly also China with a little bit of India there too.

The technological revenues in Figure 2 include all those payments that have been received on the basis of technological efforts. We observe that the divide is even more substantial with the US even more dominant, but with Europe and Japan being there and China representing still very little in this stage.

142

Figure 1   R&D expenditures

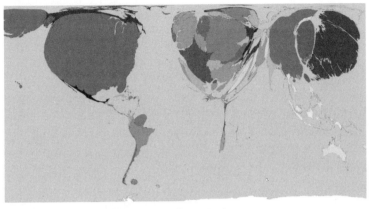

Source: Social and Spatial Inequalities Group, Sheffield University

Figure 2   Technological revenues

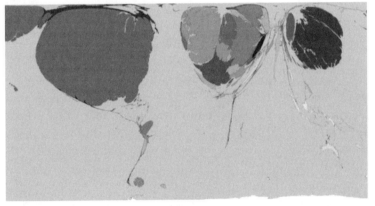

Source: Social and Spatial Inequalities Group, Sheffield University.

To conclude, the technological divide is there, and it is very significant with respect to investments in research and development expenditures. It is even more significant with respect to the immediate, direct measure of return from those investments in terms of technological revenues, which typically refer to license payments with respect to patents, copyrights, various forms of trade marks and so on.

The past, present and the future of science and technology

How should we look at science and technology in the present, starting from the past, and give some ideas about possible future developments? I can be very brief on the past. Industrial research and development is something that is very well recognized in most of the literature and in policy debates today. The 'knowledge investment action plan' in the Netherlands shows that research and development expenditures will always emerge as a central policy concern, whether with respect to private or to public R&D expenditures.

The strong focus on industrial R&D, though, is a relatively recent phenomenon. It is a phenomenon that has emerged with the industrial revolution. Before the industrial revolution, clearly there was technological research as there were continuous improvements with respect to tools and machines. Works were carried out by engineers and mechanics in ordinary workshops, and the development work took place alongside the production work.

This type of inventive work can still be recognized: we only have to go to research labs to identify it. It is also very interesting to see what they do at home. There is still a whole lot of experimentation on a small scale being carried out by most of the people involved in technological work. What became distinctive about modern, industrial R&D was its scale, the way it was organized in research laboratories, the instrumentation they used and the equipment that suddenly became available. Suddenly you had a dramatic shift in terms of the science base of that sort of R&D. That is what the old Dutch economic historian Joel Mokyr calls the 'tightness' of knowledge[6] and as such of science and technology.

But it is important to remember that the older 'arts and crafts technologies' in all the different sectors continue to exist side by side with these new industrial technologies. Given the way they were being used, however, they show something like a gradual shift. We started to get much more technical recognition to high tech sectors with strong R&D investment, as opposed to sectors that could very well be important in the engineering sense and carry a lot of older techniques and crafts, but that were considered to be low-tech intensive.

These typical classifications became very popular in the literature, and that became to some extent the basis of what you could call today industrial technology policy with its obsession with how to strengthen national technology competitiveness. You could observe this not only in the Netherlands, but in Europe as well. This was a shift that took place in the 1960s and the 1970s, when most industrial policies were aimed at international adjustments from a global perspective and with a view to some kind of international division of labour. Sectors where productivity growth would not be so substantial would be adjusted downwards versus other sectors with more growth potential.

That debate led to the development of the idea of sunrise industries, starting with Etienne Davignon's support[7] for political and/or economic reasons, of those new high-tech sectors and industries. It led also to the ultimate political sign of nationalism in the technological sense, which was the famous so called 'three percent Barcelona Research and Development/GDP ratio'[8] and was a target that arose from the concern that Europe would be very significantly behind the US and Japan with respect to those knowledge investments.

Going back to what I mentioned about Ulrich Beck: what resulted is a very nationalistic view that the R&D investments in each of these countries would lead to higher productivity gains, to stronger competitiveness and to more welfare within the national boundaries. We all know of course that that is anything but the truth, and that when you talk about R&D, it is rather the opposite.

The present: new characteristics of innovation

It is interesting to observe that suddenly we do not talk anymore about R&D, but instead we are talking now about innovation. Innovation has entered the political debate in the most dramatic way. I would say that with the Lisbon summit and what came after it, this translates into all kinds of new policy instruments. In the

Netherlands, you can think of the innovation platform and various other political ways in which one has expressed this concept as a much broader notion that also reflects to some extent a fundamental change.

I would argue that traditional, industrial R&D is very much a process that is relatively well established and well documented, whereby researchers are carrying out progress along very clearly-defined trajectories with very clear criteria of progress, with an ability to say where one has been and where one has arrived, as opposed to what was initially planned, and a clear way in which one can evaluate progress. That was what Dick Nelson calls an ability to hold in place, to replicate, to imitate: what I have done in the research lab I can transfer into commercial exploitation. That involves a whole new set of technologies, in engineering fields in particular. Those have to be developed in order to get something that has been produced in a research lab on a small scale to be turned into industrial production on a larger scale. That gave birth to new fields of chemical engineering and electrical engineering, electronic engineering, etc.

By definition, this is a very strong cumulative process where one learns from natural and deliberate experiments. This is something that takes time, and is a slow process whereby think tanks are continuously underlying this process with providing tightness in terms of scientific proof. My claim is that ICT has changed this quite radically: that ICT has to some extent opened this up in the most dramatic way because suddenly it brings in different circumstances in which those technologies can be tried out. It leads also to some extent to flexibility.

The role of users

In short, the changing external environments over time, over sectors and in space make it very difficult to evaluate the research process. You have, to some extent, trial-and-error research and trial-and-error innovation. In there, though, there were a couple of elements that were crucial, which is in particular the role of users. The role of users becomes now absolutely central, and not just users as passive consumers as with technology, where you typically have the beta users. Now you have users that can interact, who feed back and interact and tell you precisely what is working and what not in the particular new technologies or with respect to innovations.

This has led to a shift also at the policy level from, you could say, industrial technology to innovation policies in general. These policies address a much broader area of what we are typically used to. They typically do not address only the R&D activities within research laboratories, but also a much broader set of activities. Some of those could be routine activities that formerly were not part of the industrial R&D. They now include what engineers are doing in their departments, what possibly the people in the marketing divisions are doing and what designers are doing. All of that is now part of the innovation policy.

The outsourcing, the open innovation aspects, the aspects of being carried out by parties that are not part of the industrial research and development efforts, which will provide research with new ideas, deliver subcomponents and deliver ideas, are all becoming part of the same concern for innovation policies. And some of the elements, such as design engineering, which traditionally are outside the R&D department, become more crucial as well.

I have already mentioned the importance of interaction with users, and to some extent at the innovation side we are now confronted with a blurring distinction between the innovator and the user. Sometimes the users are becoming themselves the innovators. You see this most clearly in the open software community where they are talking about a 'cooking pot model'.[9]

The distinction between the real technical nerds, the inventors who have the good idea and the users who come up with particular usage which nobody thought of becomes very much blurred. One can be part of a community in an increasing number of fields, not just the open source software community. It is becoming very popular also in the biology field. As an organizational method, it is becoming increasingly popular as a way of organizing knowledge and research activities.

Research on the move

Now what does this all mean? The picture of the future that I would like to outline here is very much one of global research and local innovation. It is very clear that at the research level, universities and public research institutions are increasingly becoming part of international research communities. They will interact with other researchers worldwide. This is the community in which one operates according to some of the principles I already mentioned, such as in the open source software community. What becomes much more important, however, at the level of innovation are the local context conditions which direct developments. This is what I call and would like to debate: research on the move.

The most fascinating area we are confronted with today, also from the development perspective, is the notion of the global sharing of knowledge as a source of innovation. The idea of having 'collaborative innovation' in all of these countries that are part of my original picture of the technological divide with very low R&D expenditures is becoming very interesting to firms and organizations located in the North. The physical concentration of R&D in the North could go hand in hand with a much more collaborative innovation process, but it will require a number of conditions.

It requires first of all access to knowledge, not just in terms of having legal access as users but also in terms of being able to change that knowledge, to replicate, adjust and improve that knowledge, specifically with regard to local conditions.

This brings to the fore the crucial role of various communities of practise: local users, implementers, possibly non-governmental organizations and others. The role of the local public sector in this could very well be in setting the fences of the commons, in nature but also in innovations, in 'creative commons'. In other words, what we get is a much more global picture with, on the one hand, a very strong unequal distribution of R&D activities and R&D investments, but, on the other hand, much stronger global collaborative interaction.

Conclusions (1)

My first conclusions on this will be the following: knowledge sharing shifts its attention away from the purely technological aspects of research to the broader organizational, economic and social aspects that are today in many cases a more important factor behind innovation. This is reflected to some extent in the much greater popularity of the term 'innovation' than 'research and development', in the West, in the North and in the South.

Innovation is, at the same time, as relevant to poor countries as it is to rich countries. This holds a priori for countries with large, young populations where the potential for innovation, once users and consumers are identified as sources of innovation , can easily be enhanced. In doing so, innovation is becoming less driven by R&D and at the product end by the continuous search for quality improvements, typical of the old mode of technology progress identified with the high-income groups in society, but now by broader user needs across society. At the same time, such innovation demands might feed back to R&D departments in new ways, further globalizing the impact of research. This is really the core of what I would like to put forward as a hypothesis, i.e., that the underlying changes that I have described above challenge quite fundamentally research activities in our countries, including the Netherlands. You could say that research in the past has been governed by nationalism, focussing on research within borders. The EU is the most beautiful example of this 'research within borders': Europe is considered as 'l'espace de recherche Européen'.

The Lisbon Treaty fits to some extent with this view. It was a sort of correction on the EU institutional set up. You had the competition policy, which did not necessarily provide growth and innovation dynamics. It created, on the contrary, a lot of legal uncertainty with respect to national research policies of its member states. You had monetary and fiscal policies with the growth and stability pact under the Maastricht Treaty, which again did not provide anything on technology. So for me the Lisbon Treaty is the culmination of fifty years of European cocooning.

The challenge today is what I have called the 'recherche sans frontières'. Research is becoming increasingly global. But in most applied research fields it is driven mostly by the developed world, while many of the most challenging research questions are often taking place within developing countries.

Broadening the scope

I am shifting the discussion here from fundamental, basic research to applied research. But even in applied research, whether we talk about the research carried out in technical universities or in the framework programmes within the EU, most of the resources and demands are coming from within the developed world whereas the most challenging research questions are from within the developing countries.

There is a need to increase and to broaden the scope of research activities to include much more systematically the various groups of practise, but also what I regard as design possibilities of collaborative innovation processes with various research communities in developing countries. As organizations with a wealth of user knowledge, local community expertise and non-for-profit interest that gives a voice to all these people who have needs, and where there are clearly tremendous needs in terms of innovation, NGOs could well play a significant role there as initiators of research for development projects. From an innovation/research perspective this is probably the most interesting element: it is expensive to be poor and it is expensive to service the poor. This provides a perfect business model for innovation in those areas.

Alternative models driving product innovation

Most of our product innovations in the developed countries have been driven by a very simple kind of model. This model was based on how I can convince the average consumer that he needs better products and more quality features to the products he consumes today. The way this was done is by looking at the professional users, identify their needs, bring them into the products, consider them as new technical quality improvements and then, through the marketing division, convince the average consumer that these are the product characteristics that he needs.

So all of you are probably now running around with a watch that says it is water resistant up to 50 meters deep. I know that I am dead after 20 meters, but my watch will still be working! We will probably be sitting in cars where we have sound from our audio systems in cars of a couple of square meters wide which could serve as an audio system for the hall that is used for this lecture! We will have calamity images on 3D television sets that are used for surgical operations while we use them, sitting on our sofa, watching TV. We will go and buy a tennis racket that was used by Björn Borg when he won his first Wimbledon title. We are tempted to buy the same racket so that we might be able to pass a couple of balls across the net!

In each of these areas the technological and the quality improvements have become the standard way of product innovation, and the design and the marketing elements have just been elements whereby the typical beta user, or the fashion model or the sportsman or the movie star, etc., are the typical images to which we as average consumers look at and then want to have the same product features.

An emerging innovation development paradigm

That model has worked extremely well in the past, but doesn't work anymore because of globalization. The competition in these products is shortening so much that the time to reap monopoly rents out of these additional quality features is too short to pay for research needed to continue along this quality improvement trajectory. In other words, professional use demand has directed innovation very much to the top of the income pyramid. This has allowed us to add continuously these product quality features. In a global setting, this has offered tremendous opportunities for growth expansion. The new classes, the new emerging high-income groups in India and China, have offered tremendous opportunities for these new and high-income goods. But to some extent, also you very quickly come to the limit of your global market because there are of course competing firms also starting to produce these goods.

In the absence of any kind of Keynesian redistribution policies, there is a search on the part of the business community to find solutions elsewhere. Remembering Fords T-model, the solution might be in finding products that are standardized, low quality and cheap, but that contain a major innovation element.

Challenging characteristics in developing country contexts

Developing markets appear to raise some of the most motivating research and innovation challenges. The first of these challenges is autonomy. Most of our innovations are heavily dependent in infrastructure. In all developed countries, the range of product and process innovations introduced have always been dependent on constant and high-quality access to energy, broadband, roads, water, sanitation and so forth. But if you go to a situation where you don't have those high-quality physical infrastructures, suddenly your whole research and innovation pattern changes quite abruptly, because suddenly you now want to develop products that have autonomy in them. It is no surprise that mobile communication diffused so radically differently and very rapidly world wide, and, in particular, in countries in Africa. In other words, in contexts where you are missing the physical infrastructure that you typically find in industrialized countries, you will find very rapid diffusion of technologies that provide some kind of autonomy, in this case in access to energy.

So being unwired to high-quality infrastructure is actually a phenomenal area of research motivation and research interest. Where you see this, of course, is with the military in Iraq and Afghanistan. To be autonomous to physical infrastructure, whether that be energy, water, clear drinking water, etc., becomes suddenly a major motive to start research on decentralized systems that provide you access to freedom of movement, so to say, exactly like the motorcar at the time, but now with respect to energy. Think of the various forms of putting in solar captures in clothing.

A second characteristic in the development context is simplicity of use, which is essential given the low education levels. You cannot start to explain when education is lacking; you even have to assume that people are illiterate in the real sense. So you must find design techniques that correspond to simplicity in use. Which big firm has used simplicity in use as its new credo? So you have a shift from the sophisticated beta users, the nerds, to the needs of the digital illiterates.

A third characteristic that is typical in the developing country context is the fact that you do not have or cannot have maintenance or repair infrastructure. Once broken down, the goods will be lost. Again, what is a better application than from cradle to cradle in such environments?

Finally, you have environments with extremely high-income inequalities and strong needs in urban slums and poor, rural villages, with little current purchasing power and high living risks. Hence, you have low willingness to invest or borrow money in the long-term.

How do you solve this? Again, look at the whole area of micro-credit and micro-insurance, and how it has developed and is coming back and is starting to be developed in New York and other developed environments. In short, we are witnessing a dramatic transformation in elements of motivation in countries with totally different contexts and environments, and which are not based on this trajectory of innovation (as we have known it here in the developed world that is rich in infrastructure).

Innovation for development

This brings to the forefront a number of interesting insights that I would like to call innovation for development, whereby the role of local communities as professionalized non-governmental grass-roots organizations becomes absolutely crucial. Strategic alliances are emerging between NGOs, multinational firms, banks, microcredit financial institutions, etc., that are carrying out activities that are not part of traditional high level R&D centres. The innovation process is now being reversed: you start with trying to find a very good description of a problem, then look first at the design and ultimately arrive at the fundamental research on how to solve this problem. The outcome of this might then flow back to the research lab in the West.

In short, what you are witnessing is a whole set of new flows of technology from the South to the North that are reinvigorating and motivating the development research community in the highly developed world. I can guarantee you that in a number of fields – in the medical field, the food field, nutrition, in firms and research laboratories and in organizations within universities that I visited – you find exactly the kind of inspirations and reinvigoration I referred to.

Sanitation in India

I will not go much further into this, but I will show you one example, which is sanitation in India. Sanitation is one of the most dramatic problems in the developing world and is also reflected in the Millennium Development Goals and still unsolved at this moment in time. The Indian government provides subsidies that try to change the dramatic figures on the lack of coverage of sanitation in schools and households. Now, despite all the subsidies, the fundamental problem remains that you don't get a shift in the incentives with regard to the behaviour of consumers, in this case the users of toilets. In this sense it is to some extent a question of designing a market for toilets for the poor. The reason is that toilets for the poor are considered as merit goods that must be provided by governments or charitable NGOs.

As Shyama Ramani[10] has put it, there is a strong preference in the bottom-of-the-pyramid group to use scarce revenues for other essential goods or entertainments goods that provide temporary relief. With a couple of NGOs, we have tried to develop a micro-insurance project by adding an element of insurance to microfinance institutions.[11] Clearly the microfinance institutions are very interested in life insurance: it is their interest that their clients have life insurance. You are talking about very small amounts of money. It is a policy that is very easily implemented and with quite some success. The issue is now: can you add an element of health insurance that is linked to the use of sanitation. This is something we are thinking about, with a Dutch NGO, WASTE.[12].WASTE is working with something like sixty microfinance institutions in India as well as a number of research institutions in India and Tata AIG. I hope they still survive in the current situation as an insurance company. They provided me with this picture, which gives you an idea of the sort of products they try to develop in terms of financial and insurance products for the various parts of the income pyramid (see Figure 3).

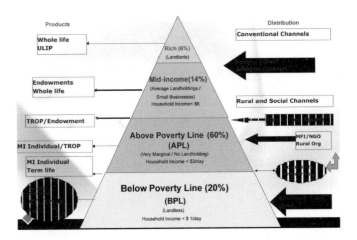

Figure 3   Rural life markets – products and distribution
Source: TATA AIG

People living below the poverty line are very difficult to address because it is practically impossible to develop any of the products I mentioned in the area of health insurance or life insurance associated with microcredit. By at least addressing the people above the poverty line, and making sure that they don't fall back to below the poverty line, you can adjust to some extent and therefore develop an insurance policy that could actually have a significant impact on your overall health expenses. Additionally, it would also solve at least partially some of the consequences of the financial crisis.

Consequences of the financial crisis

This lecture series is like a road show: it goes on and I am sure that the next lecture will give a different story from what Michael Spence[13] gave you in January and Rick van der Ploeg[14] before him, and it will be interesting to look back at their slides in a couple of years to see how correct or wrong they were in their predictions. With respect to the financial crisis, let me add my personal view, which is that I think that we are witnessing a double squeeze. There is nothing new to this, but it makes that your banks are not any longer functioning as tools by which you could address the crisis. You are basically dealing with dead bodies. I have written a paper on this and put it quite bluntly there by comparing the financial system and banks with black holes in astronomy: they are absorbing funds and are no longer sending out any economic energy in the sense of any credits. The result though, is that we are witnessing also a declining financial sector in small countries with domestic repatriation of financial services, a reduction in their profitability given their risk aversion, and a rapid reduction in employment despite heavy state involvement. In other words, you are moving from some kind of positive, towards a negative self-reinforcing externality effect. This is, as Joe Stiglitz has put it[15] a kind of non-linear feature: in the last eight years, you have had the positive element with increased leverage in a very significant way, with financial innovation, with rising asset prices. And then suddenly, at a certain moment in time, there is this collapse that leads exactly to the opposite: a self reinforcing negative mechanism with banks from an internal logic trying to restore their solvency, with commercial paper markets collapsing into itself and trying to solve their internal problems, and with economic contraction leading to further contraction.

On the crisis and the needs for knowledge investments, it is very interesting that in the Dutch debate, but also in the G20 debates in their preparations in London, the discussion remains very much focussed not on the global imbalances, to which the Dutch economy contributed quite significantly by the way, and not on the environmental and the sustainability nature of the global crisis, while in my view global access to knowledge is central to the current crisis. There is a clear demand in emerging and developing countries that depend on technology transfer and access to technology. Global access to markets raises the return to knowledge investments in the Netherlands and the global and environmentally sustainable growth crucially dependent on the rapid diffusion of technology in the current era. If there is one area today where the technological nationalism of the last century is totally at odds with the needs of today, it is in the area of environmental technology.

It is in the interest of us citizens of the developed, rich part of the globe to have technology diffused as rapidly as possible. It makes no sense to have notions of technological nationalism or technological competitiveness with respect to these sectors. The issue here is that we dramatically reverse and change the tech-

Figure 4 The global knowledge challenge

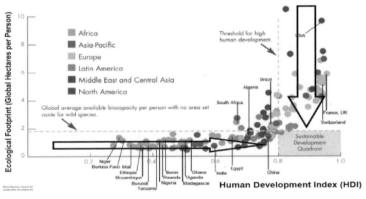

Source: WBCSD.

nology and innovation policies from the national obsession with technology competitiveness to this new global view. This is the ultimate global knowledge challenge.

In Figure 4, on the one hand you find the Human Development Index, on the other hand the ecological footprint as measured by

Figure 5   Crisis scenarios

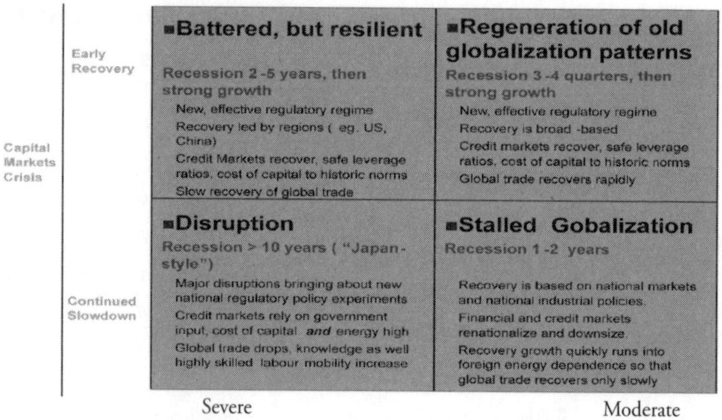

	Severe	Moderate

Early Recovery	**■Battered, but resilient**
	
	Recession 2 -5 years, then strong growth
	  New, effective regulatory regime
	  Recovery led by regions (eg. US, China)
	  Credit Markets recover, safe leverage ratios, cost of capital to historic norms
	  Slow recovery of global trade
		■Regeneration of old globalization patterns
		
		Recession 3 -4 quarters, then strong growth
		  New, effective regulatory regime
		  Recovery is broad -based
		  Credit markets recover, safe leverage ratios, cost of capital to historic norms
		  Global trade recovers rapidly

Continued Slowdown	**■Disruption**
	Recession > 10 years ("Japan-style")
	  Major disruptions bringing about new national regulatory policy experiments
	  Credit markets rely on government input, cost of capital *and* energy high
	  Global trade drops, knowledge as well highly skilled labour mobility increase
		■Stalled Gobalization
		Recession 1 -2 years
		
		Recovery is based on national markets and national industrial policies.
		Financial and credit markets renationalize and downsize.
		Recovery growth quickly runs into foreign energy dependence so that global trade recovers only slowly

(vertical axis label: Capital Markets Crisis)

Source: McKinsey Global Institute

the World Business Council for Sustainable Development. Countries are listed according to these two criteria. There are two fundamental technological challenges. One is to bring back the rich countries into a sustainable development quadrant in terms of the distribution of their production and consumption. The other is to bring developing countries into the sustainable quadrant by making sure that these emerging economies are not just growing up to much higher ecological footprints.

Figure 5 shows a framework with the different sorts of crisis scenarios, developed by McKinsey Global Institute. It is actually interesting that only if the crisis would be severe and if you have a severe economic global recession that you could hope that there might be such disruption in your system that there would be new national regulatory policy experiments, that you would have shifts in terms of global trade and that knowledge as well as skilled labour mobility would become the engines of your global society. To put it in other terms, putting names on the four scenarios: the no-change scenario, as also Arnold Heertje[16] mentioned, will lead you very quickly back into unsustainable growth associated with high oil prices, raw material and agricultural price increases. Crises will reoccur also in new areas, such as water, health, environmentally induced migration, and the like.

Figure 6 Global development

		Severe	Moderate
Capital Markets Crisis	Early Recovery	**■Balanced growth** Redirection of global financial flows in a more balanced way Growth in US and UK savings, reduction in reserves in China and S -E Asia – new role for IMF Stronger representation of emerging countries in international financial organizations Growing international trade conflicts	**■No change** At first rapid recovery Limits to unsustainable growth (oil price, raw materials, agriculture increases) expressed in re -occurrence of crises in new areas (water, health, environmentally induced migration, ...) Rising inequality and exclusive growth, resulting in unsustainable social exclusion, increased security costs
	Continued Slowdown	**■Knowledge globalization** Dramatic slowdown in trade of goods, with severe structural unemployment & new specialization patterns emerging New priority on global implementation of environmental technologies High skill labour and knowledge mobility	**■Financial nationalism** Focus on protecting national savings, going for national and international "trust" investments (local banks and global "community" banks) Regional disparities with growing labour migration pressures Financial global imbalances limit national growth opportunities

Source: McKinsey Global Institute

The balanced growth scenario still has an early recovery feature with regard to capital markets, with a redirection of global financial flows in a more balanced way and with some more positive elements in terms of some kind of redirection of imbalances. We see this in terms of growth in US and UK savings, for example, and a reduction in reserves in China and South East Asia, a new role for the IMF and growing international trade conflicts and a much stronger representation of emerging countries in international financial organizations. In a much more severe continued slow down of the capital market crisis and a moderate economic recession, you will end up straight into financial nationalism as you can observe already today. There will be a focus on protecting national saving, going for national and international trust investments, a more important role for local banks, and global community banks like Triodos Bank and others will have very specific niches at the global level. As a consequence, you will see very strong growing regional disparities with growing labour migration pressure and financial global imbalances that limit growth opportunities. You pay the full costs with declining globalization.

The fourth and most severe scenario is, of course, one in which knowledge will be the factor of globalization. There will be a dramatic slow down of trade in goods with severe structural unemployment and new specialization patterns emerging, new priorities on global implementation of environmental technologies (which becomes to some extent the access-to- knowledge element), and high-skill labour mobility and knowledge mobility in order to serve, maintain and support that knowledge.

To conclude (2)

In addition to the conclusions I presented before, I conclude that in a growing number of areas the overconcentration of research expenditures in the Northern world will also lead to a slow spreading of knowledge in general, and that is particularly the case in the area of energy-saving technology where a fast proliferation of knowledge is important. There is also a need for multidisciplinary research programmes on appropriate innovation, which can be compared to some extent with appropriate technology, in the areas of local food production, local energy efficiency, water management, transportation, logistics, urban mobility, and migration. And finally, there is a need for adjustment of our financial system with more focus on local knowledge impact.

Notes

1   See Soete, 2007.
2   See Maddison, 2007.
3   See Beck, 2005.
4   Izurieta and Singh, 2008.
5   See Soete, 2009.
6   See Mokyr, 2005.
7   See Mackintosh, 1986.
8   See European Parliament, 2000.
9   See Ghosh, 1998.
10   See Ramani, 2008.
11   See http://www.merit.unu.edu/permalink.php?id=439.
12   See http://www.waste.nl/
13   See Spence, 2009.
14   See Van der Ploeg, 2008.
15   See Stiglitz, 2010.
16   See Heertje, 2001.

References

Bech, U. (2006) *Power in the Global Age*, Malden, MA: Polity Press.

European Commission (2009) European Research Area. Available at:
http://ec.europa.eu/research/era/index_en.html.

European Parliament (2000) Lisbon European Council 23 and 24 March 2000:
Presidency Conclusions, 2000, Brussels: European Parliament, available
at: http://www.europarl.europa.eu/ summits/lis1_en.htm.

Ghosh, R.A. (1998) Cooking pot markets: an economic model for the trade in
free goods and services on the Internet, *First Monday*, Volume 3, Number
3. Available at: http://firstmonday.org/htbin/cgiwrap/bin/ojs/index.php/
fm/article/view/580/501.

Heertje, A. (2001) Some Observations on Recent Growth Theory. In: Kuper,
G. et al. (eds.), *Coordination and growth: Essays in honour of Simon K. Kuipers*,
Dordrecht: Kluwer Academic. Pp. 249-253.

Hippel, E. von (2005), *Democratizing Innovation*, Cambridge: MIT Press.

Izurieta, A. and A. Singh (2008) *Does fast Growth in India and China harm US
Workers? Insights from Simulation Evidence*, ESRC Centre for Business
Research - Working Papers Nr. 378, Cambridge: ESRC Centre for Business
Research, Cambridge University.

Mackintosh, I. (1986) *Sunrise Europe: The Dynamics of Information Technology*, with
a foreword by Etienne Davignon. London: Basil Blackwell.

Maddison, A. (2003) *The World Economy: Historical Statistics*. Paris: OECD.

Maddison, A. (2007) *Contours of the World Economy*, 1-2030 AD, Oxford: Oxford
University Press.

Mokyr, J. (2005) Long-term Economic Growth and the History of Technology.
In: Aghion, P. and S. Durlauf. *Handbook of Economic Growth, Vol. 1b*,
Amsterdam: Elsevier, pp. 1113-1180.

Ploeg, R. van der (2008) Growth and Volatility in Developing Economies,
Society for International Development Lecture.

Ramani, S. (2008) Playing in invisible markets: Innovating to harness the
economic power of the poor. The 2nd Charles Cooper annual memorial
lecture, Maastricht: UNU-MERIT.

Social and Spatial Inequalities Group (2009) Research and Development
Expenditures: Map No. 165, , Sheffield: Sheffield University, Available at:
http://www.worldmapper.org/display. php?selected=165.

Social and Spatial Inequalities Group (2009) Royalty Fees: Map No. 168, Social
and Spatial Inequalities Group, Sheffield: Sheffield University, Available
at: http://www.worldmapper.org/display. php?selected=168.

Soete, L. (2007), Recherche sans frontières, Paper presented at the "Conference
on the Economics of Technology Policy" Monte Verità, Ascona,
Switzerland June 17-22, 2007.

Soete, L. (2009) *Malthus' Revenge*, UNU-MERIT Working Paper 2009-030,
Maastricht: UNU-MERIT.

Soete, L. (2010) *The role of community research policy in the knowledge-based economy: Post-2010 strategies for research policies: Experts view collection*, Luxembourg: Publications Office of the European Union.

Spence, M. (2009) Long Term Growth and Short Term Headwinds for the Developing World, Society for International Development Lecture.

Stiglitz, J. (2010) *Risk and Global Economic Architecture: Why Full Financial Integration May be Undesirable*, NBER Working Paper 15718, Cambridge: National Bureau of Economic Research. Available at: http://www.nber.org/papers/w15718.

Saving the African Farmer: Agriculture, Sustainable Development and the MDGs

Vijay Paranjpye

Whatever kind of definition you give of sustainable development, it cannot do without agriculture. It is the basis for all later development. Most economists accept, although grudgingly, that agriculture is the primary sector and that the industrial and other, tertiary sectors all result from the growth of that basic sector.

The importance of agriculture is not new. What is new, however, is that, in the last six years, it has gone off of the central stage. How could something like agriculture, which is the basis of all social development and which is central to the Millennium Development Goals (MDGs), get off the agenda?

Until about the year 2000, we seemed to be on track with agriculture. At the time of the World Summit on Sustainable Development in Johannesburg in December, 2001, we formulated development goals and said: whatever might happen elsewhere, we will pursue those goals because they are meant to be the objective for this millennium and not only for this year. And yet, we forgot about this because something else had become more important. That 'something' was the war on terror, of course. I do not wish to go into it, but that war took over everybody's psyche and it became a syndrome out of which people could not extricate themselves. I have no intention of saying who was right or wrong, but it derailed this whole effort to reach the MDGs.

One reason has to do with climate change. I feel that Joke Waller, whom we remember today, would have been dismayed by the way in which the world is proceeding to tackle the climate convention. It is not tackling the climate convention by changing lifestyles or by reducing consumption or by reducing fossil fuel consumption. Instead it is doing it by increasing consumption of alternative forms of energy, including biogas, and not by replacing energy consumption from fossil fuels. It simply adds consumption of other, alternative forms of energy.

There was another reason why the efforts to reach the MDGs were derailed. The international global budget started to get diverted into issues that were contradictory to the achievements of the MDGs. Growth was supposed to be inclusive, but inclusive for whom? Who should it include? Of course the have-nots, the poorest of the poor! Without going into detail, it is clear that in the years after 2002, the allocation of financial resources and economic efforts have been diverted away form the MDGs. As a consequence, the amount of official development assistance (ODA) being spent on agriculture has gone down.

The fact is that, between the years of 1990 and 2004, ODA for agriculture has declined from 12 to 4 percent of total ODA. That is, ODA funding for agriculture has actually declined in real terms. I was surprised to see this figure in the reports of the EU: allocations for agriculture went down from 7.9 billion euros in 1990 to 2.9 billion euros in 2007. This is a clear indication that, over time, agriculture has been dismissed. This was confirmed by figures from the World Bank in their 2008 report on agriculture.

Food for biogas

Even 11 or 12 percent of ODA for agriculture, in my opinion, is not such a big figure, because the achievement of practically every one of the MDGs would require substantial investments in agriculture and related sectors. But the EU general report on agriculture and development in 2007 states that 4.5 million tons of food grains in Europe are being used for producing biogas, without wondering about the purpose for which it is being used. Now, Europe used to be the place that talks most of feeding the people of Africa. Why are they putting all of this grain into gas in order to burn it? Does that not contradict the European policy on development goals? There seemed something wrong with it, so I checked it out, but apparently the figure is correct.

Then I read that in the US in the last two years, 2006-07, 80 million tons of maize has been used for producing ethanol and for biogas. So Europe, with only 4,5 million tons for biofuel, is not doing too bad! The purpose is to achieve this so-called 20 percent reduction in CO_2 emissions from fossil fuels for automobiles. So what we essentially are talking about is the conspicuous consumption of petroleum. Instead of petroleum consumption being reduced, its consumption is now encouraged if you only add 20 percent of biodiesel or biogas or bio-whatever!

Now, I am not talking about the late nineties, I am talking about the year 2007. So what is the US giving us in terms of a message? That we want to feed the Africans who are poor and starving, but that we can, at the same time, afford to burn 80 million tons of food grains – maize – that is the staple food of Africa?

Back to Europe: another 1 million hectare, besides the 4.5 million tons of food for ethanol production, is used to produce a total of 3 million tons of rapeseed oil for biodiesel. This makes a total of 80 million tons from the US, plus 4.5 million tons of food grains and 3 million tons of rapeseed, while again we are all talking about and struggling with the question how to feed the Africans! While the excuse is renewable energy and satisfying the requirements of the climate convention, which will eventually have some effect in 2050 or 2099, people are starving in Africa. So my quick submission is that we cannot somehow reach those climate convention gaols without burning food. That is what I understand, and I think that people need to think about this very seriously.

What alternative?

All of the producers of biogas in Holland and Germany know that it is possible to produce biogas not only from grain, but also from straw. That is the rest use, which begets a smaller quantity but you get at least something. If you subsidize it, you can encourage farmers to grow more grain because by selling straw you are increasing the value of the crop and in doing so you are satisfying both: you are producing more food, which is *not* used for producing biogas, and you are producing straw which *is* used to produce biogas. But then there would be a counter argument: by using straw for biogas, you reduce the food for the life stock. But that is not too much of a problem because there are lots of products from which to produce straw: grasses, cereals, corn, everything.

So science and technology is available. We in India have practised it ourselves, but I will come to that eventually. It is possible to produce biogas without using the grain, but it requires an extra effort to shell out the corn and to remove the grains. Now government policies have been wrong in this respect: they have banned all kinds of things, I don't know how many kinds of things they have banned in European agriculture, but they have not banned and said: 'If you want to produce biogas out of food land, take the grain out, use it for food and then you can use the rest to produce biogas'. There is no problem in that because what you do is: you take out the gas, and the NPK (nitrogen, phosphorus and potassium in fertilizer) still remains. So you can put it back into the farms of the same farmers, without having lost any of the manure or any of the organic material or fertilizers. So it is possible to keep the food chain going by doing this.

I am not here to propagate organic farming. I am just saying: if you take food lands and use the straw to produce gas, the straw could still be used for compost. While composting normally, what everybody does in agriculture, you capture the straw and use it. When you use it for producing biogas, there is no loss of NPK, and the soil again gets back the entire nutrient value. So it gets back to the farm and it keeps the energy cycle intact.

The Indian experience

Why is Europe not doing it? That is my question, but I am not here to talk about Europe. Let me talk about India and what we have done there, and which has surprised many people because India is a problem-ridden country. It is huge, it has many religions, languages and cultures, everybody is quarrelling, 22 or 23 percent is still living below the poverty line, our politics is as disturbed as in any other chaotic democratic country and there is corruption, inefficiency and all kinds of things, but there is one thing that we have not done: we have never derailed agriculture from its mainstream, centre stage position. Food has to be on the table, and therefore its production has to be on the centre stage. Let me give you an example: ODA for agriculture has fallen from 11 to 4 percent, but the Indian government's budget to support agriculture has moved up enormously. Our planned initial investments used to be in the order of 20 percent of the total budget in the first two plans. They became larger and are now close to 40 percent. That is huge! And that is why in 2006-07, when there was low productivity everywhere else, we produced a record crop of 270 million tons of food. This implied an average growth of 4.6 to 4.7 percent, which is pretty good. Our imports of food have been next to negligible. Imports and exports are roughly balanced. We are not net importers of food.

Fortunately for the world, China and India have not been net importers of food, with a population of 2 out of six billion worldwide. Europe also is producing a lot, but Africa is not producing its own food and we all have to do something about it.

Now, how much is 270 million tons? Just to give you a comparison, the European Union, 27 countries, produced in the same year 258 million tons. That is about 20 million tons less than India. Of course, in population we are close to a billion anyway. I am not saying it is a big deal. I am saying in terms of equivalent output of food, that is an advantage and it moved from 51 to 270 million tons as a consequence of major, massive support of agriculture. This happened to sugar as well. In the same year, 2006-07, we had a huge sugar crop.

Until about 2002, India had what used to be called in the old days 'the Hindu rate of growth', i.e., a slow, crawling rate of growth. By about 2001-02, it had shifted to 3.6 percent in real terms. That was good: 3 to 4 percent is still at this moment the European rate of growth. Then we had two bad years, in 2003 and 2004, when suddenly the production dropped. But in the last three years, there has been enormous growth because of major capital inputs. As a consequence of this, notwithstanding the bad years in between, the total economy was growing in the last eight to ten years more than 5 percent on average with rates of 9.5 percent in the later years.

I am not here just to praise Indian agriculture, but I am here to state that if you do not derail and belittle agriculture, then, even in times when the world markets are collapsing, the financial markets are collapsing and the banks are collapsing, and when there is bad feeling everywhere, if your agriculture is doing OK, your economy will be stable. This is very fundamental. Why was this happening in countries like India and China? Let me give you a couple of reasons.

Eighty percent or more of the population of India and China has nothing to do with investments, shares and stocks, with speculative markets, credit cards or plastic money. They know nothing about it. They don't lose. When markets move up and down suddenly, they don't suffer from it. And what they produce is real stuff.

There is another reason why, in the last year or two, or even in the last year and a half, things were a little better in India. Yes, it is true: there were many companies that had to close down. There were some diehards that had to close down, but what did those people do? Why did they not collapse? What they did was this: instead of laying off 5 or 6 percent of their workers, they reduced everybody's salary by 5 or 6 percent. Right? So there are a lot of companies and banks in India who said: 'Well, to absorb the international market shocks, we will not lay off people but everybody will get a little less'. Now, in a market kind of situation this makes sense. It makes market sense because the companies said: 'If we throw out a thousand people, ten thousand people who we are related to them are going to curse us. There is going to be bad feeling, whereas, if everybody gets December bonus – we don't have Christmas but we celebrate all functions in India, so also Christmas – well, you would get a little less bonus but that would be the same for all people, across the board.' What was the result? There was a feeling of pride rather than bad feelings, because people felt that they had contributed to the effort of absorbing this shock.

What happened to the farmers? The farmers said: 'what crisis? We don't know anything about it!' They were not affected at all: 60 percent of the population is in farming, so what does it matter? Because they do not have stocks and shares or have speculated in the construction market, they are not bothered. Now, I am not saying that this is a great thing, because it is not an advantage. I am just telling you why India was not so much affected by the external shocks. Being poor also helps sometimes!

On the other hand, in a country like Germany, almost 60 to 70 percent of the population has something to do with the markets and the banks and the stock market. If a larger percentage of the economy is involved in the processes where there are huge ups and downs, naturally there will be larger ripple effects of the shocks.

This is what I would call resilience economics. The Indian economy with its slow growing, 'Hindu rate of growth', also has this resilience. There, most of the people are not earning high incomes and big salaries, and therefore to them it doesn't matter really too much.

But there were other problems. We had a deceleration of growth for some years, and we had problems because of excessive irrigation, excessive fertilization and excessive pesticides in the irrigated areas.

Looking at the map of India you will have noticed that 60 percent of the arable land in India is rain fed and not irrigated, and therefore no pesticides and fertilizers are used. So this is the area where, by default, agriculture is organic. By default! There are about half a million acres, or 458,000 hectares to be precise, which are doing what in Europe you call "certified organic farming", with all the tests and so on and so forth to get this label.

India is the largest producer of organic cotton for example, and this is a surprise. In spite of the Bt cotton invasion (using a biological alternative to pesticides), fortunately Bt cotton could not colonize India. The Indian pests beat the Bt cotton. It mutated by disguise and, therefore, the cotton yields in Bt cotton failed in many places. So the farmer said: 'May be you have a lot of claims, but let us go back to our good old cotton'. So, fortunately, Bt cotton failed in India. Therefore you see this massive shift back again from chemically driven, Bt, genetically modified cotton, to normal cotton. Some of these things that happened in India were happening either by accident, or for historical reasons or simply by the failure of certain kinds of technology.

What problems do we have in India? Sixty percent of our land is still clean. It is not polluted, not poisoned. I heard yesterday from some of my friends that in Holland and Germany the land is saturated with chemicals. The nitrates have reached the groundwater and it has become so rich in nutrients that they don't know what to do with it. Now this same problem we faced in the 1990s in three states in India, only three states, where there was substantial agricultural land under chemical farming. As a consequence, they got the conventional negative return on investment or a negative return in terms of output per input of fertilizer. This started in the early 1990s with the result that each time now, the Punjab farmers and the Punjab State have to put in a larger quantity of fertilizers and a larger dose of pesticides in order to produce the same quantity of output. As soon as this happened – luckily there was no government policy, the absence of policy is sometimes very nice – the farmers decided on their own that, if this is happening, let us not get into this rubbish. Therefore most of the Indian states did not jump onto it.

The other thing that happened was that the government did not give support to other cereal crops, that is, poor man's crops: lentils, sorghum and corn. None of these were subsidized. The only thing that was subsidized by the government in terms of fertilizers and pesticides was wheat, rice and sugarcane. That is all. Only three crops were subsidized and we spent huge numbers, thousands and thousands of crowns were spent, and that is a lot of money. Billions of euros were spent for subsidizing these lands. They did, however, produce the surplus output that saw us through the 1960s, 1970s and 1980s and sorted out food scarcities at that time. We could then stop importing grain from Australia and the US within about six years' time. So it did have its merits in those days.

But the point is, we need not have continued with it. We could have stopped at the point when the problem was solved and then shifted back to normal agriculture, not 100 percent organic, not seed-certified organic, but normal organic.

Saving the African farmer

Now, I have spent a lot of time explaining that agriculture in India has been the country's saving grace. But I have no illusion that India and China, notwithstanding what everybody says and what the World Bank reports, will be big economic powerhouses. I have no such illusions. I do not think they have any chance of getting out of the clutches of the WTO and the American/European market system, and I don't think we will reach that position. But what we will do certainly in the next twenty years is survive and sustain the economy, and reach rates of growth of 7, 8 or 9 percent. That we will continue to do no matter how many upheavals there will be all over the place.

But this talk is not because I want to talk about India and agriculture, but because I think we have solutions for Africa. Africa is not different from Asia in terms of its land, its people and its poverty. What is different is that they did not have political stability or cooperation of the sort that would enable them to enrich their agriculture, because their agriculture failed and because people did not concentrate on their part. There were UN missions for all kinds of things except for developing the agriculture in Africa.

I feel this is an extreme statement – and I like to make them sometimes – but the failure in agriculture was due to the fact that people were too busy kicking out dictators. They wanted to stop their fights, to support colonialists or to fight apartheid in South Africa or whatever. In the meantime, nobody was making serious efforts for supporting and developing the agricultural lands that are plentiful in Africa. There is more agricultural land in Africa than in India. We Indians would have loved to have that kind of land availability in India. In India, a big farmer has about 2.5 hectare of land while the average landholding is about 1 hectare or less.

Fortunately, since there are millions of these farmers in Africa, and their numbers are not falling as they are in Europe, there are lessons for Africa. Their lands are still in good shape, but they are barely producing one ton of food per hectare or even less. Many lands are not producing at all. Investments in agriculture are required, but not investments by taking to chemical farming and selling at high prices, because that is what failed in India.

What is the problem with chemical farming? I am not so much worried just now about the environmental arguments. If, as a farmer, my cost of production continues to increase so rapidly as a consequence of my purchase of chemical inputs, energy and power –all that is required for the new hybrids and the chemical farming – the price differential between the selling price and my costs becomes so small that it can not be sustainable. That is the main problem.

Why are the prices low? It is because the government says: 'All the poor people need to buy, and so we have to suppress those prices'. So for the farmer who produces food, the profit margin becomes very small. In certain cases they just get them knocked out, and either they commit suicide or they build up major debt. Those debts are in real terms very small, but for a small farmer a debt of say 200 Euros is a very, very big debt. That is the kind of debt they have.

So what is wrong; what is the answer for India or Africa? From this point I would like you to pay a little more attention: make the farmer independent! And how do you make him independent? Allow him or teach him how to produce his own fertilizers, allow him to produce his own seeds, allow him to run his own farm by generating power and allow him to harvest his own water in his own land. That does not require rocket science or investment policies: it requires delinking him from the market system. This is easier said than done, because every seller of fertilizers and pesticides – and in Holland you know this better than I do – will say: 'You are such an idiot if you do not use my fertilizer, you don't know farming, so you take this fertilizer and grow some more crops'. In other words, in order to maintain food security in India or Africa or the world, the farmers must die because you make him to produce food at very high costs, and you are giving him a very low price. In the bargain, he is sacrificing his being a farmer so the international food security targets are met. That is ridiculous. We should delink him from the market. By market I mean market agriculture, or industrial agriculture, as it is known in Europe.

How should we delink him from the market? I will now use the same example that I used to discredit biogas. If for this 60 percent of our arable land we are able to produce biogas without touching the nutrient cycle, then the purchase of straw gives him that extra price support without there being government subsidies. Right now it is up to the government. It first has to collect the taxes, then it has to pay the farmer, enrich him, and so on. This did not happen: if ten rupees were collected for the farmer, he might end up with only one or two. Instead, the right subsidy comes through his own production of straw: he gets back the manure, and the biogas produced is available for pumping up his own water, for his own light, for his own electricity.

Why is this important? In India and in Africa we are short of energy. In Africa, Uganda and Kenya – everywhere – people would give their left hand to get some substitute for imported oil. So this is a great possibility: support his organic agriculture, you don't even have to call it organic, by helping him to contemporize his techniques of organic farming, use his straw and keep his nutrient cycle intact. Has this been tried? Yes! We have tried this with a population of 15,000 people in a valley where the biogas is now being installed and produced by farmer enterprises through the use of its straw. In Africa, they can use another product that is extremely useful called the Sudan grass or the Nipia grass. We found that this grass has far more biogas potential than all the other grasses like wheat, sorghum, rice, etc.

This is just one example. Precision farming in agriculture is another. I am speaking of precision cooperatives of buyers and consumers, without there being a premium on the organically produced bango or rice or grain. It is an illusion that all organic farming is about premium prices. It is not true that all organic farming has to be expensive. Not true! This is normal farming, which gets back its nutrients without having to pay for it. So the farmer's production costs fall as a consequence. Even for the same amount of grain that he produces, his income rises. This is the only way to make him independent of the international market and international market prices.

What should Europe do?

I do not want to dwell on it in great detail, but in 2005 some of us actually got a patent for doing this exercise and it has huge potential. Even in Europe, 4.5 million tons of grain could be saved and sent to Africa. You could have produced the gas with the straw, and then you would have done both: obeyed the climate convention in such a way that Joke Waller would have wanted, and fed the poor at the same time. So Europe should shift in the next twenty years gradually from non-sustainable agriculture to sustainable agriculture. Why do I say 'gradually'? Because I am not one of those illusionists who say that within two years or five years you can quickly move without any losses.

I would say it would take fifteen, twenty or even twenty-five years to move back to reason. Because all farmers and all governments know that the phosphate mines will be exhausted in about twenty-five or thirty years. So out of three key chemical inputs, one will be gone, and with petroleum, the other two will also go. So why wait until that point?

Within the next fifteen to twenty years, Holland might want to decide that many more lands will go out of production. But I know that in Holland, that will be impossible because there is a nexus between the huge food chain suppliers and the fertilizer industry and politics. I don't know what exact nexus there is, but you do and you need to sort it out for yourself. I would say that you must have a long-term plan to shift out of this and to reduce consumption, that is, the net consumption of energy, and not replace it by this 20 percent of biodiesel which is actually just encouraging more consumption of diesel.

If the whole of Europe and the US would decide to do that, that would mean a lot of money to be ready to be shifted. And India and China can contribute by sharing their technology, and Latin America can contribute by sharing its biodiversity. All that was stolen out of Africa many years ago can go back into Africa from all countries, not just from Europe and the US. Asia can contribute as well.

If what I am saying actually happened, and we expect it to happen by 2015 or 2018, we would have a surplus stock of at least 40 million tons of food grain, which is roughly half of the total output of Europe today. And that much output is enough to feed 250 million Africans for one whole year. That is how much it is. So it has to be an all-front attack

When I met Mr. Pronk some years ago, I said to him 'you are talking nonsense if you are not going back to organic farming in agriculture of the kind I just explained'. The fact of the matter is that national politics need to have a longer time horizon if it doesn't want to fall into the perverted logic of short-term profits.

Now let us look at the other MDGs. If you want to support agriculture, you need to support water: water security, sanitation and water for food production: all three need to be taken care of. If you want to do decent agriculture, farmers need to be educated. And if farmers are to produce good organic food, the women wouldn't die while giving birth to their children. In other words, we should try to sort out the MDGs by attacking them as if they were one goal. If there is no sanitation, just see to it that people will be provided with new toilets, if the children are dying, just give them medicine: that is not the way to do it.

It is too expensive to attack these goals piecemeal. Instead, bolster up normal agriculture, which requires huge amounts of investment in water, and make access to water, energy and food available. It is access to food in the normal situation that we have to make available, not investment. That is the bottom line.

If we want to save Africa, we have to save the roots of Africa, we have to save the soils of Africa, we have to save the gene banks of Africa and we have to save the farmers of Africa, both men and women. In Africa, the men are either dead or fighting or making politics or doing anything else like migrating, whatever; the women, poor women, get left behind to look after their land. If you want to support the women, you don't have to carry a gender flag and go shouting all over the place. You have to give women work that makes sense, and food for the children. So agriculture again:

if we are able to get agriculture back onto the main stage, and if ODA funding can move from the present 4 percent to 15 or 20 percent of total ODA, or at least bring it back to the 11 percent it was before, now these will be good signals and show that we are serious about the African food crisis.

Food as a Strategic Commodity

Comments by Cor van Beuningen

The importance of agriculture indeed contrasts sharply with the decrease in the percentage of ODA that has been spent in agricultural development over the past fifteen years. Also, I agree on the derailment of the pursuit of the MDGs by the war on terror, and the need for increased focus on Africa, a resilient agriculture, the importance of second and third generation biofuels, the use of less fertile and waste lands and a gradual shift to sustainable agriculture. I would like to reinforce this argument by focussing on the geopolitical consequences of the neglect of agriculture.

As Amartya Sen pointed out in 2001 in his book on poverty and famine, we know that, often, food shortage is not just that: it is an absolute lack of food. There are other, political factors involved including social inequalities related to the mechanisms for the distribution of food.

Food shortage is also related to power relations, politics and conflicting interests. At the same time, food shortages, real of perceived, increase conflicts. Food shortage is a likely cause for new conflicts, both between countries and between groups of people within countries, especially in the developing world, with possibly disastrous consequences for human lives and livelihoods. So food shortage can both be a product of social conflicts as well generate and increase social conflict.

What we have seen in just the last two years or so is that the so-called 'new scarcities', including the scarcity of food, has led to a political redefinition of particularly energy and food. In the eyes of present day politicians and states, they are considered to be more than just economic goods. These commodities have been redefined as strategic goods, that is, goods that are directly relevant to the national security and sovereignty of nations. National governments feel obliged or legitimized to meddle in affairs that until only very recently were left to the market, at least in Europe. National energy and food security have suddenly become *chefsache*, deserving of direct political control and intervention by political leadership.

Of course, the awareness of the peculiar nature of food in the sense that its production is bound by natural constraints, and also that food shortage implies immediately problems for the economy, society and the individual, and the awareness of the strategic and military qualities of food, probably is as old as politics itself. As far as the European Union is concerned, this awareness was very much alive until well into the twentieth century. Of course the Treaty of Rome, the European Community for Coal and Steel, the Common Agricultural Policy originally focussed on food security for Europe. The de-politicization process only started in the eighties with the privatization of utilities and the liberalization of markets for energy and water. The political definition of food was questioned for the first time only in 1986, the first Uruguay Round of GATT, now the WTO, and only in the 1990s were energy, food and water stripped of their political definition and transformed into economic goods just as any other good.

Now, in the last two years, at the international level energy and food are defined as strategic goods in a geopolitical sense, i.e., as important assets in international power relations. The possession and actual control over and access to those goods affects the behaviour of politicians and states to an almost unprecedented degree. Leaders of energy rich countries display a new, almost imperial self-confidence, and energy and food certainly turn out to have strictly military qualities. Suddenly leaders talk about the energy weapon and the food weapon.

Countries that depend on energy from elsewhere go as far as it takes to get hold of them. So we talk about the scramble for resources or even the search for oil. In fact, what we witness is an ongoing process of geo-politicization of international relationships and at the same time a reversal of the globalization process. The pace of this process is breathtaking by any standard. This world, two years after the book of Thomas Friedman, 'The World is Flat', is anything but flat. National boundaries do matter as much as ever before. National governments play again centre stage in the economic realm and international relations are redefined as geo-political power relations.

The promise of globalization was that everybody would be a winner through the twin process of niche specialization and increasing interdependence. Of course, when all the stakeholders would share an interest in economic integration on the globalized world market, international power politics and rivalry would lose its meaning and gradually come to an end. Actually, however, the reverse is happening: geo-politicization is the antithesis of global-ization, and geo-economics is subordinated by geo-politics. The global market for entrepreneurs has been integrated and super-seded by the geo-political arena where again national governments play the main character. They are not dealing and negotiating; they are into the power game.

This geo-politicization of the power relations driven by the combined effect of the new scarcities of food and energy and, of course, now the financial crisis and the prospect of a deep economic depression is taking place in a very particular period of the world history. The period is one that is characterized by a tran-sition in the world order of a uni-polar system as we have known since 1989, to a multi-polar system. The uni-polar world was ideo-logically dominated by western liberalism and it was geo-politically dominated by the US as the sole superpower. This period is coming to an end, but the outlines of the new world are not clear. Ideologically, the new world will not be dominated by liberalism, I suppose. Economically we know what it will look like. We know that in about fifty years' time ,China, the US and the EU will each account for 20 percent of world GDP, followed by India with about 10 percent and then Japan, Brazil and Russia with each about 5 percent.

Now, how will this new economic configuration be processed? In the ideological, political domain nobody knows. Will the new world leaders be willing and able to ensure a peaceful transition to a sustainable new world system? Or not? What is clear is that we face many problems and enormous challenges: food shortages, scarcities, the financial crisis, economic depression, maybe security and poverty, climate change and loss of biodiversity. The problem of this moment is that two years ago we would think that the size and the urgency of these problems would provide more than sufficient motive for world leaders to undertake far-reaching collective action and come to binding agreements on non-voluntary institutionalized forms of global government. What has happened over the last two years is that each of those problems, instead of bringing people together, instead of bringing world leaders together, are proving to be a trigger for deepening polarization and increasing conflict.

The scarcities have produced polarization. They have produced a redefinition of international relations in terms of power relations and the willingness, the preparedness and the capacity of world leaders to be reasonable and to come to agreements on how to deal with and tackle the world's problems, including food shortages, has been decreasing as a consequence.

So we are left with a double problem: not only are our problems increasing, but also the capacity and the willingness of key stakeholders to tackle and deal with these problems have decreased.

The Global Relevance of European Social Values

Ad Melkert

It is tempting to consider the worldwide steep economic crisis as the crest of the wave of globalization that has defined so much of our thinking and our lives throughout the past decades. As sailors know, getting caught in the crest might cause you to capsize. A steady hand at the tiller is required to steer out of the storm and set a course for quieter waters.

The crisis that has engulfed the world is far from over, despite increasing inclinations by strong interest groups to go back to business as usual. However this is not what is going to happen, simply because the fault lines that have been laid bare are too deep to jump over. Of the many factors at play, there are two fundamental impacts that I would like to mention as reasons why just reverting to good old times will not be possible: first, the breakdown of the global agenda dominance by the G7 of 'industrialized nations'; and second, the resurgence of the recognition of public interest and the necessary role of the state. Their game changing impact will not go away with time. Let me briefly elaborate on both, as they are interconnected and will lead me to the main point that I would like to explore in today's presentation.

In July there will be the next annual meeting of the G7. In the course of recent years, creeping changes already affected the set up of the Group, first with the inclusion of Russia under the G8 misnomer, and then with an almost standing invitation for other leaders, in particular China, India, Brazil and South Africa – though only for parts of the agendas and dinners served. This time around it will be clear that, regardless of whoever shows up on whatever photograph, the G7 has virtually ceased to exist as a driving force of the global agenda after around thirty years of service in leading the postcolonial– some would like to say neo-colonial – world order from the north. The game changing impact of the crisis has come forward in the need to formally sit around a much bigger table, bringing the Group of 20 together and encompassing most of the key players of this moment not hierarchically, but rather recognizing their mutual interdependence. There is no doubt that around and from this Group a new architecture of global governance will evolve, highly imperfect as the terms of reference for the meetings that took place so far (in Washington and London, with a September follow-up in Pittsburgh) have been. The gravest consequence of this imperfection is the ongoing exclusion of the majority of states, particularly low income countries, and the ignorance of established frameworks of multilateral governance like the UN, IMF and World Bank, which are very much the products of the post World War II architecture and by now following and not leading to face today's global demands. However, despite serious shortcomings, there is a promise in the convening of the main global actors at one table. On the one hand, it could provide a credible buffer around the American-Chinese entanglement that has emerged as the nucleus of a new world order, yet it should not be allowed to ignore the rest of the world in decisions with potentially high global impact. On the other hand, any effective way of governing the globe, steering the ship out of choppy waters and discovering new shores of hope at the same time, requires a forum with requisite authority, visibility and credibility, the absence of which has been painfully felt in the worldwide incapability to avoid the big losses of a crisis foretold.

This is an important notion when looking at the second fundamental impact revealed by recent events. What we have seen is a complete about-face from the sacrosanct market rhetoric in the past three decades. That era started under political guidance by Reagan, Thatcher and the likes and met with broad political following and support to the detriment of the recognition and decency of the public cause and egalitarian principles for organizing society and global interdependence. Many have been forced to take a hard look at their conviction that the best state was a sleeping state, and now quite often entertain second thoughts about deregulation of what ought to be regulated for protecting and advancing the common good. The resurrection of Keynes and state fiscal intervention has been nothing less than spectacular, particularly in the US where the primacy of market dominance and private entrepreneurship and risk have been carried by solid majorities for a long time. It is probably right to be sceptical on the extent of true internalization and acceptance of the about-face. After all, it turns out that quite a few banks or car producers balk at conditionality as soon as they come to realize that their rescue cannot be just in the form of a blank check. And as things go, many would like to forget the anxieties of this period as soon as the stock market rallies again and profits bounce back up. What will remain though is an awareness of revaluation of the moral and normative role by mandated public authorities without which companies could not have survived, confidence would not have been restored and safety nets would not have existed. This awareness, bringing together a widely stretching spectrum of converging interests and views, offers a unique opportunity to identify and pursue the values that would strengthen cohesion in society, trust between nations and effective authority of global governance – all interconnected and indispensable conditions for social progress and justice.

Against the backdrop of these fundamental game changers, it is a welcome challenge to explore the value side of past and future of globalization. Globalization will not go away and, frankly, should not go away as its reversal through renationalization of economic, cultural and political action would bring us back to the past instead of forward to the future. However, as it has become crystal clear that systems governing globalization do not exist or have not stood the test, it is very relevant to explore the values that can bring and hold citizens and nations together. As I speak the echo of president Obama's speech in Cairo is still ringing, with its key message intensely focused on exactly that. Given the tremendous receptiveness for his message all around the globe, I sense that many people are longing for more than technical responses to their deep lack of social and economic security. Are we ready to cement the fate of individuals and regions, of winners and losers, of insiders and outsiders in a construction of common destiny? Or will we go back to 'might makes right' and the survival of the fittest as the way forward to growth and prosperity – marginalizing the disadvantaged?

Assuming that the crisis has now, indeed, paved the way for a renewed recognition of the public interest and for a more representative architecture of global governance, it may be realistic to see the end of the monoculture globalization model as the beginning of a multipurpose global equilibrium practice – replacing the private interest by the common good as its objective. In order to see how realistic this could be, let us take a moment to assess some relevant facts that have emerged in different parts of the world in recent years. In particular I would like to take a look at the areas of healthcare coverage, state pension rights and direct income support in different parts of the world.

In most countries, access to and quality of health services show wide disparities. In rich and poor countries alike the issues are both related to highly political issues of how to organize and for whom to organize a system of efficient delivery. The US way of organizing the system, largely driven by private interests, has turned out to be a recipe for very high costs and selective coverage. This coverage issue is also very pertinent in many middle-income countries. In Brazil and Argentina for instance, huge gaps exist depending upon employer contracts or workers' unions' arrangements. In China, high user fees discriminate heavily between the haves and the have-nots. In South Africa, state support contributes to 40 percent of all expenditure on health for delivering services to 80 percent of the population – leaving just 20 percent benefiting from more than half of total resources available. With a few exceptions, such as in Thailand, most developing countries show a pattern marked by wide differences between those included and those excluded.

State pension systems show a similar overall pattern, further complicated by different ways of securing revenue from pension contributions; a highly relevant aspect as the crisis has shown when erasing huge savings of countless people who were looking forward to benefit from their hard work and saving efforts after retirement. On top of that, in quite a few lower or middle-income countries, the pension age is rather low for limited groups of privileged, often state functionaries, thus contributing to the unsustainability and exclusivity features of the system.

Direct income support has been on the rise in quite a few countries, after a long period of marginalization as part of the traditional advice by international financial institutions, including World Bank and IMF. For example, in India there are good reasons to attribute the recent election results to the emphasis on rural employment and income guarantees that have reached millions of very poor people. It may make the point that even at a relatively low level of national income, it is possible to start cementing a floor of income entitlement that not only serves as a protection against starvation, but also might be an incentive to very small savings that could be the start of a micro credit contract.

In the same context, there have been significant initiatives in a number of countries, like in Brazil ('Bolsa Familial') and Mexico ('Oportunidades'), to provide through 'conditional cash transfer programs' money to poor families contingent upon certain verifiable actions, generally minimum investments in children's regular school attendance or basic preventative health care. They, therefore, hold promise for addressing the inter-generational transmission of poverty and for fostering social inclusion of targeted groups. These include in some cases internally displaced people (Colombia) or the disabled (Jamaica). Importantly, these programs have become part of regular budgets, accepted also as part of public expenditure frameworks with the blessing of World Bank and IMF. This could lay the foundation for expanded programs of more general welfare entitlements. Along this line of evolution, it would be a good example of initially small development projects gradually transformed into scaled up programs eventually leading to welfare system arrangements of a structural nature.

In short, the key challenges emerging from all three areas mentioned are: how to make the formal economy –with its high entitlements and exclusive thresholds of access – and the informal economy – with the near absence of individual rights and entitlements – converge? And how to sew together the patchwork of disparate facilities and entitlements and fit these to a system providing safety and opportunities for all? Obviously, that is not just a technical question. Rather, it is a value-driven challenge to the active aspirations of a unified society or to the passive acceptance by a divided one.

Let me mention here the interesting case of a middle-income country one step further up the ladder of inclusive arrangements, Chile, which is often labelled as part of the group of emerging market economies but is increasingly a showcase of an advancing social economy. Last year I had the privilege to contribute to the work of a special Advisory Council established by President Bachelet that has produced an authoritative account on the social future of Chile under the title 'Towards a Fair Chile: Jobs, Wages, Competitiveness and Equity'. I would like to summarize here my input into that discussion, trying to capture the relevance of European and Dutch experiences and views in the context of an economically booming, yet very unequal and on average still under educated country, though a country with the advantage that it can and wants to build on a strong institution to foster common direction of policies.

Building an equitable society requires a non-ideological acceptance that three pillars are indispensable under any circumstances: i) economic growth based on the strengths of the market economy; ii) political stability relying on consensus based institutions; and iii) universality of access to the labour market and appropriate social security arrangements, fostering an inclusive society. Equally it requires the rejection of three fear factors that continue to fuel strong advocates of one-sided interest representation and information. First the myth of a trade-off suggesting that expenditure for social policies will necessarily diminish economic return; second the ghost of taxation as the enemy of entrepreneurial success; and third the fear of globalization as the recipe for a race to the bottom of social standards and norms.

The discussion took place against the backdrop of the historic achievement, unique for the Latin American continent, of the introduction of a universal state pension (the 'General Old Age Pensions Act') for all Chileans. With the individual entitlement still at a very modest level, the essential progress lies in the bridging of the gap between insiders and outsiders in the labour market.

Thus, the case can be made (and that is what I did in Santiago) that this breakthrough is essentially recognizing values that in the post-war reconstruction of Europe have glued an increasing number of countries together around the notion of the responsibility of the state to recognize and support in an inclusive manner social rights and aspirations of all citizens based on the principle of equality. Universal coverage of health and disability risks and universal entitlement to a minimum income including after retirement reflect those values. Their implication extends to the understanding that the revenues from individual performance can be subject to limitation or taxation on the basis of public interest considerations. The recent heated debates about income norms and moral dos and don'ts in a society of equals show that something has gotten lost after the decades of reconstruction of Europe. The current crisis offers an opportunity borne out of necessity to revisit the fundamentals that enabled Europe to rise from the ashes and to foster a more inclusive type of society than in most other parts of the world.

However, there is no reason at all for complacency as the struggle to keep the values alive and well puts high demands on policy makers and the public debate. The distinction between the formal and informal economy is not the domain of developing countries only. Illegal residence and work in many European countries de facto creates an informal economy situation with exclusion of most of the universal insurance entitlements. In the US, the illegal workforce adds to the patchwork of situations due to absence of universal coverage and entitlement. Needless to point out the harsh unequal consequences, often even despite contributions by illegal workers to social funding. And the issues go beyond that. The 'British jobs for British workers' statement by Gordon Brown made a point of the insecurity in society that is affecting fundamental values of equal treatment. Harassment practices in quite a number of European countries emphasize the harsh distinction between being in and being out. The impact of such statements and facts stretches as far as the beaches of Senegal, Libya or Somalia with desperate people embarking on voyages of despair to find their fate decided on inhospitable shores or in relentless waves. And it extends to the support for development aid, which is vital to too many people in spite of the skepticism of some. I would like to mention two examples here.

Increasingly, key donors are providing support to countries for post-conflict recovery and reconstruction purposes. Examples include DR Congo, Liberia, Sierra Leone, Cote d'Ivoire, South Sudan, Afghanistan and quite many other places. There is often a potential of strong short-term gains, starting from the rock bottom of absence of services, institutions, security and justice. Whilst quick wins should not be confused with long term development requiring patience and stamina over a long sustained period of time, there is much evidence that without progress in delivering of services and provision of livelihood, the chance of resumption of conflict increases. Simply put: the role of aid is indispensable as it can make the difference between peace and war.

Another striking example goes back to earlier global economic crises and their impact on developing countries. Through these examples we can learn what in today's circumstances should be the way forward, despite negative economic growth and budget cutting exercises in donor countries that affect the levels of Official Development Assistance. Indonesia went through a severe crisis at the end of the 1990s, seeing its domestic expenditure drop in real terms. However, health spending paid by aid rose from 10 percent in earlier years to 24 percent during the crisis, creating an important buffer to sustain health services. In contrast, in Peru (during a comparable crisis ten years before) public health expenditures fell by more than 58 percent without any countervailing compensation from foreign assistance. While both countries suffered adverse impacts on child health, in Indonesia the impact was minor. In Peru, however, there was a sharp increase in the infant mortality rate, resulting from a combination of the collapse in public health expenditure along with a reduction in private health spending. Again simply put: the role of aid can make the difference between life and death.

When considering the core of 'European values', I would certainly argue for including the role of Europe in public development assistance as part of an elementary understanding of solidarity, promotion of stability and contribution to market creation – a combination of moral choice and economic opportunism. Often the choice of areas of support, particularly state and institution building and delivery of education and health services, reflect European traditions for better or sometimes for worse to recipient countries.

So far so good. However it is far from self-evident that applying the values as described can be economically sustained, or that it can continue to rely on electoral support. I must admit that I had to overcome some hesitations to speak about 'European values' in a political and economic climate that does not appear to entice a large number of politicians, opinion-makers and voters these days. I am highly concerned about the mood in Europe and the rising risk of renationalization of the common good, which might lead to increasing cut-throat competition with eventually more losers than winners.

Still, history of progress is part of a long journey, with many ups and occasionally deep downs. For keeping the right direction, it is important that we understand the roots of an unprecedented period of European peace and prosperity, achieved over a period of more than sixty years. It is also important that we remain open to welcome or support fellow citizens from poorer neighbouring areas as friends instead of foes. Let us not regress in giving in to the rejection of values that constitute the very basis to include and protect many of the people that used the European Parliament elections to express their insecurity about today's political and economic conditions. That is why it is worth every effort to advocate for and advance the European value proposition. And to address the deeply underlying electoral divisions that lie in the distinction between the cooperative, collective, public-private partnership approach on the one hand and the privatization of opportunities, risks and ultimately values on the other hand.

Ever since the privatization drive started in the early 1980s, the size and scope of the public domain have often been identified as obstacles to growth and prosperity. It is a valid question whether a solidarity system can be sustained over time. The Dutch experience suggests that this should be permanently an agenda priority, reconciling long-term trends with short-term adjustments in order to keep the balance between reservations and entitlements right. However, it should be pointed out that, despite those decades of ideological opposition, some of the most compelling facts demonstrate the opposite of the 'obstacle' ideology. There is abundant evidence that a conducive investment climate can go – and to an extent should go – hand in hand with clear frameworks of regulation and enforcement. How, otherwise, could there be an explanation for the consistent high ranking of Norway, Sweden, Denmark, Finland, Netherlands and Switzerland as countries of good business practice and opportunity? Why would Germany and France have managed to remain key industrial competitors despite quite loaded regulatory practices? How did Singapore, Vietnam, Malaysia and China rise to economic success? So why is it that the Anglo Saxon version of capitalism has been allowed to make such inroads into the fabric of societies around the globe, denting solid post-war institutions and arrangements in Europe and affecting traditional values in Asian societies? The global culture of capitalism has become very much adjusted to the style, language and customs of Wall Street and the City of London. Yet, Britain and America harbour considerable societal inequalities, lagging Europe and Japan in both social and physical infrastructure. And within the EU, Ireland led the race to the bottom of corporate taxation only to find itself confronted with an unsustainable bubble of short-lived luxury. Now more than ever the pressure is on that unrefined model to adjust to social and environmental realities. The reality of pollution, climate change and disaster surge; the reality of under education requiring renewed investments in schools and public university access; the reality of pockets of deep poverty and insecurity amongst middle classes: they all demand determined and binding public action and authority, nationally and internationally.

To be sure, global culture of capitalism has been a driver of important change to the benefit of many poor peasants or urban dwellers seeing their sons and daughters improving their life standards through tough labour. Emigration has been the source of surging remittances that are providing more and more regular income to millions of families. And larger developing countries with larger markets are seeing the two sides of brain drain and brain gain that on balance helps them integrate into the global economy.

Rather, the problem is the sustainability of capitalism in its raw version. Decency and security of jobs and income, and – as a simultaneous consequence and precondition – solidarity across society are not the adversary but the complementary of thriving economies. In ideological terms, it is the appreciation of the moral imperative that polarizes hard-core market protagonists against ideal-driven social advocates. In practical terms, it should by now be understood that the gap between the two is much narrower than either side would be pleased to admit. Essentially, globalization should be associated with progress; the contrary of falling back into a petty self-interest definition, nationalism, chauvinism that all have been or are breeding grounds for polarization and war. In the response to the crisis, the European Union is walking a fine line between keeping the momentum of integration intact and responding to national concerns in very national ways in order for governments to maintain legitimacy. However, for globalization to equal progress it is of the essence to broaden the scope of the measurement of its success so that it will go beyond the superficial security of impressive national product growth figures, will attribute authority beyond the corporate and financial world and will substitute the fiction of national sovereignty by a mandatory delegation of power to representative and accountable multilateral global governance.

Now that at this point in time we have to learn to live with growth, debt and inflation figures that are hard to reconcile with what we were used to, it is time that we embrace other figures on equal footing as measurements of the success of our action and of the prospects for our life. The world has made remarkable progress in recognizing the need for carbon emission ceilings as a yardstick to change our way of life for safeguarding conditions of life for future generations. On the social side, it is time to recover from the backlash that widely discredited the twentieth century historic achievements of labour regulation, social security and universal pension and health insurance coverage. Moreover, the notion of job rights, not by way of a static entitlement when there is no demand for work but as recognition of the need to serve society and boost the market economy in making labour supply and demand meet, would deserve revived attention and support. I have never understood why a report by the IMF announcing half a percent decrease in global output tends to raise the highest alarm levels in capitals, whereas references by the International Labor Organization to ten, twenty or close to 100 million more unemployed job seekers is taken note of like one learns to live with many rainy days in an otherwise moderate and comfortable climate. But how is it that a production system can be of value to people that are exempt from contributing? How could an economy benefit from the input of all talents if hundreds of millions are banned to the sidewalk of dark informality? And how can the fabric of society maintain coherence and strength if insiders and outsiders mistrust each other's efforts and opportunities? We should therefore be guided by parameters of inclusion alongside parameters of economic and financial solidity and conditions of ecological sustainability. And we should incorporate values of fair access and participation into our standards of performance measurement and public policy priority setting.

The confusion and disorientation of the time that we are living right now offers us a long-sought opportunity to plot a new course to quieter waters of this wider understanding of the interaction between economic growth and the common good. It also puts pressure on establishing the systems and levels of governance that helps the world on its way up from deprivation, poverty and despair to dignity, prosperity and accomplishment. This combination of a global equilibrium agenda and a global governance structure is a powerful one. The new prominence of the G20 enables more than ever before the representation of the very poorest in global decision fora that matter. Social values are regaining the place at the table that had been lost because they were neglected or simply taken for granted. Private entrepreneurship and profit making, whilst remaining necessary drivers of growth, are being reassessed as part of their contribution to coherence of society and quality of life.

An interesting test case, with repercussions far beyond the borders of the US, is going to be President Obama's efforts to take on many vested interests opposed to public interference in the organization of health risk solidarity. How to organize this will have to be a master class in bringing a value proposition (inclusion of every American under insurance) to an accepted system. The New York Times put it last week this way:

If the President embraces a tax on employee benefits, he may infuriate labor and the middle class. If he insists on a big-government plan in the image of Medicare, he could lose any hope of Republican support and ignite an insurance industry backlash. If he does not come up with credible ways to pay for his plan, moderate Democrats could balk.

Whatever the outcome, it will resonate in Europe and, if indeed universal coverage would be the result, would be of influence in many Asian and Latin American countries.

Let me conclude. In a world of American-inspired cultural dominance and of Asian-driven economic innovation, Europe has something precious to offer that it should not underestimate, let alone be careless about. It is the recognition of solidarity arrangements and consensus institutions as necessary preconditions for an inclusive and stable society, as an economic asset instead of a liability and as part of a winning combination and not a trade off with entrepreneurial initiative. These values are universally relevant and should be universally applied. Without further initiative, the economic crisis of our own making spells disaster for years to come and setbacks in many of the poorest countries, including for people that thought they had entered the land of the middle classes. So, let inclusiveness guide the way domestically and abroad. For in today's world there is not and should not be sovereignty to draw borders between human equals and their aspirations.

A global Development Agenda

Nancy Birdsall

It is a privilege to be in the Netherlands, which once again ranks highest among the 22 countries on the Commitment to Development Index (CDI). Along with many of my colleagues in the US and the Center for Global Development, I have always considered the Netherlands as the centre of sound and sensible policy on development. I have also happily noted that the Netherlands is a champion for women's concerns and rights throughout the world.

This lecture is partly based on a recent publication by the Center for Global Development, called 'The White House and the World', which presents a global development agenda for the next US president. The book bespeaks very much the Center's mission, which is to focus on improving the policies of the rich world and the major global institutions – the IMF, the World Bank and the UN – that are influenced primarily by the countries of the rich and affluent world. The essays in the book cover a range of issues just as does the CDI, from which I shall also draw. The CDI provides a ranking of the development policies of 22 rich countries while taking into account seven policy areas, which are averaged for an overall score. I urge you to investigate the CDI on our website.

Development is not just about aid. A core message of the Center is that there is much more to development policy than foreign aid itself, although aid is obviously very important. In our new book we examine migration, propose action on climate change policy, advance approaches to regional development in Africa, global health issues, education and so on. Before I turn to our recommendations to the incoming US administration in those areas, let me set the stage in a broader sense of the changing global order.

The White House and the world: A global development agenda for the next US president

It is time for development gurus to realize that we are living in a different time, and that we have to adjust to a big change in the world. This is particularly true for the US because it has a history of being a superpower, indeed a kind of hyper power, and now it has to adjust to a world in which it is less dominant. It should still take leadership on many issues, but it has to be a leadership in a different style.

The reason for the necessity of this new style of leadership is the deep tectonic shifts in the world: specifically the rise of Asia, particularly China and India. The reality is that the US cannot lead anymore by simply pushing other countries around. There has to be something different.

There are many other factors leading to this changing universe. One is that by 2050, today's emerging market economies will be twice as big as the G7 countries. The economies of the BRIC countries – Brazil, Russia, India and China combined – will, in another couple of years and at current growth rates, be larger than the US and the Western European economies together.

This is also true from a population point of view. As we go forward, there will be an increasing lopsidedness in a world where most of the people will be living in what we now call the developing countries, compared to the G7 countries. By 2050, those of us in the traditional powerful nations will be fewer than two billion, and in the rest of the world there will be more than seven billion. In just a few decades, the middle class population in developing countries will be larger than the total US population. In short, we are living in a time when developing countries matter a lot more.

But there are risks as well, and a key message in the US setting (and I think in Europe as well) is that developing countries will not be able to contain their problems within their borders; these problems end up mattering to the world as a whole, much like the US expression that what happens in Las Vegas doesn't stay in Las Vegas.

There is a whole list of issues that do not honour borders. Issues such as the avian flu, which was incubated in Vietnam but was a health risk to all; deforestation in Brazil, Indonesia and the Congo, which is, of course, a great contributor to climate change which will affect everyone in the world and especially the poor; energy vulnerability and instability in the Delta region of Nigeria, which affects gasoline prices around the world; and drug trafficking that stretches across borders and respects no national boundaries. Mexico, Colombia and Afghanistan are large producers of illegal narcotics, and people across the globe are victims of this industry's insidious effects.

There are also political and economic risks associated with the rise of ill-conceived populism in countries like Bolivia, Venezuela and Ecuador. And, of course, there is the terrorism issue and the instability posed by fragile states: the 'swamp'. This term refers, among other things, to the circumstances that incubated the 9/11 hijackers, but now with the Mumbai tragedy last week we see that the rise of Islamic terrorism is a problem for the world and not just for a few rich, western countries.

Against this background we can see that developing countries are beginning to matter more – both in terms of opportunities as well as risks. With that in mind, the recommendations on US development strategy in 'The White House and the World' can be thought of in terms of four themes.

The first one is that the US, and I would say this is true for Europeans as well, should build on its strength, its business acumen and its scientific and technological strength in order to invest more, including at home, in ways that benefit people who are poor in developing countries. The second is the importance of continuing to press for open markets in order to share prosperity, and under that heading we conduct research on trade, migration and investment policies. A third theme for the US is the pressing need to modernize foreign assistance programmes. The fourth theme is multilateralism and the need to move towards a much more cooperative approach to a whole set of development issues, in particular those dealt with by the World Bank, the IMF and the UN. Given the nature of the trans-national and transcontinental risks that I mentioned earlier, multilateralism is a big agenda item for the Center. After all, it was the WHO that helped contain Avian Flu, UN peacekeepers that helped stabilize West Africa and the IMF that will be called upon to put out the current financial fire.

I know the extent to which the United States embraces a multilateral approach to development is of special interest in Europe. Will the new administration support international institutions other than 'coalitions of the willing'? Is the US willing to put itself into the position institutionally where it is also subject to the rules of the game, i.e., where it has to play along and cannot pick and choose when it wants to take one initiative and not another? Will the US put much more emphasis on participation and reform of international institutions?

At the Center, we have done a lot of work on a key problem in the World Bank and the IMF, which many of you will be familiar with. Namely, it is the problem that developing countries have very limited voice and limited votes. For the most part, in the multilateral banks and at the IMF, developing countries are very much underrepresented while the US and Europe continue to hang on to their privileged access to determine the leadership of the World Bank and the IMF. Additionally, China and India ought to be given more voice and recognition at these institutions.

Let me turn now to some specific topics we address in the Commitment to Development Index, focusing specifically on the Netherlands and the US

The commitment to development index: some key topics

Climate change

Let me show you where the Netherlands is on the issue of climate change in the Commitment to Development Index: it ranks fifth of the 22 countries we rank. On this particular measure, the US ranks at the bottom. It is a really pressing development issue for us in Washington. As you know, and as we have shown at the Center in a couple of books on this matter in the last few years, the climate change problem will create a much greater burden in the developing world, with much higher costs in welfare terms than in the rich world.

The US has CO_2 emissions per-capita of 20 tons per year, whereas in Europe they are about 10 tons, in India less than 2 tons and in China about 5 tons. So we recommend investments of twenty, thirty or even forty billion US dollars per year in clean energy research and development, in particular in solar/thermal and other renewable energy sources where developing countries may have a comparative advantage. These investments should push the whole industry to go down the learning curve to the point where these new, renewable energy sources can be competitive with traditional fuels.

Trade

I will next turn to the issue of trade. On trade, the Netherlands does quite well in the Commitment to Development Index: it comes fourth. The US is doing better here and as you see, although the US is not doing great, you Europeans are a little bit worse due to the Common Agricultural Policy. But let us look at what we recommended to the US for its trade agenda.

First, we recommend that, as a development policy even more than as a trade policy measure, the next president should pick fifteen to twenty countries in the world, for example developing countries that are low-income and relatively small and vulnerable, and announce permanent duty-free, quota-free access to the US market. This would expand on existing preference programmes like the African Growth and Opportunity Act and something like Everything-but-Arms in the existing trade approach of the EU to developing countries. But, again, we should make these preferences permanent and irrevocable, and take away all the conditions and complications, like rules of origin, that needlessly complicate matters and make it more difficult for many developing countries to exploit preference programmes.

Second, we suggest that the US review its farm policy, which is of course as huge a problem there as it is in Europe, and which has undermined the Doha development round of trade negotiations.

Third, we suggest that the US support transfers that help countries to develop safety nets for their domestic losers. The idea here is that in a bilateral agreement on free trade, there should be an explicit reference to the possibility of transfers from the rich country, the US, to a developing country in order to help the developing country cope with its poor farmers, small retailers or workers in industries that are going to loose their competitiveness because of open trade.

Migration

In our book we recommend 500,000 visas to be issued for skilled migrants to the US each year instead of the 100,000 currently being issued. In the US, to get a skilled visa you apply and annually it takes about seven hours for all of them to be assigned. As a result, Bill Gates, among others, has testified several times to Congress that this doesn't make any sense. As he has pointed out, Microsoft has moved some of its facilities to Vancouver in Canada because it wasn't able to bring in the skilled and talented engineers they needed and wanted to hire.

We also recommend at least 500,000 temporary visas for unskilled workers. That would represent actually the number of unskilled workers who enter the US annually, many of them illegally. We recommend bringing in the same number of immigrants, but making them legal. And we recommend working towards bilateral treaties, for example with Mexico, under which Mexico would take the responsibility for the return of temporary migrants with the incentive that that would then generate or enable another round of temporary migrants to enter the US.

Conclusion

The problem in this world is that rich country politics always trump poor countries' needs. A good example of this is the recent Farm Bill, which many of my development-minded colleagues and I deem a deeply flawed piece of legislation that demonstrates a problem in the US. It's been called the 'Iowa problem' because it was there that this problem first came up. Iowa was the state with the first primary of the presidential campaign, and it is also the place where a lot of corn is grown, i.e., where there is vested interest in corn-based ethanol production. The effect of this is that candidates feel compelled to accede to the requests of the farm lobby, even at the expense of good policy. Yet again, politics determines policy.

I say all of this to underscore my message: we are at a very delicate moment, and it is very important for development advocates to be noisy and creative, and to help our governments over the hump in the next couple of years. Times will be tough for everyone, and we need to use all of the tools at our disposal to ensure that poor countries and their needs are not pushed out of the way by the priorities of rich countries.

Responses to questions

Foreign aid and the broader development agenda

Most of you will know that president-elect Obama, in his campaign speeches and in his campaign documents, has endorsed the Millennium Development Goals (MDGs). But more interesting and more problematic is the question of the US endorsing the 0.7 percent of GDP for foreign aid. It would be terrific if we were getting anywhere close to 0.7 percent, but I am not sure that we will. Obama said during his campaign period that his administration would double US aid. US aid is currently about twenty billion US dollars, which is not quite 0.2 percent of GDP. So a doubling might imply getting to something like 0.4 percent of GDP.

It was unfortunate that in the 2008 vice-presidential debate, when candidate Biden was asked about how to cope with the fiscal burdens, the one thing he chose to mention was that their administration might not be able to honour immediately what it had promised about foreign aid. What he actually said was that we might not be able to double it in the first four years or something like that, but it is amazing how many people heard that foreign aid would be cut. Even if aid were cut in half, the fiscal effect would be trivial compared to the cost of the stimulus package and given the overall budget of the US. This should give you a sense of the politics surrounding foreign aid in the US: for both parties it is invariably the first item on the chopping block.

As I said, focusing on the broader picture has been a deliberate choice from the founding of the Center. We use this broader lens to drive home the importance of foreign aid quality as well as quantity. We also use the bigger picture to underscore that there are other issues that matter as well, reminding in particular the American people that there are multiple ways in which what they do or don't do matters tremendously for poor people around the world.

The Center was founded by coincidence just one month after 9/11 in 2001. At the time I would have guessed that our biggest challenge was to just get development onto anybody's agenda, anytime, anywhere, because during the nineties development almost completely fell off the political agenda. That is the way we began, realizing that it would be a struggle just to get development thinking incorporated into the legislative agenda in the US. As it turned out, 9/11 changed things a lot in the Bush administration. Among other things, the administration got very engaged in the fight against AIDS and, because of the United Nations Monterrey, Mexico conference in 2002, it was pushed into what turned out to be a great announcement and a good idea: the founding of the Millennium Challenge Corporation. A lot of things changed in the intervening years, but I have to say that, in the US context, it is important that we have this broader agenda because in this time of crisis it is likely that there will be minimal attention to more aid.

A new world system

I already mentioned the need for reform at the World Bank and the IMF, and giving more voice and vote to China and India. We also need to engage China and India on international security issues, including staffing and financing of peacekeeping operations, climate change and infectious diseases: all of these global challenges I have mentioned. We don't have them at the table now in a serious way, and I believe that, with regard to some of these development issues that are, in fact, global in scope like climate change, there is a huge opportunity to bring them to the table. But only if it is for a discussion among equals.

For example, one of the things we recommended in our earlier work is that there be established at the World Bank a large trust fund for the provision and financing of global public goods. Contributions to that fund could come from these new rising countries as well as from the traditional Western powers, and the voice and votes at the table should be related to contributions, maybe on some sliding scale. If you are a low-income country, for example Malawi, and you contribute, you may get twice the weight that you would get if you were the US or the Netherlands. The idea would be to engage those countries to help them move faster to a position of sharing in global stewardship.

Prospects for a more collaborative approach by the US

Now that the US is no longer the superpower in the world, it will have to face its partners in a different way. What are the prospects for a more collaborative approach by the US? I think Americans are really hoping for a return to a position of respect in the world. Certainly all the signals coming from the transition team and president-elect Obama are that there will be a major effort for a change in style at least, maybe also in substance, but certainly in style, to reject what was seen as the unilateralist and arrogant style of the Bush administration. Some of that got better at the margin in the second term of President Bush, but there is a real thirst in US political and diplomatic circles for a change.

What will be more challenging for the US is sharing power in a different way that involves giving up a little bit of existing apparent power in the long term interest of everybody, Americans included. That will be tough politically. We will see what happens. A lot will depend on attitudes on Capitol Hill. I think that for the leaders of countries like the Netherlands, in interacting with the US, it is very important to encourage cooperation, to encourage the multilateral approach, not only with the administration on the executive side but with key members of the Congress as well.

A human rights based approach to development

Hillary Clinton has several times referred to Eleanor Roosevelt as her role model. The question is whether she and the administration will include a rights-based approach in the development agenda and what will, more specifically, be her sexual and reproductive rights agenda. We are very hopeful that she will move as quickly as politically sensible to get rid of the present gag rule and get back to a more reasonable approach on reproductive rights.

In general we are very hopeful that the entire foreign policy will be better on human rights and on reproductive rights, and better than it was during Bill Clinton's administration. At the Center, we haven't done much on the human rights approach to development, but maybe it is something we should think about more, because, certainly, the more I think about it personally, the more I see its merits.

The effect of the financial crisis on developing countries

At the beginning I mentioned risks and problems that were transnational. Right now we face such a problem in terms of a global financial upheaval. Developing countries will certainly be deeply affected by the financial crisis, and that is a terrible tragedy.

The effect of such crises is always asymmetric: the rich gain more during the boom and the poor and incipient middle class in developing countries will be hit very hard as they were in Asia, Brazil and Argentina during the financial crises in the late nineties. I was on a panel with Mary Robinson, the UN High Commissioner on Human Rights in Doha, and she made the point that this financial crisis is the responsibility of the US and to some extent also the UK and the Europeans, yet she had not heard anybody say sorry to the developing countries who are going to be hit hardest. In the emerging market economies, where the financial links are stronger and who are already being hit first, the poor in those settings will lose out tremendously.

At the moment the poorest countries – Africa, Central America – are being hit: remittances are down and, of course, trade and exports are down. The difficulties that will be faced in the rich world will be magnified in terms of welfare losses in developing countries.

At the Doha meeting there was, of course, a lot of discussion about the need to ensure that foreign aid commitments are being honoured, but, frankly, I think that there is a very large risk that they will not be honoured. At the Center, we did some quick analysis of what happened to aid flows in earlier crises. After the financial crisis in the nineties in Japan and the banking crisis in the early nineties in Sweden and Finland, there was an initial dramatic decline and only a very gradual return of aid flows, not quite to trend, except maybe in Sweden.

The above history relates to single country crises. Currently we have a global crisis that requires a global and multilateral solution. There will be a tremendous focus on our own problems in the rich world. I already mentioned migration and trade, and I will continue to hammer on those issues. One of the reasons is that, particularly on the trade side, there are some risks with the new Democratic administration, and we looked for a way to help it to at least avoid doing anything really bad – to kind of hold the fort and find something positive to do. That is why I mentioned some kind of early, even if somewhat symbolic, step like announcing to give fifteen very poor countries perfect, open access to the US market. The administration will be able to say that these countries only constitute 1 or 2 percent maximum of all imports into the US so this would not risk US jobs.

PART 2

From crisis to sustainable development

Towards a Healthy Financial Sector in Developing Countries

Jan Kees de Jager

Economic growth and the common good are two issues that are very close to my heart. Economic growth is the essence of my day-to-day work as state secretary for finance, and the common good is something that underpins my political convictions. It is a great honour to be invited here to present the vision of the Dutch Government on international poverty reduction, especially in these times of economic crisis. For the Dutch Government, the position is clear. It must support developing countries and work with them. Together with them we must find solutions that bring back sustainable growth, particularly in these difficult times. We have given our word that we will not slacken in our efforts and we will call on other countries to join us.

The crisis

First I would like to discuss the crisis we are in and its consequences for developing countries. A recession of the current scope and depth has not occurred since the 1930s. Above all, it is a global crisis that has left its mark on all four corners of the world. It began in the American housing market but quickly spread to engulf us all. Governments and central banks throughout the world have been forced to take action. By doing so, they managed to avert a complete meltdown of the financial sector. The worst danger seems to have passed, but we now find ourselves on the slow and sometimes painful path back towards a healthy financial sector: one that fulfils its vital economic function without taking excessive risks.

It was first thought that the crisis could be confined to the financial sector and the rest of the economy would be left unscathed. But the collapse of Lehman Brothers a year ago and the subsequent nationalization of ABN Amro and Fortis made it clear that the rest of the economy would also be hit hard.

The global community was quick to respond to this new reality. Following their life-saving interventions to shore up the banks, many governments, including the Dutch Government, took sweeping measures to stimulate the economy. These measures seem to have worked in the short-term and it looks as though the economic freefall has been brought to a halt. The outlook for next year is generally optimistic but the recovery is still fragile.

The consequences

Developing countries are suffering more than most from the current crisis; the recession has hit them hard and the already frail growth in the developing world is coming under severe pressure. Given the problems in the developed world, many donor countries have become less concerned about the plight of developing countries at a time when their support would be very welcome.

As I have already said, the Netherlands remains committed to development cooperation and will keep its promises, also during this crisis. We cannot stress the international context of development aid enough. In this respect, the crisis also offers opportunities: global problems need global solutions. We should look upon the current challenge as a means to strengthen international cooperation. It is an invitation to tackle problems together.

Joint action

If we make the comparison again with the 1930s and the Great Depression, we can see an immediate and obvious difference: eighty years ago nearly all countries turned inwards, and a wave of protectionism swept over the world with direct consequences for the global economy. This time, the response has been completely different. Countries are looking to each other and are trying to work out solutions together. Admittedly, there are signs of protectionism here and there. But they seem to be limited and everyone agrees that joint action produces better solutions. This is partly because of the presence of the international policy framework and international institutions that did not exist in the 1930s. There is no denying that the credit crunch is a serious threat. But there is a great willingness to take joint action. The IMF and the World Bank are playing an important role in reversing the crisis, and the G20 has turned out to be an important forum in which a very mixed group of countries are together showing leadership. For the first time in history, everyone is at the table and there is a sense of interdependence.

The role of the financial sector in developing countries

Besides the global nature of the crisis and the international dimension of a solution, the crisis is a financial crisis. Paradoxically, the financial world, where the crisis began, also holds the key to economic recovery. In the first place, the financial sector in developing nations is small and at first sight the damage seemed to be limited. The small size of the financial sector, however, is in itself a problem as well: it restricts the access to credit of many people in developing countries. If people cannot borrow money at reasonable cost and have no alternative but to borrow at exorbitant rates in the informal economy, many potentially productive projects will be deprived of funds and economic growth will be nipped in the bud.

Over the past years, one often-heard the call for free access to financial markets. This idea of improved access went hand in hand with a drive towards liberalization and deregulation. A sea change is now taking place. It goes without saying that the role assigned to supervisors and regulators has become far more important in the past year. The question is: How can we tackle the underlying problems of lack of access to financial markets without losing sight of the vulnerability of financial institutions?

Princess Maxima has been asked to become an advisor to Ban Ki-moon on the question of how to improve access to financial markets. The challenge is to offer people in developing countries inventive solutions without exposing the economy to even greater volatility and shocks. A good example of this is microfinancing. By providing relatively small loans on a local scale, this financial innovation can give people a direct chance to improve their own lives. Not by providing one-off aid, but by giving them a way to satisfy their own needs. By lending them money to buy farm equipment, enlarge a shop and so on.

Cooperation with local private parties is the key to microfinance. The knowledge of these private parties and the local networks are a crucial input for a balanced development of the financial sector in developing countries. The danger we are facing now is that the crisis in donor countries will put an end to many microfinancing projects. If so, a one-off shock might have long-term consequences. The commitment of the Netherlands has not waned in light of the crisis. In 2009, the Dutch government has pledged around 100 million to financial sector development. FMO is an important partner in this effort. Recently, during the G20 in London another fifty million has been earmarked for trade credits for developing nations.

New instruments

Another, more recent innovation that the Netherlands supports is the provision of new forms of insurance to large groups of people in developing countries. Lack of access to doctors – like lack of access to loans – can have far-reaching consequences for people and their productivity. If people have to save to pay for insurance, they have less money to invest. And many people are not even in a position to save. Health insurance means people have to save less in case they become ill.

Setting up health insurance funds can help spread the risks, and relatively minor ailments need not lead to long-term health problems. By working together with private parties, a considerable improvement can be brought about in the lives of large numbers of people. These are examples of inventive ways to use development aid to improve the quality of life. A better spread of risks can bring about substantial improvements.

The Netherlands is not the only country to recognize the importance to developing countries of access to financial services and products. The G20 in Pittsburgh starts tomorrow, and the G20 Financial Access Initiative will be on the agenda. This initiative considers the crisis's impact on access to financial services for the poor and small businesses. Its chief aim is to increase the use of branchless banking and small business finance.

New initiatives

The Netherlands is already playing an important role in small business finance by taking part in Small Enterprise Assistance Funds, which take equity interests in small businesses in developing countries. The Netherlands wholeheartedly supports the establishment of a Global Small Business Capital Fund. A second initiative is to set up a global, diversified currency fund modelled on the existing Currency Exchange Fund (TCX) that was launched in 2008 and operates from the Netherlands. The fund would give local banks better access to currency hedging instruments. This would in turn make it easier for local businesses to be granted long-term loans.

Conclusion

Even if we have not looked on the financial world as a source of stability in the past year, we must not lose sight of the primary function of financial institutions. The uncertainty caused by poor access to credit and insurance has an enormous impact on investments and thus on personal productivity. The shared challenge we are facing is to realize the enormous potential for personal development that is latent in developing countries.

The present crisis has an impact that is felt throughout the world. The landscape of the financial sector is changing rapidly. So, we now have to commit ourselves to a stronger financial sector in developing countries also. Especially now we need to fall in step internationally. Together we are now faced by the opportunity to build towards a healthy financial sector in the developing world.

Panel I

Diverse Approaches to Economic
Growth and Development

Economic Growth and Social Protection for the Poor and Vulnerable

Shenggen Fan

Food and financial crises hurt the poor

Economic growth, agricultural growth and social protection for the poor and vulnerable are particularly important in addressing the recent food and financial crises. Even before both crises hit, hunger has been on the rise in the last decade. Mainly due to the food and financial crises, the number of hungry people around the world increased from 873 million from 2004–06 to 1,020 million in 2009 (see Figure 1). This sharp rise in hunger is in stark contradiction with the 1996 World Food Summit (WFS) target of reducing the number of hungry people to no more than 420 million by 2015.[1]

High and volatile food prices have severely undermined the food security and livelihoods of poor people. Since the poor spend 50 to

Figure 1   World hunger, 1969-71 to 2009

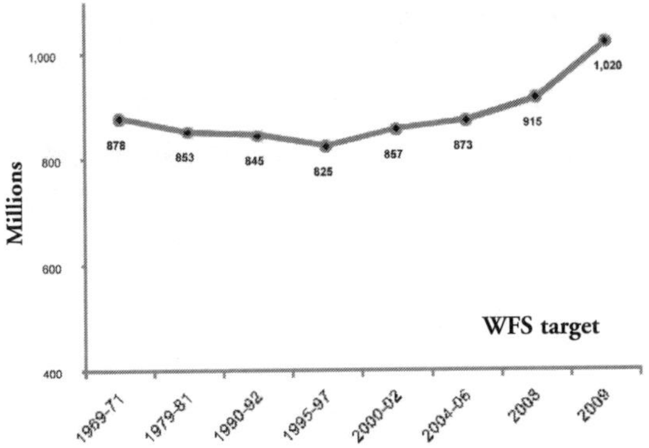

Sources: Data from FAO (Food and Agriculture Organization of the United Nations). 2009. State of food insecurity in the world 2009. Rome; FAO. 2009. Hunger. Available at: http://www.fao.org/hunger/en/.

70 percent of their household budget on food, food price increases as well as wages that did not adjust accordingly caused their purchasing power to decline. Thus, a doubling of food prices as observed during the food crisis hurt the poor and vulnerable dramatically. In response to the food price hikes, poor households in distress cut back on the quantity and quality of food consumed, sold their productive assets, and withdrew their children, especially girls, from school. These limited coping strategies employed by the resource-poor have severe consequences for their long-term productivity and well-being.

Slow economic growth and recession added to the burden of the poor and vulnerable. Global economic growth plunged from about 8 percent in the pre-crisis period to 2 percent in 2009 (see Figure 2). The only good news was that some of the emerging economies continued to grow, although at a much slower rate. In contrast, a majority of the Organisation for Economic Co-operation and Development countries experienced negative growth rates. In addition, foreign direct investment fell significantly with the financial crisis leading to a shortage of capital for agriculture (see Figure 2). The capital crunch resulted in higher debt burdens for farmers, especially smallholders. In India, for example, an increasing number of poor farmers struggling with their debts were put in precarious situations. The economic downturn also led to reduced employment and lower wages of unskilled workers. In China, more than twenty million migrant workers had lost their jobs as of early 2009.[2] Many had to return to their hometown to engage in agriculture. Remittances, which act as a buffer against income shocks for poor households and contribute to economic growth, also declined during the financial crisis (see Figure 2). Substantial declines in remittance inflows occurred in some of the Central American countries such as El Salvador, Guatemala and Honduras.

Economic growth for hunger reduction

Economic growth is a necessary condition for poverty and hunger reduction. Empirical evidence shows that in Bangladesh, a 1-percentage point increase in GDP results in a decline in poverty of

Figure 2   Financial inflows and GDP growth, 1990-2009

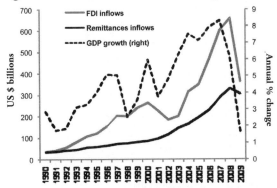

Sources: Data from IMF (International Monetary Fund). 2009. World Economic Outlook database. Available at: http://www.imf.org/external/pubs/ft/weo/2009/01/weodata/index.aspx; Ratha, Mohapatra, and Silwal. 2009. Migration and remittances data. Available at: http://siteresources.worldbank.org/INTPROSPECTS/Resources/334934-1110315015165/RemittancesData_Nov09(Public).xls; UNCTAD (United Nations Conference on Trade and Development). 2009. Foreign Direct Investment database. Available at: http://www.unctad.org/Templates/Page.asp?intItemID=1923; and World Bank. 2009. World Development Indicators 2009. Washington, D.C.

0.73 percentage points.[3] Figure 3 shows that a clear correlation also exists between economic growth and hunger. The proportion of the people undernourished and suffering from malnutrition declines as per-capita income increases. Another illustration of the fact that income growth and hunger reduction are strongly correlated is that a 10 percent increase in the income of very poor households increases their caloric acquisition by 5 percent,[4] showing an elasticity of caloric intake of 0.5. Income growth and pre-school malnutrition, however, are loosely correlated, which suggests that the direct effect of income growth on pre-school nutrition is low. Nonetheless, targeted programmes aimed at pre-schoolers are needed given that such programmes have high economic returns. In addition, since the first two years of a child's life are crucial for physical and cognitive development, nutrition interventions must be introduced during this period in order to prevent childhood malnutrition and enhance future productivity.[5]

The role of agriculture in pro-poor growth

Agriculture-led growth is particularly crucial for reducing poverty and hunger. A study on Ethiopia shows that a 1 percent annual

Figure 3 Hunger and GDP growth in developing countries

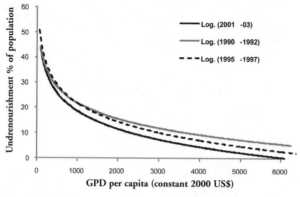

Source: von Braun, J. 2006. Emerging Issues in Developing Countries' Food and Agriculture: Challenges for policy and research. Presented at the International Fund for Agricultural Development seminar. Rome, September 22.

increase in per-capita GDP growth, led by growth in agriculture, reduces poverty[6] Another study shows that at least one agricultural extension visit reduces poverty by 9.8 percentage points and increases consumption growth by more than 7 percentage points.[7]

Table 1 R&D investment and impact on poverty and output growth under poverty minimization

	R&D allocation (million 2005 US$)		Change in number of poor (million)	Agric. output growth (% points)
	2008	2013	2008-2020	2008-2020
Sub-Saharan Africa	608	2,913	-143.8	2.8
South Asia	908	3,111	-124.6	2.4
Developing world	4,975	9,951	-282.1	1.1

Source: von Braun J., S. Fan, R. Meinzen-Dick, M. W. Rosegrant, and A. Nin Pratt. 2008. International Agricultural Research for Food Security, Poverty Reduction, and the Environment: What to Expect from Scaling Up CGIAR Investments and "Best Bet" Programs. Washington D.C.: IFPRI.

Public spending is one of the most direct and effective mechanisms to promote agricultural growth and poverty reduction. The developing world is currently spending about five billion US dollars on agricultural research. If this amount is doubled to ten billion US dollars by 2013 over the next five years, the number of poor people will be reduced by almost 300 million (see Table 1). Increased investment in agricultural research will also increase annual agricultural growth by 1.1 percentage points. This impact will be particularly strong in Africa, which will see a reduction in the number of poor people of nearly 150 million as a result of a doubling of agricultural research investment. Annual agricultural growth is also expected to increase by 2.8 percentage points (see Table 1). The impact will also be large in South Asia where the number of poor people will be reduced by about 125 million and annual agricultural growth will increase by 2.4 percent.

In addition to economic growth, effective social safety nets are needed to decrease poverty and hunger. Social safety nets can promote economic growth and reduce poverty and hunger by:

i   creating individual, household, and community assets;
ii protecting households assets when shocks occur;
iii helping households use their existing resources more effectively to cope with risk;
iv facilitating structural reforms of the economy; and
v   reducing inequality.

So how much is spent on social protection? At current levels, Germany, France and Sweden spend 7 to 8 percent of GDP on health. Austria, Greece and Poland spend 11 to 13 percent of GDP on pensions. But on health, pensions, and social assistance, developing countries spend very little. Pakistan, Peru, Colombia and Chile, for example, spend less than 1 percent of GDP on social assistance.

Social safety nets are particularly important during food and financial crises. Many governments have effectively used safety nets to mitigate adverse impacts, though political constraints sometimes limited the responses. China, for example, undertook a stimulus package of about 600 billion US dollars, including spending on social safety nets. However, some of the programmes are aimed at large scale investment in agriculture, but do not directly target the population. Others programmes consist of direct income transfers to poor people. In China, a minimum protection scheme was launched to make sure that everybody has minimum access to income in order to help cope with the current food and financial crises. But some other governments did not expand safety nets as much as was expected.

The time of crises is a vital period to re-examine the role of social safety nets, in particular regarding securing access to food. Social protection programmes should focus on the most vulnerable such as children, women, excluded groups, disadvantaged groups and the poorest. Pro-poor social protection and nutrition interventions – both protective and preventive actions – are urgently needed. Protective actions, for example, can be in the form of cash transfers, conditional and unconditional, and employment-based food security programmes. These schemes can ensure that poor people have immediate access to food and to cash. Preventive actions, for example, school feeding and early childhood nutrition programmes, can help keep children in school and enhance long-term productivity.

Scaling up social protection programmes remains challenging but achievable. Policymakers need to start with the existing institutions and choose an appropriate scale for the programmes. The tax base should be strengthened to provide funds for social protection. Information and incentives should also be improved in order to target the poorest and vulnerable. Also crucial for effective targeting is broad-based political and stakeholder support. Public-private partnerships can enhance the delivery of social protection and the private sector can play a crucial role in achieving this goal. Drawing on global lessons, in particular from Asia and Latin America, is also very important. Asia's strategy in the past was to use broad-based growth in agriculture or large-scale overall economic growth for poverty reduction. This is necessary, but not sufficient. Latin America, which has been implementing targeted social protection programmes for a long time, has lessons to share with Asia and the rest of the world. Thinking across institutions such as markets, microfinance, and insurance is also essential when designing social protection programmes.

In sum, strategies towards inclusive growth are needed to accelerate economic growth and to increase its pro-poor qualities.

Social spending and its effectiveness should also be accelerated so as to effectively target the poor and vulnerable.

Notes

1   FAO (Food and Agriculture Organization of the United Nations). 2009. More people than ever are victims of hunger. Press release, June 19.
2   BBC News. 2009. Chinese migrant job losses mount. Available at: http://news.bbc.co.uk/2/hi/asia-pacific/7864293.stm.
3   Klasen, S., and M. Misselhorn. 2006. Determinants of the Growth Semi-Elasticity of Poverty Reduction, Proceedings of the German Development Economics Conference, Berlin 2006 15, Verein für Socialpolitik, Research Committee Development Economics.
4   Hoddinott, J. 2009. Poverty, hunger, and agricultural growth. Presented at the Agriculture and Food Security Roundtable. Washington, D.C., June 12.
5   For more details, see Hoddinott, J., J. A. Maluccio, J. R. Behrman, R. Flores, and R. Martorell. 2008. Effect of a nutrition intervention during early childhood on economic productivity in Guatemalan adults. The Lancet 371 (610): 411-16; Ruel, M. T, P. Menon, J-P. Habicht, C. Loechl, G. Bergeron, G. Pelto, M. Arimond, J. Maluccio, L. Michaud, and B. Hankebo. 2008. Age-based preventive targeting of food assistance and behaviour change and communication for reduction of childhood undernutrition in Haiti: A cluster randomised trial. The Lancet 371 (9612): 588-95.
6   Diao, X., B. Fekadu, S. Haggblade, A. S. Taffesse, K. Wamisho, and B. Yu. 2007b. Agricultural growth linkages in Ethiopia: Estimates using fixed and flexible price models. IFPRI Discussion Paper 00695. Washington, D.C.: IFPRI.
7   Dercon, S., D. O. Gilligan, J. Hoddinott, and T. Woldehanna.

Crisis in the international system and Africa's development

Benno Ndulu

Africa has in the last couple of years come a long way in terms of development efforts that have been applied across the region. Our development strategies have gone through a long evolution. African countries have not been alone in moving from focussing initially on concerns with regard to market failure and the adoption of dirigist strategies, and then moving on to the next stage where we were mostly preoccupied with government failure and pursued liberalization alongside other parts of the world. The pendulum redressed in a way that saw the state again playing its supportive role with regard to the market.

That was one string. The other string was our attitude to cross border flows of goods and services and capital and moving from inward looking strategies early on, to being part of the globalization process in production, trade and capital later on. With the new reality that we are operating in, global interdependence has played a big role in the design of the development strategies in the region.

Consequences of increased global interdependence

Three major aspects of global interdependence are crucial. One is that economies have become much more interdependent. Production takes place more or less in a globalized factory. I think Adam Smith, if we had a chance to wake him up, would be surprised to see how the division of labour has become part of a globalized process, not limited to a single factory. Trade has grown much faster than production and the international financial flows have dwarfed national savings and financial intermediation.

The second aspect of interdependence is that economic and financial actors are now unconstrained by borders, significantly weakening the role of the nation state. Some of the multinational companies operating in our countries are much larger in power and influence than the countries in which they are operating. This is the new reality that we have to face in Africa.

The third aspect is that contagion has become a powerful tool for propagating booms and crises across borders, and this is what we have seen now: systemically important economies are more influential than in the past. What happens in those economies now has a bigger influence across the world. We have seen that African countries have largely turned out to be victims of the crisis, which started in the systemically important countries. So it is not enough to secure your own economy, as one had wanted to believe, because it is ultimately the interdependence that has turned to propagate the crisis.

African vulnerabilities to this interdependence stems from four factors. One is the extent of the exposure of domestic production to external demand and, in turn, dependence of African countries on primary commodities and natural resources. Second is the degree of dependence on foreign savings to finance investments (FDI and ODA). Third is the extent of dependence on imports for domestic production, and this is true for both primary and manufactured products. The fourth vulnerability is weakness from acting individually as small countries and markets when the rest of the world is forming defensive blocs through economic integration. These features make African economies much more vulnerable in the context of this interdependent world.

The upside of globalization

But there is an upside to globalization: it is not all grey. We have seen countries in Asia that exploited the interdependence to record unprecedented growth and poverty reduction. African economies themselves have also benefited greatly. About fifteen countries have grown at more than 5.3 percent over the last decade; twenty-one countries have grown at more than 5 percent in the last five years; we have seen inflation go down to single digit levels before the food and oil crisis, which is a big achievement. We have also seen a significant build-up of international reserves from the boom in exports, which has helped to cushion to some extent the effect of the crisis. More than two-thirds of the Sub-Saharan countries have also seen both investments and revenues increased. FDI raised from eleven billion US dollars in 2000 to fifty-three billion US dollars in 2007. The revenues to GDP ratio also increased.

All of these gains are now under threat, partly because of the crisis. Although African countries, in most cases, have weathered rather well in terms of the financial sector, the global recession has had a major impact. From weakening demand for commodities with global recession, to a slow down in capital flows (FDI and ODA) which has widened the financing gap and reduced access to credit. There are those that had already started to turn to sovereign issuance, to borrow in the world capital markets, but which have had to postpone this because the spreads suddenly widened very significantly. Inflation has threatened the sustenance of growth and the high cost of finance has intensified financial risks. We have seen also a very rapid outflow of some of the reserves that had been build up, particularly with movements of hedge funds that have taken profits and externalized. And these are real, major threats of the gains that had been made today.

Africa's main concerns

What are the main concerns of Africa from the crisis? One is that it endangered the whole sustainability of the growth process that we had begun. We fear that, if proper action is not taken, there might be a repeat of the 1980s, when the global recession translated into almost two decades of lost growth. I will come back to that.

We also fear that it will undermine the macro stability that had been achieved rather painfully over the last two decades. We also fear the erosion of progress in social well-being, particularly in education and health. There is a real danger that there will be a push back toward achievements of the MDGs. But most worrisome for us is a threat to social and political stability if safety nets against vulnerabilities, particularly jobs and food, are not provided. And that would cause a long-term problem.

So how are we coping with this? First, I think the focus of most interventions have been on weathering the storm so that we can continue with genuine development after the crisis has played down. Here our first priority is protecting jobs, mainly in the exporting sectors and those linked to them, ensuring availability of food at affordable prices, which is the food security challenge, protecting life savings programmes that show results (such at HIV, malaria and tuberculosis) – we are protecting these at any cost – and sustaining macro stability and protecting the banking system from client distress.

In Africa we are facing a real danger that we will have pressure on the banking system, starting from the global recession, which weakens the growth in the exporting activities and builds up non-performing loans in the banking system. It is important that we prevent such distress, because that will again lead to another round of credit freeze and subsequent reduction in growth. Finally, it is very important to protect investment in infrastructure. We cannot afford to have a stop-and-go process as we had in the 1980s. We need to keep all the capacity for growth in investments going.

We are aware that the global response is important in the sense that our recovery will very much depend on the recovery in the systemically important countries. So we appreciate the importance of the bail out schemes underway in these countries, knowing in fact very well that once they recover, we in Africa also stand a good chance of recovery.

But these schemes should avoid protectionism, which will close out those economies that, for trade, are dependent on their natural resources. This should add, of course, to the pre-emptive measures to make sure that such a crisis does not return. Pre-emptive measures should focus on correcting regulatory failures like effective surveillance and strengthening the global regulatory institutions and players, including hedge funds and rating agencies.

We should be committed to an early conclusion of an ambitious and development-oriented Doha Round. Shareholders need to agree to increase the financing capacity of the Bretton Woods

Institutions and Regional Development Banks to provide trade finance facilities. Development partners should be encouraged to provide technical, financial and political support to the Aid for Trade Initiative.

Is de-globalization an option?

De-globalization is definitively not an option for Africa, because we know that there is a very strong statistical relation between African and its trading partners growth. So there is no way in which African countries can proceed in terms of development without that linkage. Secondly, African's strong natural resource base makes it world market-dependent, and that is the most important resource that it has. But we can change the terms of engagement over time.

How will we be able to build resilience to external shocks? One way is via diversification of our economies and reduced reliance on primary commodities. This is one thing that we have always tried to pursue. Second is better integration of our production and consumption processes, including adding value. Third is a reduction in aid dependence and enhanced domestic savings mobilization, which is quite important for building resilience. Fourth is diversifying our sources of foreign savings, building on our recently achieved creditworthiness by having access to capital markets. Finally, more effective regional integration to enhance the connectedness of our economies and our global influence as a bloc is required. And development partners will do well to support us in the process of this building of resilience to shocks.

A Latin American Perspective on the Financial Crisis

Alfredo Valladão

As a Brazilian, I can tell you that Brazil may have another way of looking at the crisis than some other countries. As a matter of fact, it has so far lived quite happily with the crisis. And I would also like to say that, dealing with the crisis, we should not throw the baby out with the bathwater.

We have to be conscious that in the last fifteen years, the world may have had the fastest growth in the history of mankind, a growth that lifted around 800 million people out of poverty. That means an advance in poverty reduction by 600 million. But there was more than that. In many countries, including my own country, the inequality index, the Gini coefficient, got better. Even in Brazil, one of the worst performers on equality, the Gini coefficient improved. So we could say that in the last fifteen years the whole 'financial party' did more for development than forty years of development aid!

Secondly, this advance was possible because of at least three things. Firstly, as Benno Ndulu said, trade was very important; second: very cheap and available credit; and third, the information technology and transport innovation that we got in the last twenty years. This permitted a very important new thing in the world economy – the fragmentation of the production chain of value that resulted in a big increase in interdependence of production all over the world, a boom in global consumption and a boom in global foreign direct investment.

A crisis of confidence

The problem with this very fast growth and interdependence is that people started to think about the sustainability of this process.

I think that the crisis, therefore, is less of a financial crisis and more of a crisis of confidence concerning the sustainability of the process. One year before the Lehmann Brothers broke down, we already had this huge inflation of commodity and energy and food and mineral prices in the world. This was a mark of a lack of confidence that this growth could go on forever. People all over the world were questioning whether there will be enough food, minerals, energy, water and clean air if we keep going on with that rate of growth and with new people coming into the market.

This doubt about the sustainability migrated from natural resources to the soft spot of the financial system, which was the sub-primes, then to the whole financial system, and then to the production system.

What to do?

Thinking about what to do, we all know that growth is not enough. But without growth, nothing is possible. As Benno Ndulu said, we cannot turn the clock back on interdependence. Perhaps we could, but if we did that, it would mean spreading poverty all over the world, including to the rich countries.

In this kind of systemic crisis, there are always more or less three solutions. The first is a very efficient and feasible solution. It is a global war: you destroy a lot of fixed capital, you kill a lot of people, and then you can grow again very fast. This was the kind of solution that we had in the last two centuries. It works, but it is not very palatable.

The second is to try to impose slow growth. That could be efficient, but I don't think it is feasible. How are you going to tell two-thirds of mankind, including the Chinese, the Brazilians, the Indians and the South Africans: 'Look, now you are going to grow slowly. Because your great grandchildren will have a stake in it, you have to stay calm, keep on with poverty and then, in two or three generations, you are going to be rich.' That is absolutely impossible in the world of today. Nobody will buy that.

You also have one last solution that some economists call the Schumpeterian creative destruction leap, which is to have fast growth, but with less intensive use of natural resources. It is what the G20 call the ecological economy. It is a tall order, but it may be worth trying.

Fight protection first

But first we have to fight protection. It is not true that there is no danger of protectionism. There *is* a danger of protectionism. Just look at what the US did with the Chinese tyres. Everybody is doing that kind of thing. We have to fight it, because we have to deepen the interdependence of production and consumption. For that, we have to first complete the Doha Round, strengthen the rules of the trading system and then open the way to discuss the real challenges to trade in the future.

These challenges are first what I call 'creative managed trade'. When you have, for example, Gulf States buying land in Africa and then taking all the production of this land back home and not to the world market, that is bad for the world market and for food security in the world. We have to fight that countries that buy a chunk of energy in one country can refuse to put it on the world market. Instead, I have heard that the Japanese have a programme of buying land whereby the food produced on this land will be put on the world market instead of taking it to the national market. Now this would be something interesting.

The second big challenge to trade is export taxes on commodities. This is coming up in the world today and is really bad. Every country is trying to introduce this, and it is a kind of reverse protectionism. In the WTO, they don't have rules for that. They have rules for not imposing import taxes but no rules for export taxes. I know that Europeans, for example, are very worried about this because Europe is very dependent on raw materials.

The third challenge is what I call green protectionism. We have already seen this when Sarkozy said that we have to have a green tax on the border for countries that don't have a carbon tax. This is very bad. You could start a trade war on this.

Protecting the poor

In addition to what I have suggested about trade, there have to be some policies in both poor and rich countries to soften the blow to the minority of people who are displaced and suffer from this interdependence. You can not just say: OK, interdependence is good, we get richer, so we have to accept what it takes. But there are people who are suffering. It is a minority, but you have to have civic policies for this minority. This means also that the politicians should make speeches and go public defending trade, defending openness as well as introduce policies to soften the blow. They need to educate the public, particularly in rich countries.

Dealing with the financial system

The next set of recommendations is concerning credit. Everybody agrees that we need more regulation in the world financial system today. The problem is: where do you put the bar on regulation? You have to cut the excesses. You cannot kill the goose with the golden eggs, however. The more regulation you put on, the less riskier the system, and the more expensive and less available is the credit. The less regulation you put in, the riskier the system, but the more available and less expensive is the credit. So this is what we are discussing about in the G20: where exactly do we put the bar? This is not a technical issue. This is a political issue.

Risks and rates of growth

In societies like in Europe, we are getting older. We are prosperous. What we want is work. We don't want risk. We want stability, even if it is with slow growth. So we want more regulation! But if you are a poor and young society, what do you want? You want a booming economy. You want more risk, less regulation and more credit. As I said, this is what we are discussing in the G20: where you put the bar on regulation.

Another problem with credit is the crowding of markets. Next year, or the next two years, Europe and the US will go to the capital market to finance their huge deficits and bailouts. By doing so, they will crowd the credit markets. This is bad for all developing countries, for Foreign Direct Investment, etc. This should be tackled instantly. But how can we do that without hampering access to credit for poor countries?

Migration and remittances

A side issue of credit, strange though it is, is migration. For old societies, migration is absolutely necessary to compensate for the greying of these societies. Everybody, or at least every economist, knows this. We also know the problems that these societies have in accepting this migration. But migration is also very important for remittances. They are today very important as a source of credit for development. I think that it is time to start looking for negotiating pacts on migration between North and South. Also for Latin America, this is very important, this migration to Europe, even more so than to the US.

Democratization of credit

Another set of recommendations concerns sustainable growth. The first thing to do is to find an alternative to the American consumption locomotive. As you know, all this huge growth in the last fifteen years was possible because of the US market, which represented 35 percent of final consumption in the world. If you add the UK consumption, which is 7 percent and Europe, including the UK, you get two thirds of world consumption. But the US will not continue to consume at that old level. Now the Chinese, for example, today consume only 2 percent of total world consumption. So, even if the Chinese would double their level of consumption, that will only be a blip in global consumption.

So we will have to find ways to make other people consume more if you want to keep up economic growth. But that means one thing: democratization of credit. People will have to have more access to credit. But in a lot of societies, like in China, India and

Brazil, this is complicated. These societies still have a clientelistic way of distributing credit.

Democratizing credit means democratizing power and that is complicated, but may be we could discuss these things, for example opening up our countries to foreign banks and introduce more competition for credit inside our different countries.

Ecological economy

What is ecological economy? If you really look at what happened in this crisis, you had a 15 to 20 percent drop in consumption and production. This 20 percent was sufficient enough to calm down the commodity markets. We may keep it like this, but then we will have slow growth. So the problem is how to get back this 20 percent in a more sustainable way. If we talk about green economy or ecological economy, we are talking about this 20 percent or 15 percent of GDP, we are not talking about the whole economy. This 20 percent means a tremendous effort in terms of credits and innovation. This is what we call the Schumpeterian creative destruction process. This implies the introduction of a lot of new technology, a lot of new businesses, improving the quality of buildings, introducing new software so that the production processes will be cleaner, and so forth. You have the whole world for this.

But in this process, there is one challenge that we should be worried about. It is what I call a new green gap between rich and poor. Countries on the rich side have the technology and the money to engage in this. But if there is no way to negotiate some transfer of technology, obviously with the provision of a fair return of intellectual property, we will get again a kind of war between the rich and poor countries on this new economy and on the new 20 percent economy that is coming up.

To conclude

It is not true that you can achieve all this without the engagement of more people and more countries. The G8 is not enough anymore. As for the G20: we don't know yet how exactly this will work. But it is absolutely important to give more voice to more players. Everybody more or less agrees to that. But the devil is in the details. We all know that if we want to give more voice to India, Brazil, China, etc., in the IMF, this means less of a voice for Europe. How are the Europeans going to get their act together on this? But it is not only Europeans who have this challenge. These new players also have a challenge. If you want a place in the IMF, a voice in the World Bank, a voice in the Security Council of the UN, what for? To do what? What are you going to propose? You have to make your hands dirty. You cannot just stay alone and criticize. You have to take responsibility.

We all know that if you are not at the table, you are on the menu. But if you are at the table, you have to take responsibility to cook the meal and be criticized if the meal is not to the taste of a lot of people. Let's face it.

The Asian Perspective to the Crisis

Jan Willem Blankert

The patient is doing fairly well, thank you very much! As you may know, Asian economies are already recovering, it seems, even if there could still be a 'double dip'. For the time being, the news is rather good, just as it is from Latin America, where apparently there is great resilience.

Two years ago, decoupling was still in fashion. Then, when other countries were drawn in after the recession, coupling was again in fashion. What we see today, I think, demonstrates that there is, whether you call it coupling or decoupling, at least less interdependence than we thought. Singapore, for example, is coming out of this recession, Indonesia is having 4 percent growth and China will have something like 7 or 8 percent growth. Productivity is improving, and it looks like things are not too bad.

The Association of South East Asian Nations (ASEAN) is dealing with the crisis by being open to all economies in the whole world. But on top of that, it is strengthening its regional integration, not only as ASEAN but also with its free trade agreements with Australia, New Zealand, Japan and China. The free trade agreement with China will go into force on the 1 January 2010. I would call it a major development when these two regions: China with its 1.3 billion people and ASEAN with 570 million people will be linked in a free trade agreement.

For ASEAN, I must say this is a daring operation. There is always the considerable opposition of textile workers in Indonesia, for example. There may be delays, there will be exemptions, but it will be coming no doubt and it will be cementing regional integration. So the message from Asia and ASEAN is to keep the trade channels open.

Distrust and nationalism may lead to protectionism, but vested interest may be even more important. Distrust and nationalism is what you see in certain political parties in the Netherlands and in other countries as well that preach xenophobic hate. But even those parties are not always protectionist. Their views are more of a cultural thing. Protectionism, on the other hand, comes much more from vested interests, e.g., from shoe makers in Europe, from steel makers in the US that have not followed the technological developments, and from agricultural lobbies in the European Union. It is impressive to see the list of beneficiaries of European handouts from the European Agricultural Policy.

I am afraid I am preaching to the converted, but let me just repeat this: borders lead to costs. In the EU, even in the 1980s after we had already a custom's union, we discovered that we were wasting 5 percent of GDP annually by not yet having a single market. That set us on the path to a single market.

ASEAN and China are working in that direction, ASEAN in the first place for itself. They are not yet talking about a single market but integration is the word. Of course, the strange thing with protectionism is that it always comes in the form of a tax. Nobody calls it a tax, but it is nothing else but a tax. Where trade takes place between individuals, firms and citizens of different countries, governments interfere on behalf of certain citizens, usually others that are not involved in that trade, to levy a tax. What you can see throughout history, with China today, Japan twenty-five years ago, Germany in the nineteenth century, all this protectionist talks and fears are always going by. In the end, the countries always integrate; they normalize and get into the mainstream.

I think it is good to remember the time of Japan bashing. I would almost say: who has heard of Japan these days? Unfortunately, so.

Europe may be in a better position than the US to face the competition from China, but leaving that aside, I am very happy to hear from Mr. Ndulu as representative of Africa that de-globalization is not the way to go.

The World Economic Forum, which is not particularly well known for being biased against market economies or against the

233

US and the EU, has produced a report entitled 'Enabling Trade', in which 121 countries in the world were listed on a number of criteria like border management, i.e., on how easy or difficult it is to pass the border. But they were also ranked on the basis of access to its market: for example, on how easy it is to sell a product on the market of that country.

Even if it is only a listing that is based on opinions and information from WTO, UNCTAD, market operators, etc., it is at least better than just a talk in the pub. It could be improved, perhaps, but I have not seen it heavily criticized. But who would have thought that Burkina Faso, when it comes to market access, is performing much better than, for example, Germany and the Netherlands? You will see El Salvador at the top with, not surprisingly, Singapore next. The US is 49th, and Germany is ranked 89 out of 121 countries. Syria is very last, while India and China are also very low.

Maybe my trade colleagues in the European Commission will not be happy if I draw your attention to this, but this is public knowledge. I think, upon seeing this information, that we in the West still have a long way to go to open our economies to other countries.

Panel I: Discussion

On slow growth, inequality, labour migration and the role of agriculture

Valladão:

I don't believe that *slow growth* can be a solution because he doesn't believe that governments can impose the level of consumption and control the desires of the people. I even do not think that controlling the desires of people would be a good thing. The good thing is to produce what people want in a way that is less hungry of natural resources and less destructive for the natural environment. It is a philosophical question. We talk about governance today but we don't talk about global government because that may very well be a very totalitarian government. What would be the legitimacy of this global government? If you have a global government with nothing else, without proper checks and balances, will that government be allowed to decide for all people what to do? I don't think it would be possible to manage that politically. Global government is sometimes seen like a technical thing: you put together institutions that will more or less do the job with no interests for itself. But there is nothing like that! So there is no interest in such an arrangement, neither in big countries, nor in small countries. We have to solve this international governance in a political way.

I agree that we should do more research *on equality* at the global level. I believe equality at the country level is getting better, but between countries it may be getting worse. In Brazil and some other countries in Latin America it is getting better for the first time in history at least.

235

With regard to *migration*, the question is how to create an opportunity for skilled people to remain in their own country. Why are they leaving? Because they have no opportunity to use their skills, and because their countries did not modernize their economy. These countries have to create the opportunity for these people to stay and use their skills. At the moment they are leaving because they are not well paid. Look at the Indian people that went to the US. Now that India is growing, they are coming back!

I suggested applying the ecological economy to the 20 percent of the economy that was wiped out by the crisis. That is because I think we should be realistic and start somewhere.

Right now you have a long period where we have to try all these new techniques in order not to fall back in another crisis. That is why we have to have this limit of 20 percent. We could try to do it with 90 percent, which would be beautiful. But that would be just a dream. So let us look at what we can do and start with that 20 percent. Let us do it and not just talk about it.

Benno Ndulu:

I tend to agree with the argument that with globalization of production and with emerging economies creating more opportunities, reverse migration might probably become reality. We have seen that happening in India, in China, and the skills that have been nurtured at an earlier stage, wherever they have been working, would become more important for those countries. So it is good to create opportunities and to make good use of those skills. I think reverse migration is a reality for the future.

We need to look at *resilience* in terms of trade and growth also from a longer-term perspective. In the short-term you may have fast growth with high volatility and end up actually just capsizing the economy. In Africa, many countries have seen periods of very rapid growth but, because they were not able to sustain that growth for a long time, more or less they were capsizing and not making any progress. There might be some trade off in the short-run, but I think in the longer-term through resilience you build much higher growth trajectories. For that you certainly will have to build up your domestic resource mobilization process and, over time, when you have enough strengthened revenue collection, growth can become self-sustained. That opens the opportunity for a country to reduce its dependence. As a matter of fact, we have seen in the last decade a few countries that were able to reduce the dependency of their budget on foreign aid with more rapid growth. It is possible to do it.

The other way is really to open up channels of sourcing foreign savings. No country actually can progress without foreign savings, whether it is FDI or otherwise. We know that the US is depending on foreign savings from China. So the question is not to close doors and to diversify your sources of finance so that you can have a less risky concentration of foreign finance.

Shenggen Fan:
Why is agriculture not going anywhere? In the 1960s and 1970s, agriculture played a very positive role in terms of promoting overall economic growth and poverty reduction in Asia. The green revolution really occurred, but during the 1980s and 1990s, because of structural adjustment programmes, the government support for agriculture declined dramatically. That is probably the reason why agricultural production stagnated. But now we see some good news. In Africa, many countries have committed themselves to so-called Comprehensive Agricultural Development Programmes and to allocate more budget support to agriculture. The higher the allocation to agriculture, the more agricultural growth will be accelerating. So we see some good news but it probably is not good enough. We need to continue to focus on agriculture.

Migration, I think, is an interesting topic for debate. From an economic point of view, resources, including human, physical and capital, should move to where the marginal return is highest. So why do we have migration? It is because returns to labour are different in different places. So what should we do? We should take away these barriers, whether they are across countries or across regions within a particular country. When you take down these barriers, the labour productivity will converge across countries and within countries. So the living standards will converge and your income inequality will come down. Why didn't it happen yet? It is because of the barriers.

Take China for example. In China, regional equality was higher before the reform than after because everybody was campaigning and nobody was paid. Everybody was equally poor. Although after reform everybody was better off, some people got much better off than others. So inequality increased. How do you reduce inequality? By far the best solution is by taking down all barriers to migration. We see now people moving from poor to rich areas, while capital is moving from rich to poor areas, because the return to capital is higher in poor areas while the return to labour is higher in the rich, coastal areas. That is why you see a convergence of labour and capital productivity in China.

This applies also to cross border migration. In America, in the US, you see a lot of unskilled labour migration from Honduras and Guatemala, which in the US helps to relieve the shortage of unskilled labour. Honduras and Guatemala in the meantime have a good source of income from remittances. That actually also helps to reduce inequalities.

It is true that in the developing countries we have not done enough to produce jobs for the skilled people. That is why they move around, looking for opportunities and a better return to their education. There is nothing wrong with some people moving from the Soviet Union to the US or from Poland to the UK, because there are opportunities there. By taking down barriers on migration or capital or trade, inequalities will eventually go down.

Jan Willem Blankert:

I would love to take away the barriers against migration, but what to do in the case of Jamaica? If they train nine doctors, one stays behind and eight move to other places. And how do you solve the European dilemma if you take away the barriers against immigration from Africa?

The problem of *the double dip* can be translated into the problem of who should cut more in its energy consumption, China and India or the West? China and India tell the West with some justification that they should cut more because in the past they had already used their share. Let us not forget that China has three times as many people as the US and is still consuming less energy. China's growth comes, of course, with a cost because China's growth is still very dirty. But I am convinced, and you can see it already, it is fast getting cleaner, faster than anywhere else in history. Hopefully fast enough for saving the climate, because I am a pessimist on climate. All these reductions we are talking about are only adding less to what is already there. That is the problem that we will not be able to solve. But that is not China's fault.

On the Gini coefficient: we have seen *inequality* between countries decreasing but within a number of countries inequality is increasing. If you would be able to calculate worldwide Gini coefficient, it would be decreasing with a small amount. Interestingly the Gini coefficient for China and the US are exactly the same.

On MDGs, sustainable growth, raising agricultural productivity and climate change

Jan Willem Blankert:

I have no clear view on whether or not to review the MDGs. I would stick to them as long as you can, even if they seem beyond reach. To take a completely different example: ASEAN is aiming to reach a single market by 2015. I personally think this is over ambitious, it is unattainable, but it is better to stick to the goal until you are at the deadline and to not revise the goal far before the deadline. Try to stay with the goal until the finish.

On green and slow growth, I think the issue is finding ways for *sustainable growth*. They make us believe that there are possibilities for solar power, and that it can grow in all sorts of ways even without creating more pollution. According to the guru of new materials, Amory Lovins of the Rocky Mountains Institute, you can still have your beer and your air conditioning but with 95 percent less energy than you use today. Should you believe him? He actually makes these things at his institute, but you have to pay a little bit more. So I tend to believe that there is at least a technical solution.

Shenggen Fan:

Until the recent financial crisis, progress on MDGs at the global level was on track, but that was mainly because of the contributions from China and India. With many African countries, there was a large range of variation. Before the crisis, the poverty rate had been going down. In 1990, the poverty rate there was about 45 or 46 percent. Around 2003 or 2004, it had increased by one or two percentage points. So at the global level it was on track, but it varied by country and by region. Particularly in Africa, progress on MDGs was not on track, and the financial crisis will probably has set back that progress even further.

On the question of whether we should revisit the MDGs, I tend to agree that we shouldn't. It is a target; a goal we want to achieve. We may over achieve it or achieve only 90 or 80 percent of it. What is important is that we are making progress and that we stay on track.

It is true that agriculture will play a crucial role in achieving the first MDG on hunger and poverty. Again, the focus has to be on Africa. Africa is making some progress in the last four to five years. Agricultural growth has accelerated somewhat. The governments have committed to increase their budget allocations to agriculture to 10 percent. It was only 4 percent when they made that commitment in Maputo in 2003, and it is now going up to 7 percent on average. They are moving in the right direction. Their commitment has to continue. The G8 has recently committed twenty billion US dollars to agriculture, but I think the national governments should also commit themselves, not only the donors.

Now the question is how do we spend these committed resources, the 10 percent of national budgets and the twenty billion dollars, which should be invested in agriculture? Should it be in research, in irrigation, in rural infrastructure, and how do we combine some of the so-called social safety nets with productive investments and with some of the priorities these countries have to focus on? There is no one-size-fits -all strategy; it has to be in parallel country strategies.

I think that if the governments are committed and if the donors are committed, that many African countries still have the potential to achieve the first MDG. 'If' means that the political will has to be there, government leaders have to commit themselves to develop agriculture, to focus on food security. That is a basic condition for the overall economy to take off.

Ndulu:
We know for sure that without making progress in agriculture, you cannot address issues of poverty in Africa. But I have a slightly different view on how to do it. We have stuck too much to the model of taking support to the smallholders without thinking about reorganizing agriculture. I think we need a new strategy that should be a combination of agribusiness, small holders and processors as a package. Whether it is tea, sisal or coffee, wherever you have had large firms work hand in hand with small holders, we have seen them use their creditworthiness as a way of channelling credit to the smallholders and tying that with processors. Research would show clearly that you have had definitely bigger impact and that income earned becomes four times bigger per household if you are part of an out growers scheme, as opposed to be purely on your own. That is a striking difference. The question then is how you support that combination where you have private capital and small holders. We have always thought only in terms of delivery. I think the organizational solution is going to be the answer.

Does that mean collectivization? It is not exactly that. Let me take an example: sugar cane. There is a plantation, there is a company, and they have a factory that processes sugar cane to make sugar. They have an out growers scheme of smallholders who receive support of different kind. They get credit, they get extension services, and they get also access to mechanization.

Working within that framework makes a huge difference compared with those who work on their own. This is happening not only in sugar cane, it is happening in coffee as well, where you can collectively also define the standards. It is happening definitively in tea, where you need the link between processing and production. To a large extent, smallholder credit has failed partly because they were not credit worthy. But as part of that scheme, the big guy there actually has that creditworthiness, so he can get access to credit. We need to think outside the box, we are too much married to the traditional models of providing support.

On MDGs, I think attainability is not the issue. The main focus should be the delta, the improvement and the progress. We need to take stock after the crisis of what is needed in order to breach some gaps in terms of speed of attainment. But we don't need to overhaul the goals. The goals remain novel. I think we need to be realistic by leaving states to come to it on their own in their own context, to make a review of the attainability and the importance of sometimes even prioritizing within those goals. You can't just do all of them simultaneously very well. That is also part of the strategy. So we need to be much more flexible in the way we proceed.

Valladão:

As a Brazilian, I know the importance of agriculture. Brazil is now an agricultural superpower, and a lot of agricultural firms work in the way you do with out growers, even in soya, which is a big thing. There are huge regions in Brazil where medium-sized farmers are linked to soya processors, which are in turn directly linked to the world market. But coming back to the question of slow growth, I do not know the answer. Nobody knows. What I know is that in the industrialized countries, growth is already low. Very low. Too low in a certain sense. The question is global growth, but you cannot compensate slow growth and fast growth. For global growth climate is the biggest challenge, but I do know that any enforced solution is impossible. Because there are too many different ways of looking at it. Just look at what is happening in Copenhagen now with the American Congress, etc. So how do you balance these things? You have public opinion. That is important in all of this. And you have to try the technical solution. You *have* to do it.

But if we don't have a legitimate power structure capable of enforcing a solution, so we have to take care of what the political reality is. We don't have a legitimate power structure, and maybe it is even nice we don't have one, because I don't think it would be legitimate and democratic.

The more we get to the catastrophe, probably the more the minds will be focussed on how to get out of this predicament. But

242

we won't get out by an enforced solution. You cannot say to Brazil, to the Chinese people, to people who are hungry, to people who are poor, that they should stop growing for the sake of the climate.

On regional integration, the global political reality and two-child policy

Ndulu:

In the context of the African continent, I think we do not have a choice other than to integrate, getting better connected, creating stronger markets, taking care of those that are land locked, because of the high cost of crossing borders if you do not. I think the bigger challenge is in the integration of factor markets that was referred to in East Africa right now. We are moving on fairly quickly on most fronts, but when it comes to land, it is a different issue. Unfortunately the way it is configured, among the five countries of the East African Community, there is only one country that had land. All the other countries have their land already grabbed. So integration means sharing Tanzanian land and Tanzanians have raised the question: what do you bring to the table? I think on the side of the labour market, most likely we would be able to achieve something more easily than on the issue of land. I see regional integration as a way of resolving a whole range of development issues across that region. That connectivity in terms of investment and infrastructure in softening barriers for mobility of both people and goods and services is fundamental. All regions are moving in that direction anyway and it would be unthinkable for African countries to not also deal with that as a major issue. By the way being landlocked is probably a much bigger problem in Africa than in any other region. When you look also at how small countries have been divided, likewise. Tanzania has borders with about 8 other countries, and if you will have to have for every border a different relationship it is absolutely too costly.

On a *global two-child policy*, my own view is that we should get there by necessity rather then by design. Over time the demographic transition will take care of that. Let the demographic transition do the job and let us not speed up that process by decree.

Shenggen Fan:

One word about the global political reality. At the global level, we do need to work together. Wherever we should design a sort of governance structure or architecture, let us make sure that the structure, the architecture is inclusive, and also make sure that everybody is accountable for this. For example, climate change is a serious issue. The argument of China and India that is based on per-capita consumption in comparison with US total emissions is nonsensical. They really need to come to the table to negotiate on which way to go further, on what is the next step to move forward. Otherwise we may have to wait for another who knows how many years? With the Copenhagen Convention coming in December next, China and India will have to think in terms of global emission, not only on per-capita emission basis, because the incremental emission will come to these countries also. So, for sustainability reasons they will need to grow, but their growth should be clean. They realize this already and they are thinking about it. It is part of their economic stimulus package: a massive investment in environment, a massive investment in cleaner energy. China now ranks second after the EU as largest investor in clean energy. It probably will take time but the issue is there, they are ready to take this up. The wider global platform really helps to introduce some mechanisms to make everybody accountable, not only on climate change but also on security, on safety nets, on trade, etc.

On *family planning* we should not force anybody. Reproductive rights are a basic human right. As the economy keeps growing, the people will naturally reduce the number of children they have. As the costs of having children increase, people will start to look for quality instead of quantity. I don't think it would be advisable to force people to just have one or two children, even though my own country had that kind of policy for a certain time.

Jan Willem Blankert:

Regional integration is a way of countries working together that allows you to approach globalization in a more pro-active way. ASEAN, by the way, is looking at the EU practise of organizing social safety nets whereby 0.5 percent of GDP going from the rich countries to the poorer regions to help them to cope with the integration problems. It is still a while to go but they are looking at the EU system.

Alfredo Valladão:
There are a lot of things you can do with integration, but you have to realize that it is not politically neutral. In planning regional integration there are asymmetries. For example, in South America, Brazil represents 70 percent of Mercosur on the basis of territory, etc., so it is very complicated for Brazil to accept deep integration or supranational institutions, like in Europe. It is more like in Southern Africa with South Africa in SADCC. It is difficult to manage that.

One last word on global governance: I agree with your pessimism on politicians, but I prefer to be an optimist, if only for one reason. Pessimists suffer all the time; optimists suffer only at the end!

Panel II
Innovative Approaches to Finance and Development

Lessons from the Crisis

Nanno Kleiterp

In this panel, we will focus on the lessons we learned from the financial and economic crisis and how to deal also with the other crises that have a much larger and lasting impact: the water, energy and the climate crises. By doing so, we hope to find answers to the question of how we will create much-needed change to reach sustainable growth. We will touch upon three levels, the macro level concerning financial markets, the meso level dealing with the banking sector and the micro level of individual companies. Three speakers in our panel will share their lessons, but I would first like to take the opportunity to share a few of my own thoughts on where I feel change is needed.

The macro level

At the macro level of financial markets, we have learned one thing the hard way. That is that markets are not perfect. We have to realize for once and for all that we have to deal with these imperfections. But what are these imperfections?

First of all, we should realize that the interest of society is no longer the sole responsibility of the government, but also of market participants. If participants of financial markets only focus on shareholder values instead on stakeholder values, and on short-term profit instead of long-term goals, they should lose their license to operate. Fortunately, we have also seen that some financial market participants, especially in emerging economies, have suffered less from the crisis.

Secondly, public goods such as clean air and water do not have a price, so we use them freely and irresponsibly in financial terms.

It is cheap to use scarce resources such as water and clean air. It is cheap because the environmental and social costs of actions are often externalized onto the general public. On the other hand, it can be more expensive to produce them in a sustainable way, because financial markets still lack sufficient incentives to support superior environmental or social performance.

The third imperfection is the fact that financial market actors can basically get away with anything. Or in economic language: we have to solve the problem of moral hazard. Governments and central banks want to prevent banking instability at any cost, because of the damage to the economy. Important market participants therefore feel secure and have taken on excessive and dangerous risks. But when high losses were created, as we have seen, taxpayers pay the price and not the banks.

The meso level

Looking at the meso-level, we see that the confidence in the role of the banking sector has been undermined. This confidence needs to be restored quickly because finance is important for society, especially in developing economies and emerging markets where access to finance is still limited. Access to finance is about enabling people to realize their ambitions. Private finance will allow them to take their destiny into their own hands. By giving entrepreneurs access to financial services we strengthen the foundation for sustainable economic growth. This should get more attention in the development budgets of governments. The financial sector is at the heart of the economy, and therefore at the heart of sustainability. If banks can live up to the expectations and implement the right values, they can be the agents of change.

The financial sector has the knowledge on how to promote sustainable growth. Already in 1992, 23 of the world's leading commercial banks signed the UNEP Statement by Banks on Environment and Sustainable Development. But, more than 15 years later, the same promises are still being made. How many banks have actually proven that they really changed their behaviour and lived up to the promises they made? We do have some good examples, however they represent only a small fraction of the total financial sector. There seems to be an invisible barrier to taking action. Time is running out and making a statement or checking a box is no longer sufficient. We have to walk the talk.

But what does this mean? How can banks be agents of change? They can do this by treating sustainability as an integral part of their business. Historically, FMO, as most other organizations, has approached sustainability predominantly from the risk management perspective. However, there is a much broader perspective to treat sustainability also as good and profitable business. It has been clearly evidenced that companies in developed and emerging markets gain financial benefits from sound environmental practice, social development and economic progress. To achieve a sustainable profit, sustainability should be integrated in the investment process. There are three ways to implement this.

First of all, through the design of financial services. Banks should attach conditions to loans on environment, social and governance issues. This in itself is not new. Making sure that clients actually adhere to the conditions is another thing. The step forward is that the conditions are not only the responsibility of the clients, but also of the bank. A bigger and better step forward is to apply these conditions to the pricing of the loan and to the interest costs. This means that clients receive a reduction on their margin when they achieve defined Environmental, Social and Governance targets. FMO has started the implementation of the price incentive in the contracts of selected clients.

Secondly, there is the choice of clients. A strong focus on companies that contribute to people, planet and profit will have an enormous impact. Can any bank adopt this model? Is the sky the limit for the financial sector? Or are there also limits to the scale of banks that focus on sustainability. Triodos is a good example of a very successful bank that only chooses clients based on these criteria.

Thirdly, banks can be the agents of change in promoting sustainability through sustainable financial products and services and innovation. At FMO, we also have some excellent examples of client banks that are providing green products, such as loans for solar panels in Nicaragua and Mongolia or for biodigesters in Vietnam and Uganda. The innovation of these financial institutions in the poorest regions of the world is exemplary for those in the developed world. These banks have proven that they can be agents of change.

Good examples of agents of change are development banks focused on the private sector, like FMO. These banks support clients that aim at improving their environmental and social management systems and their governance structures. They have long-term goals and remained profitable also in this time of crisis. At the same time, development finance is very efficient and effective in its contribution to economic growth and poverty reduction. The capital paid in by governments has a huge multiplier effect because it generates a development and a financial return and is used many times over. In these times of crisis, they should get more support from governments to compensate for the decrease in capital flows from commercial parties to emerging markets.

The micro level

Finally, I would like to mention the micro level. At the micro level, we focus on the entrepreneurs because entrepreneurs are an important force for change and development. I am very happy that Vineet Rai is with us today. He actively supports entrepreneurs to transform their ideas into coherent business entities in places and ways nobody thought was possible. But these entrepreneurs made it possible, because they are fuelled by a drive to bring about change. We can ask for all the regulations and government intervention we want, but without this drive and willingness to change, we get nowhere. It is therefore up to the leaders of the companies to set the example.

If we can prove with our projects, our actions and our decisions that sustainable growth is possible, only then will others follow. I'm aware that this process of change is a long and winding road. It will not be easy. But the only time you run out of chances is when you stop taking them. If we decide today to alter our own behaviour and choices, we can become the agents of change.

Macro Lessons from the Financial Crisis

Trevor Manuel

The timing of this conference is exceedingly propitious. The G20 is meeting in Pittsburgh tomorrow, and there is also a strong voice to be heard next week at the annual meetings of the IMF and World Bank in Istanbul, and, beyond that, the December meeting on climate change in Copenhagen.

The subject of this meeting today – the consequences of the financial crisis for development – is not one that will go away, and is also of fundamental importance because of the Pittsburgh meeting.

It is important that the focus of our meeting should be on the wider challenge of globalization, meaning premise, equity and balance. Within that context the word that Professor Ndulu used repeatedly this morning is interdependence. That is, in many respects, the key mechanism to understanding how the world ought to work.

The backdrop to the issue of financing for development is important. What we need to recognize – certainly in these last 53 weeks since the collapse of Lehmann Brothers, and even since the 9 August 2007 when BNP Paribas indicated that it was in difficulty and needed an urgent injection of liquidity from the central bank – is that an understanding of what happened is key to understanding what the future holds.

What went wrong?

There are a number of questions that need to be answered: is this a crisis of capitalism or are crises inherent in the nature of the beast? Is this just a set of consequences of irrational exuberance?

Also, we must ask: what went wrong? There is a wonderful book written by a pair of Nobel laureates, Akerlof and Shiller, called 'Animal Spirits'. Basically, they say that no matter how many times you look at the markets and try to understand the equations, it is understanding people that is key to understanding how economies work and why they fail.

That is why we try to understand what works and what did not work. It is clear that there is no way that either macroeconomic policy, especially in large economies, or financial regulation stop at the border post. They don't carry passports. The failure of managing the mortgage markets in the US was in many respects a trigger, but the position of governments elsewhere is also important. It is all related to licensed institutions; indeed banks are licensed to print money, but because they are licensed they must also be regulated. If we relate to them only through agencies over which we have no control, the way rating agencies provided the necessary cover for all these institutions operating in the mortgage market, then we need to think again.

The risk of the pendulum swing

We also need to pause to take account of what the next period may bring. Of course there is a risk there. There is a risk that we will have a pendulum swing, because people start to believe that we who are in government now have all the answers. That is a huge risk.

If the next period is much like the last two decades: we are going to fail humanity. We will fail humanity if we for a moment believe that it is possible to separate the financial economy from the real economy, that the financial economy can exist for its own sake, that it can not just innovate but that it can produce and add value while in fact, fundamentally, the focus should be on the allocative efficiencies of the financial sector.

In the period ahead, all institutions will have to adjust to a higher cost of capital, to a reality that leverage will be much harder to come by, to the fact that there will have to be new checks and balances in the way in which systems operate, and to ensure that we can put in place mechanisms against excess. I realize the cynics view of this is that the only thing that history teaches us is that it teaches us nothing. Well, there is a wonderful song that was written in 1929 at the start of the Great Depression, and which was played at the inauguration of F.D. Roosevelt in 1932, and when I look at what is happening on Wall Street I still get the refrain of that song: 'Happy days are here again'. The bonus pool is back, and it is all green. Nobody needs to be concerned about these issues.

It is our responsibility as governments, as those who license financial institutions, to prevent those kinds of excesses because that kind of greed was fundamentally part of the problem. There were no checks and balances and there was no risk. There was only reward.

The economy is in the lives of people

While we frequently think that what is happening in the economy is what we see on TV programmes such as 'Squawk Box', or the various stock market indicators rolling across our screens in ticker tape, the economy is, in fact, present in the lives of ordinary people. The report of a commission created by President Sarkozy and including big names like Joe Stiglitz and Amartya Sen gives measures that we should try to introduce in economics. The report makes some very telling observations about what GDP does not mean, and how little GDP informs us about societal well-being. When we talk of development, we talk of societies, and their well-being becomes fundamentally important. So we need to think differently about all of these issues. Perhaps that report will take us forward. Its transnational experience may provide us with a better basis for analysis and understanding.

The MDGs and financing for development

At the Millennium Summit in September 2000, important deci-sions were made. The Millennium Development Goals were already a point of reference this morning, but beyond the Millennium Summit there was an agreement within the United Nations that we need a basis for financing development, and so the Monterrey

Conference on Financing for Development was convened in 2002. A very important Consensus Document was produced, and perhaps naively we believed that the world would operate differently beyond that point.

Just over six years later, in December 2008, a review conference was convened on the Monterrey Consensus Document. The review conference fizzled out appallingly. Part of the reason that that momentum, that commitment, that sense of collective decision making, was so strong at the time of the Monterrey meeting was because it was created in the wake of 9/11. The conference convened in March 2002 as one of the first global conferences after 9/11, and the world said that we have to take decisions differently. By December 2008, however, all of that was forgotten.

It is a terrible thought that people like ourselves should require that kind of catastrophe to have to make rational decisions of what we do in our everyday lives. But look at the interregnum, at the very important decisions taken at Gleneagles for example. As we prepare for Copenhagen, we should remember also that Kyoto provided an opportunity for large emitters to opt out of the agreement. And since we are here in The Hague today, let us also remind ourselves that even the ICC agreement is not a compulsory treaty for countries.

We need governments

Unless we fix the world, financing for development is not something that is going to correct itself; markets are not going to correct themselves either. We need governments, and that very important question asked this morning about how to deal with these issues without a global government is pressing. How do we deal with them? What important decisions are required, and what needs to happen to ensure that decisions taken will have some consequences? There are a number of lawyers in the room, constitutional and otherwise, who would ask those very important questions because they emanate from Roman Dutch law, which comes from *here*, and they ask: what is the point of law without consequences, of law without sanction?

How do we place the issue of finance for development back in the context of mutual accountability? This question is as important for us in the developing world as it is for other countries, and here the issue of political will is fundamentally important. I chaired a committee looking at governance in the IMF. Now, the users of the IMF are underrepresented. In Africa we have two chairs for 52 countries. A region like Europe is over-represented.

How do we square the circle? How do we deal with the fact that rights that were vested in 1944 must now be addressed? If we could, then we would also have to deal with the UN reform. And we must!

Unless we can put those issues that are so germane to globalization on the table, we are going to talk past each other while dealing with issues of equity and balance between countries. And we are sitting in a very difficult position. We are sitting in a position where wealthy countries had to borrow very excessively. The US had to borrow 1.75 trillion US dollars this year to finance its deficit. If that amount of liquidity is taken out of the savings pool, what is left on the table for these countries that Benno Ndulu was speaking about this morning – countries that have performed exceedingly well in macroeconomic terms against great odds? How do we fix that, taking account of the fact that the G20 in April committed a further 750 billion US dollars of resources for the IMF? What is left on the table?

From Monterrey, there was an initiative from President Chirac, President Lula and President Lahos of Chile on innovative sources of financing. It made a recommendation on the taxation of airline tickets. The present chair is a 'very wealthy country' in Africa. In fact, it is one of the poorest countries in Africa: it is laughable. We can't be serious about this. These are the kind of things we have to fix. We have to talk to our own conscience, because we are after all decision makers.

Conclusion

We must prevent the pendulum swing. We must understand the role of governments, because markets are not going to correct their own inefficiencies. We need to address the problems of inequality and exuberance because they have gotten us into this situation, and they are ongoing. We need to address asymmetries of information to deal with the problems. We need to address these issues of global governance and then, when we come to poor countries, one of the issues we must fix is the capabilities of states, because states must be able to deliver services.

One of the things that worry me frequently about the discourse on microfinance is that often, people must borrow to get money to pay for services like educating their daughters. But if states provide these services, then people can borrow for economic activities and other things. The need for capable states is not something that can be ignored in the context of financing for development. What is the basket of services that every state should provide and how can we ensure that states can do this in the wider context of ODA and other issues?

I want to make this plea as we deal with microfinance. We must ensure that these micro-financiers will provide access and that we don't use donor aid for that. There is the need for some start-up funds, but donor aid should not be used as the money that then gets lent because that creates distortions that are almost impossible to recover from.

We must ensure that you have capable states and that you can eliminate these policy contests that frequently impose a tax on the poor, and we must ensure that we can deal with the issue of freedoms. Perhaps it is not even at the micro level, but at the supra level that we have to repair things. If we deal with those issues correctly, the micro level is going to require a lot less attention. It is going to require a big push at the macro level to repair them, because we all understand what is wrong in the system. We need to understand that these decisions are about values and our broader commitments to society.

Sustainable Banking

Peter Blom

Let me assure you that it was not possible for Triodos Bank to make a big advertisement in the Financial Times, and then get the award for being the most sustainable bank in the world. We as a bank are too small for doing it that way, but we are very proud that, out of the 160 banks worldwide applying for the prize, we were rewarded. We didn't expect that at all. But the prize also gives us responsibilities.

What the crisis means for banking

What I would like to do now is to very briefly go through the financial crisis and what it means for banking. I want to do that because I believe that the financial crisis has created a great opportunity to what I would call a realignment of banking with the needs of society. That sounds very obvious, but the practise of banking has deteriorated in the last thirty to forty years.

As has been mentioned before, this realignment is also needed to create a true relation between the financial sector and the real economy. That is another lesson that we can learn from the crisis, and it is very interesting to see that the notion of the real economy was not very much in people's minds until only two years ago. The real economy has come alive again as a way of expressing that in the end we depend on what people produce, what services they provide, what is really happening on the ground and what the real needs of the people are.

With regard to the financial crisis, we should also realize that we can make a choice. We can either choose that this is a challenge to really change the financial system, to change the way we do business, or we can see it as just part of the deal of capitalism and continue to move on from crisis to crisis. And I must say, I am not very optimistic about what I see in the banking sector. Many of my colleagues see the financial crisis as part of the way we operate. Some of us hear our colleagues saying that they hope that we will be back, that we will restore the old situation and that we will continue as we did before. That is not a very positive sign. Interestingly enough, there seems to be more interest in the civil society to make a different financial system than in the financial sector itself.

So I think there is a real challenge for the financial world to make changes, but I must admit that it is not a very progressive part of society. As a small player, I hope we will be able to make a difference. We should at least give our best effort.

There is, and this has been ignored, also quite a bit of personal responsibility on the part of bankers. It has to do with professional ethics, and I am very happy that, at least in the Dutch banking code, there is now a bankers' oath where bankers commit themselves to the public good, to the needs of society and to serving customers. At least that is something tangible, although we will have to live up to it. But it is an important step forward.

Fundamental changes

Before I go into the practical changes that I see for banking systems, it is important to first look at some more fundamental changes in our thinking. Because the financial crisis actually starts not so much in the way banking is done today, but in the way we educate our students in universities. It is because of the reductionist thinking that students are not aware of what is actually going on in the economy. It is a certain approach to issues that is applied in many sciences, including in the economic science, that makes it possible to deal with problems one by one, going from A to B, without being made aware that they are parts of a totality of problems. I think that, in the future, also in economics thinking should follow a more holistic approach that better deals with interdependencies. We should not try to separate the economic realm from other parts of society.

Another very important issue today, and I will come back to that later, is that there is no economy without ecology. I still hear many of my colleagues saying, well, first we will restore the financial markets and then we talk again about environmental issues, climate issues and so on. I think that is very 'historic thinking'. Today, we have to connect things. If we do not do that, the next crisis will be around the corner.

As I mentioned earlier, it is very important that finance is reconnected with the real economy. I would say that the triple P bottom line for business in general is People, Planet and Profits. For banking, it is the triple E bottom line: Ecology, Economy and Equity. It is a slightly different notion and I will come back to that.

Equity is more than what we know as a class of financial assets. Equity is the intrinsic value that is behind investment, behind a loan, behind any debt instrument. The first thing that I learned as a banker in my 30-year career, and I was one of the co-founders of Triodos Bank that we started with five people, was that the value of a loan is not so much what is in the contract – the value is in the entrepreneur, in the economic context that the entrepreneur is working in and in how the entrepreneur deals with that reality. The value of a loan is, in the end, determined by people and by how people work. It is very easy to make any loan worthless, whatever contracts are there. We have to learn again that equity is something that is related to people, is related to the economy and that is related to ecology.

Changing the system

What about changing the banking system? Today, we realize that banking is not an ordinary business. We understand that now, but for many years the focus, also in the banking business, was on creating shareholder value, and that is simply not creating the right conditions for serving the economy as a banker. We learned that the hard way: governments had to come in to bail out the banks and rescue society. So we have to change the governance model of the banks. We have to move from a shareholder-based banking system to a stakeholder-based banking system. That is an important change that will probably reduce the profits of banks.

Many of my colleagues say about basic banking that you are not making returns of 15 to 20 percent; returns are probably more like 5 to 7 percent. That is the sort of return to basic banking that you can achieve. But may be that is fine because at least it is very stable.

The other important governance element in banking is to make a distinction between retail banking and investment banking. The Glass-Steagall Act is an important example in American history of making that kind of distinction. But more and more we have merged all of those types of banks, and we pay the price for that. We should realize that investment banking is something totally different than basic banking. Investment banking is about taking risks. You speculate sometimes on markets. Basic banking and retail banking is, on the other hand, about connecting depositors and lenders and providing them with a good payment system plus a few other things. But that basically is it.

You see that banks that were very close to this basic banking model and stayed very close to it have been very successful during the last year. Banking needs to be very close to the real economy. There are two strong forces in banking, and that is being local and having a clear sector focus. I think the cooperative model is a very good example of banks being local and very close to the people they serve. Of our colleague banks, the Rabobank is a very good example of a bank with a clear sector focus. It has stayed close to agriculture and also close to the communities. Also it has done quite well through the crisis.

Another notion, which is a very difficult one especially in the Netherlands where you have many big banks, is that banks maybe should not be too big anymore, or at least not so big that they fail. It is very important that we develop a different sort of financial service, one maybe more on a network basis where banks are aligned with each other and that we do not create these big conglomerates that are very hard to manage.

How does Triodos Bank fit in? Banking on values

How is Triodos Bank working in this environment? What we try to do is combine a number of agendas. One of them is the climate agenda: climate change, poverty reduction, the social agenda and the sustainability agenda. The other is transparency in finance. In finance, it is extremely important that you are transparent. People should be able to see through your balance sheet to what you are actually doing as a bank. The lack of transparency is one of the main reasons that banks got in such big problems. Transparency is facilitating the responsible bank customer.

The third agenda item is that Triodos Bank takes sustainability as a starting point and not as a limiting factor. In this respect, we are very different compared to our colleagues. A clear assignment of our loan officers is first to see how a project or a business contributes to society in a sustainable way, and then to see if we can make it bankable, not the other way around. The other way around almost always creates disappointments. In banking business, it is really healthy to start with sustainability, and of course the finances have to be OK as well.

What we experienced is that it is not easy to make a bank like Triodos Bank grow very quickly. Many people told us that we had to scale up, that we had to go to other countries. In fact we have been growing quite fast with 20 to 30 percent a year for many years. We are in five countries now in Europe, and we have relations with many microfinance systems. We have more than 500 people working in the bank. But that still is relatively small.

We try to find other ways of being different as a bank. That is why we created a global alliance for *banking on values*. It is an alliance of eleven banks worldwide, from Mongolia to Denmark, from the US to Bangladesh. What all those banks share is the values, the values we want to work out of. As banks we are very different in that we use very different models. Some have millions of customers, like Brad Bank in Bangladesh, while some have only a few thousand customers. But values are important, and that is what we share. And then you can look at the differences and see what you can do with that.

These banks are independent; that is one condition. They have at least 100 million dollars as a sort of minimum on their accounts, and that is especially important for the microfinance banks as they serve many people with not so much funds. But those eleven banks together are serving almost ten million people today and have about ten billion dollars in assets on the management.

They are all very successful, profitable, are growing very quickly and went very well through the crisis. So there must be something to them. We want this global alliance to grow with more banks and show that banks can actually serve the real economy.

Main challenges for the future

I think that the future has some surprises for us. We probably will see that very large financial corporations are going to have a very tough time, and that there will be many more smaller banks. Many banks think about starting smaller banks with different sorts of sectors, different sorts of products. You could say that it is almost like going from a monoculture to more biodiversity in finance and banking. Biodiversity creates fertility, and I think that is very important today

What I also see is that the top-down approach in making global agreements is becoming extremely difficult. Kyoto was already extremely difficult. I am also not very optimistic about Copenhagen. At the same time you see many promising bottom-up initiatives.

I am very impressed by what China is doing at the moment on environmental issues. It is not joining international agreements, but they start wind farms every week and they have a leading role in solar energy, not because there are agreements at national or international level, but because they think it is important. So for me it is a real question of whether change will come from the top down or from the bottom up.

I also see that there will be a rapid expansion, maybe even an explosion, of social enterprises in all sorts of hybrid forms, partly with social goals, partly commercial, but always in a mix. That is an important new dimension that means that we move towards a different kind of capitalism. We had capitalism in the nineteenth century, and we may call it capitalism 1.0. Capitalism 2.0 was about respecting human rights and respecting people. I think we are now in the middle of capitalism 3.0, which includes ecology and nature and that has people, planet and profits as a bottom line. So we have to work with a much more sophisticated notion of capital. Capital is not just about money; capital is human capital, nature capital, all sorts of capital. How these elements work together is what is important.

Last but not least, back to basics, back to banks. We have to make money a tool for change. Banks can be a tool for change, but in the end everybody in society has to deal with money. It is for the banks, really, to help people to make conscious decisions on how they direct their money. Only when they realize that it is with their own money that they can change their own situation will they change the world.

Conditions for Inclusive Growth

Vineet Rai

This lecture will be on an issue that has been part of my life for quite some time. My trials with development issues started around the year 2000, after I had spent a lot of time seeing people struggle. I used to see it almost as an observer. Living in India, you see poverty of an extreme nature. You see it as if you were sitting on a train and seeing people pass by. You don't participate in it.

Living in two India's

It was around the year 2000 that I came across this amusing feeling that we live in two different Indias. One India consists of very educated people who work in fairly fast-growing service industries as part of an urban India. Almost 30 percent of India is that kind of India. They are also benefiting from what the world economic boom brought to us.

Then there is another India, making up 70 percent of the population struggling to create opportunities to survive. They live in the rural hinterland, far away from our eyes, and are basically a passing movie for us and not a population that we connect with.

It is also pretty clear that if you have these two Indias living so far apart, that you are going to get problems that we possibly do not see when we are living in the city; problems that are slowly creeping towards us without us realizing it.

So when I came across this and realized that those 30 percent of the people that are educated and work in the service industries contribute almost 80 percent of GDP while the other 70 percent contributes only 18 percent of GDP, then it is pretty clear that sooner or later we would start going back, getting pulled back, if the others, the 70 percent of the people, did not start to contribute more to the growth.

Addressing the challenge

As a country, we have known this challenge for quite some time and we have used very different methods to address it. When I came here, I was thinking about the things that the government did and that had a significant impact. I thought it was a right wing coalition when the government of India played a critical role in making us self-sufficient in the production of milk and dairy products. Then, some time in the 1970s, they took upon themselves the role of bringing in the green revolution. That was again driven by the government and achieved sustainability of food production.

It was around 1991, at the time when we first met a financial crisis, that the government decided to disengage and create room for the third revolution, which has brought us a lot of success in terms of IT and IT-related service industries. This was the third revolution that the 30 percent of the population is presently enjoying the benefits from.

The unfortunate reality is that, in spite of all three interventions, those who are living in the rural Indian countryside continue to remain excluded from the growth. A lot of governments have come and gone, but not many changes have happened. This challenge can apparently only be dealt with in an approach that would be different from the conventional way of dealing with the poor, which is to give out tools and alms, to poor out donor support, etc. This is the kind of discussion that all of us have been going through for quite some time. There are three things that are shaping our response that we want to build on. We want create a more inclusive participatory growth where we have people benefit and at the same time create benefits for us as well as for them.

The success of microfinance

The first thing that happened was the success of microfinance. I am calling this an infrastructural investment and not really a financial tool because it was very difficult to deal with poor people: we had access issues. But without building roads, without creating any kinds of infrastructure, the financial infrastructure that had been built to provide microfinance has been extremely innovative. Organizations and institutions like SKS Micro-Finance, or Share Micro-Finance or Basics or Self Employed Women's Associations have had a significant impact in creating what microfinance is today in India. Similarly, the state-driven building programs like self-help groups have contributed to building what I called the financial infrastructure that allowed the poor to participate and make choices that they never had. This is a significant departure from the earlier approaches of reaching out to the poor without seeking out what they needed.

If you look at microfinance and try to see why it is successful in India, one of the key questions is how many people have come out of poverty because of microfinance. My answer is: we don't know. But that should not determine the success of microfinance in playing a role in poverty eradication. The real success of microfinance is creating those choices that are needed at the bottom.

Notwithstanding all of the criticism, which I personally believe is fairly true, microfinance has a lot of value for the poor. But it doesn't really take them out of poverty as has been proven again and again. It is an instrument that has its own challenges. For people like me, I would not like to take a 100-dollar loan at 30 percent interest that I have to repay in weekly instalments. It is a fairly inefficient product, but we have nothing else to exchange it for. Until the time we have a better alternative, we have to use it. We cannot exhort people to drop it just because it has inefficiencies within it.

The question of talent

Microfinance was one of the key inputs that we have seen come true, which is telling what infrastructure means for the poor. The second critical need, and it has been discussed in the first panel a little bit, was the issue of talent. We all know that dealing with social problems is far more complex than the problem of doing business. Unfortunately, the best talent the world has to offer works for multinational companies which have only single bottom line agendas and fairly simplistic problems to solve, while the most complex problems are left to those who do not have the best education or access to the best tools and technologies. So if you want to make a difference in solving complex social problems and promote economic growth and bring about development, you need to bring your best talent together. This is something that we possibly do not think of when we start looking at these things.

To expect NGOs to employ their best talent at the salaries they offer is a very big challenge. Therefore, there was a need to look at this challenge to attract talent differently. I won't say that I have a solution to offer, or that India has a solution to offer, but there is a fairly critical point that India, and people working in India, are looking at, which is that we are benefiting from the reverse migration of a lot of talented people.

I did hear people here saying that being economical means that people will migrate to where there are better opportunities. I think that we have to find ways of creating non-commercial incentives that are far stronger than the economic incentives. I also think that what has happened because of the financial crisis may have taught us a lesson, because just building on commercial incentives may not deliver the results for a sustainable future for you and everybody else in the world.

Social enterprises

Let me now share with you a very small example of the company that I created, Intellicap, which is supposed to be a social investment bank, a social consulting company.

We had the idea of creating a company that was to attract the best talent and sensitize them by connecting them to the problems that are sometimes insurmountable, to challenges that had not been met before, and to use their talent of dealing with finance not by being analysts in a billion-dollar bank, but by playing the role of a leader in solving the problems that may make a real difference. At the same time, they have the ownership to change the future of the institution that they are working with.

I am happy to say that we have grown from one to thirteen people in 2004, to eighty people now, and that a 2,000-dollar equity investment has now increased to eight million dollars in equity, and that we are reaching a large number of people over a period of time without loosing them. We are keeping them motivated, paying salaries that are way off the market and yet keeping their entire talent pooled together.

Maybe there is merit in looking at decoupling commercial incentives from non-commercial incentives. Challenges will remain. It is not that I am saying that we are not facing challenges, but the fact is that you can bring a lot of people from across the world to work for you if you have the right kind of incentives, and those don't always have to be commercial incentives.

The third initiative that I think has been pretty important in the Indian context has been the use of sceptic water processors. Supplying water to rural India is a huge challenge. But it can also be an opportunity. In the last fifteen years, we have seen a lot of innovation, and converting problems into opportunities has been the way India has gone. A lot has happened in the social sector.

You mentioned social enterprises of all shapes and sizes. We are witnessing hundreds of them blooming in India at this time, with some of the best talents coming back to the country and starting enterprises that none of us would ever in his life would have thought of. And that kind of talent coming back to India is really critical for any kind of economic agenda that can be created and brings development at the same time.

Lessons to learn

There are certain lessons that I took away from the time I spent in the last ten years trying to make these investments both in microfinance and non microfinance, working in companies right at the grass roots level. The first and most important is that business models need to address the needs of the people and not their wants, or, as has been mentioned by somebody in the audience: business should address the needs of the people but not their greed.

I think the problem is that most of the business is targeted at addressing the wants of the people and not their needs. Microfinance institutions in India conducted an experiment and realized that most clients want products they need. It is pretty clear that you would have trouble to be a leader in terms of mission, drift and agendas if business models are directed toward the aspiration for a product that the business wants and not that the people need.

The second lesson is that the need business is very large, and it is not that multinational corporations don't know about the need business, but it is just that it does not give returns in a very short time frame. Therefore, the need business is not very attractive for them, also because you need to be very patient for it. This is a critical point for anybody who wants to bring economic growth and the common good on the agenda. We need to keep in mind that this patience also applies to commercial interventions.

The third thing we really need to know is that, although not all social challenges can be solved by a business approach, we should still use the business approach because that would release philanthropic capital to carry out those activities that cannot be solved from a business angle. This, to me, is a fairly critical and important issue.

What is the kind of business model that is usually associated with a developing country? If you look at India, especially on the social enterprise side and the kind of business approach that is emerging, it seems that it is fairly convergent to what normal business is: if you have high risks, you expect high returns. But maybe in India investing with high risks is associated with low returns, not because this is just a trend but because this is part of transitional investing, which means that you are investing in an early stage to make a difference in a place where you don't know what the results will be. So the risks may be higher while the returns might be lower. High quality normally means high costs, but in India high quality with low costs is more the trend. If you cannot produce high quality at low costs, the chances of success are low. Indeed, those are some of the trends that we have been witnessing in the kinds of businesses that we have seen and been working with.

Maybe it is time for us to really have a look at the world the way it is. We all know capitalism and have heard about capitalism 1.0, 2.0 and 3.0. My belief is that capitalism has taught us how to create wealth, but the key challenge that capitalism has not taught us is how to redistribute wealth. We use philanthropy for that, but that is a choice we make. Is there a way we can think about capitalism that not only creates wealth but also distributes wealth while it is being created?

There is one final point I want people to think about. It is time that business and greed are decoupled. There was a time that business and greed went together, and I think we will see a repeat of the financial crisis if we cannot decouple greed from business. And if we cannot, we better start introducing courses on greed management in our MBA schools as well.

Panel II: Discussion

Are local banks able to deal with big bank issues? How does the crisis affect financing SMEs? And are we ready for green banking and financing adaptation to climate change?

Peter Blom:
The question on global banks really implies that Triodos Bank as a local bank can only flourish if the big greedy international banks continue to deal with their big bank issues. But the value added of banks should not only be in delivering credit, but also in delivering know-how. What we have seen in the last twenty years in international banking is that we have created a kind of banking that is not related anymore to the real economy, so that it is not clear what value they can add to the real economy and that they can only contribute to creating their own value by circulating money around. We really do not need that kind of banking. We need banks that deal with international payments and with international capital transactions. In that sense, we do not only need local banks, we also need specialized banks, but we have simply gone too far. Securitization is fine, having a group of mortgages put in a pension fund, that is fine, that is not a problem. But as soon as you start to create a virtual market for these packages that have nothing to do with the real economy, that create their own price, their own risks, then you are in a dangerous zone. That sort of banking is what should be limited.

Trevor Manuel:
Will it be possible to have a multiplicity of financial systems? One issue I am concerned about is that all money is fungible. What you

have seen and what gave rise to a lot of exchange rate volatility was the reality of carry trade. If indeed you had a system that lent money at very low rates to developing countries, the chances are that very seasoned operators from elsewhere would come and borrow that money, money that is likely to be utilized elsewhere at high interest rates. Those are the kinds of issues that we need to factor in: how do you, in an industry that is regulated, actually have such regulation, such quality of supervision, that you can prevent that kind of speculative behaviour?

On *financing SMEs*: We realize that there is a gap in the market. If governments wanted to fill this gap then we would need an infrastructure that we could not afford. So we actually struck a deal with the banks: governments put in place a guarantee scheme. SMEs would borrow from the banks and, because they don't have collateral, there would be government guarantees that would then reduce the interest rate burden itself.

But the banks, instead of dealing with the new clients that had opted to utilize that credit guarantee credit system, preferred to continue dealing with their traditional clients. So they removed all of the risks out of the system and then did not assist in extending SME lending to people who had been denied access. So these are fundamentally important issues that we have to realize and share the experience of. I am sure that if we applied the lessons from across the world, and give it very focussed attention, we would probably find five or six ways that we should be able to deal with these issues.

On *green banking*: I was finance minister through the crisis, I don't own any banks. I did not then and I do not now. The interesting observation, of course, was that in developing countries our financial sector held up. You know that we lived with crises earlier. Between India and Brazil, other Asian countries and ourselves, we have been talking to each other and we were learning from these experiences. But we had already such experiences before. The key difference, I believe, is that we have improved on the quality of regulation and supervision, partly because we did not have a choice. Article 44 of the IMF would set out these things, that we should take these lessons. We applied them because they are rational as well. But those who were doling out the lessons never applied them for themselves. That has been the big difference.

On the *direction of flows and aid*, we clearly need to have a wider discussion, but the problem is that the people who are the conscience of the society today go into government tomorrow, and sometimes people who are the conscience of society and run NGOs today do that because they were in the government yesterday. But what we should discuss is how financial flows and aid money is utilized. One of the big problems, one of the missing parts of globalization, is illustrated in the following example.

Take a company, Coca-Cola from the US, headquartered in Atlanta, Georgia. It sells Coca-Cola in Tanzania and repatriates the profits to the US. Tanzania would have signed a treaty to prevent double taxation with the US. Ostensibly, all taxes are only imposed in the US, not in Tanzania. Now, when a road needs to be built in the US, say between Georgia and Washington, it is just an infrastructure investment. The US government brings engineers, they design the road, ensure supervision, etc. But when Mr Ndulu, when he was the Tanzanian finance minister, needs to secure funding from the same tax pool, it would come through USAID and it would be somebody who is a USAID officer and not an engineer, because it is no longer an investment. There is something missing in the equation that we have to repair if all of these things are on the table for repair.

Financing adaptation to climate change is, of course, a fairly difficult question. I know that our colleagues from across the African continent say that they can measure the consequences of climate change. There is a strong sense that developing countries must put money down to finance adaptation. The climate change is more popular now, more fashionable than the poverty issue. The airline ticket tax scheme might work here for climate change because it is no longer a poverty issue.

But I wanted to draw your attention in this regard to another matter. I was struck the other day by the fact that some West African countries had agreed with the EU from Brussels to include the right for certain countries in the EU to fish in the territorial waters of the economic partners in Africa without any ability to oversee what is being fished, how much is taken out or what the degradation of the marine ecosystem would be. Now, this month big commitments will be made to deal with climate change, with the EU probably putting some money in for adaptation, while licensing plunder of the ecosystem. How do you fit this kind of thing in this global world?

Let me say finally that I am a bit worried with some of the debate on climate change. There is a lot of talk on carbon markets. I don't know what the price signals are and I don't know what the enforcement mechanisms are: if you polluted, who knows, who checks, who charges? Who imposes and who distributes? Maybe there is a system in Europe that exists, but does it really affect the equilibrium, does it replace what is consumed? I am sorry to ask these uncomfortable questions.

Vineet Rai:

The issue of the missing middle with regard to *SME financing* has been around for some time. The Bank of India has given advice to other banks to give out 50,000- dollar loans with low interest rates without any collateral, without much costs to the borrower. Not that anybody obeyed it. This goes back to tell us what happens to microfinance. Of course no bank wanted to lend and thus no innovation happened. It tells you that somebody has to find a way, a mechanism by which you can do this kind of lending without increasing the cost. The same thing happened with us, when we launched the microfinance product every venture capital venture fund said that if you invest 100,000 dollars in this way you go bust in five days. Well, we did not go bust in nine years. For sure you can do it. Somebody has to take the risk and start it.

The question was also if the crisis would help to get more credits to SMEs in developing countries. I am afraid it is the other way around. What is happening with the crisis is two things. One is that government deficits will increase and governments will become big borrowers and crowd out especially SMEs. It is already happening, because the easiest way for banks to earn money is by investing in government bonds. Another factor is, of course, that international banks are reducing their activities in a lot of developing countries and that most international banks are targeting the big corporations. So there is more space for the local banks to go to the big corporations.

Normally, small and regional banks see SMEs as a natural market for themselves. But what you need is more competition. If there is more competition in the financial sector then banks will have to look for new markets and innovate.

I don't have a clear answer to the question on *the Rhineland model*, which is much more of a co-opted model than the Anglo Saxon model. In India we have seen entrepreneurs that authorize themselves disproportionally, especially if they operate in a very cooperative kind of production like the handicraft industry that takes place in remote rural villages. The fact that you can pay a small amount of money to people to collect our lead and sell, means that, because you have an opportunity to create wealth, you take a disproportionally large amount of the wealth that has been created.

Is there a way to not only create an employment opportunity for the handicraft people, but also to create ownership for them right from the start? I understand that this has been tried in *the cooperative system* and that it has done very well in Holland. In a country like India, but possibly the world over, the cooperative model has been very successful if the product is easy to classify, like for example milk. Maybe in finance the model is applicable as well, as Rabobank has demonstrated. Maybe there have been reasons that we don't understand as well.

One of the risks that you can run if you set up a model like the one that we are pursuing, is that some day somebody will come and buy a ten rupee share for 100 rupees, especially if you know that it will be worth 1,000 rupees in three years time and you have the capacity to pay. There are mistakes that exist in every model; we just don't know what is the best. Coming from a very confused background we are trying to do the minimum, we are not trying to go for the best but for the better.

What systemic changes are required in financial systems? What is a fair return on investment in SMEs? What incentives are sufficient to attract the talent you need and what role can banks play in the development of the society? What role can ODA play in fostering private investments?

Trevor Manuel:

Before we talk of banks playing a role in the development of the society and do that in a way that is not rewarding risks that are not related to that goal, there are a few other things to consider. I have a sense that in the wake of Enron there was an overreaction. The emphasis on markets did two things. It introduced the pro-cyclicality in accounting systems, which came from the International Financial Reporting Requirements System (IFRRS). I really don't know if the model they used can be reinvented but I would hazard that, unless you deal with those accounting systems, this problem will not go away. In reaction to Enron, you can have a one-size fits all situation, but that size is going to be a terribly bad fit for most of what we require.

The second issue is that code of ethics that Peter Blom was talking about. You can have well-intentioned bankers, but the key issue is that they must know their clients sufficiently well to know that a promise made is a promise kept. I am sure it will leave out of play those who have not actually been active, with a small enterprise, with a good record, of whom you know that there is the commitment to operate in an ethical way, both environmentally and also in relation to the community. But very often you have to deal with a new entrepreneur, and those frequently are the ones that Peter Blom is talking about, that do not have any track record. You have to deal with those as well and because you don't also want cronyism to dominate the scene, you put it on the table and work around it. That is, I think, the approach that you should take.

The point that may have been missed is that you need supervision. Throughout the crisis our registrar of banks called me at least once every second day to give me some assurance or to give me a trend analysis, not in order to upset me. I was amazed by the quality of information that he had at his disposal and was treating with the necessary circumspection so that there was a line of sight that was always his but that allowed us to understand what was going on. And in the same way the Central Bank Governor was getting information also. In many respects that has been the point.

The key is to know that your supervision works, and that line of sight is fundamentally important. 'Bazel II' makes a lot of sense: capital against risk. If you go back to all of these strange derivatives that were created in the mortgage markets in the US, there was no capital against risk! If you take your risk and dice it in slices and then take it off of your balance sheet, that is not rational behaviour. If you ask supervisors to behave rationally, you must give them the instruments for rational behaviour.

Herman Wijffels:
But it was rational from the point of view of those who were doing that, who were dealing with these derivatives. That is also one of the issues we have to deal with in the financial system. Micro-rationalism does not imply macro-rationalism, micro-rationalism was destroying public rationality. That is the systemic issue that we have to deal with. The only way to do that is to oblige people to keep some of the risk in their books and then have high equity standards against their risks, even if that means decreasing the capacity of the financial system to finance operations. That is why the IMF yesterday issued a report advocating not going too far in raising the bar of equity against risk. There has to be a balance."

Trevor Manuel:
The argument has been: 'Don't worry about the bubbles, worry about the stream', and supervision would make sure that the stream would be regulated. You don't want your banking regulation to accept the balance sheets of ugly clients. There has to be a kind of rationality. It would be quite irrational, and it would set up the regulator to fight it, if there was no measure of how much has been diced and sliced and securitized and, in addition, had all this unregulated originative lending, mortgage lending, student lending, all kinds of originatives without any ties to the system. We have set up the system for failure. The stream was not in the place where we had been looking for it, it had in fact been diverted elsewhere, and that is what went wrong.

Vineet Rai:

Two points on the return on investment at the back of the poor. India and Mexico are very different markets. In Mexico you can charge a 100 percent interest rate. In India that would not be possible. SKS rates of interest would be 22 or 24 percent, the cost of borrowing 13 percent and the profit margin would be 2 or 3 percent. Basically, they make money on the basis of volumes, because they have five million clients. That is why they make a lot of money.

Whether they decide to scale their rates down or not, I think it is their obligation to do it. But I don't think that in the Indian context you can say that they are making money on the back of the poor.

I have a personal opinion on who is poor. In my life in the last ten to twelve years, I have met millions of poor people and I have not come across one who did not want to become rich. If you would give them the opportunity to charge interest rates, they would charge high interest rates themselves. So the fact of the matter is; when a person is poor, he should not be charged a rate of interest that actually his business can't justify. It is not the right thing to do. If that person doesn't have the ability to pay you have to use a different instrument rather than microfinance.

Peter Blom:

On the basis of our worldwide experience, I can say that the starters are often making good returns. What we have seen in Bolivia, which was the biggest market in microfinance, is that one of the first institutions and banks that were entering the market were making high returns. Then there came more competition and they were forced to be more efficient and reduce their interest rates. So competition is very important in order to let the market function and let the people have choices to go to different financial institutions. Kompataan was an extreme case: there was no competition and there were extreme interest rates.

In general what you see is, yes, returns in microfinance can be attractive and it is important that they are attractive, that you can have good returns, that you can attract capital and increase the market and have more people getting more access.

On measuring social and environmental impact: the first thing we look at before we finance a company is if it is making a return and if it is a sustainable company. Because that is the basis. If the basis is not there, it cannot be social and it can not be ecologically sustainable. We also try to support companies in order to become sustainable, and we try to measure the impact that we have on those companies in a non-financial way to prove that you really can show what also the non-financial returns are.

If you want to make as much money as you can on microfinance, then there are opportunities. Some of the shareholders of Kompathaan have become very wealthy. But that is not the reason why *we* started with microfinance. We wanted to have healthy businesses with a long-term perspective. Then you should hold back a little bit. If the financial returns around the corner seem to be very high, you have to think: does that really help the institution, the people, including the stakeholders in three, five, ten years time into a healthy development? If we go back all the time to the financial returns, we will not really change things. The financial return is just part of a global return. For the Western, European banks, I think we will go back to a situation where shares in a bank will be a bond with a little bit of an upside, as it was thirty, forty years ago. Because the risks in basic banking in Western Europe are relatively low, then also the returns can be lower. You have to work with those elements, otherwise you create huge expectations. I would not at this moment invest in a bank in Western Europe and expect a 20 to 25 percent return. That will not be the case in the coming ten years, even not in ABN AMRO Bank.

Nanno Kleiterp:
FMO is a case in point when you talk about leveraging to private sector investment by use of ODA. Capital of FMO is not ODA, but you can use forms of guarantee to leverage ODA. Being more creative in using revolving funds is another good opportunity to leverage ODA money, especially if you provide it to the financial sector. When the government puts capital in development banks, if they remain only slightly profitable, you see that this capital is used several times over.

FMO doesn't get any new money for its core business today, we don't receive new contributions from the government, apart from the funds that we are managing on behalf of the government. But we are doing more than one billion of new financing on the basis of capital of 600 million euro that was created over twenty years ago. So, yes, I am convinced that more can be done and FMO represents a very efficient way of using ODA to stimulate capital flows to the private sector.

Trevor Manuel:
The FMO's point is surely that you need a mediator. Ostensibly, in Africa the African Development Fund should be able to do more if they were able to enlarge the pool of funds they have at their disposal and if they could improve on the level of support from their donors. African countries had difficulties to fund the ADF and after we were able funding it, the other donors didn't want us to simply be party to decisions because you had to be a non-regional member. That has been sorted out now.

But I think it should be possible for other pools and funds to find their intermediaries. Even if it were possible to identify that you wanted to have oversight of a partner in say Tanzania, it should be possible to do those kinds of things. But it means that we must try and expand on the capability of what exists so that we can get money into nooks and crannies where it won't normally flow.

Hermand Wijffels:
During my stay as Executive Director at the World Bank, my vision of its future was that it would evolve into an institution that is, of course, financing development in developing countries, but doing that in a way that is crowding in private capital. That could be done by giving guarantees, but also by creating consortia for financing infrastructure or whatever in developing countries. That is the way forward. We can also use that in financing climate change issues. That might also be helpful.

If I were a representative of a developing country and would be asked to have a view of, for example, the future role of the African Development Bank, I would also want it to not only finance on its own account but also to try to crowd in private capital. That is a real possibility and an opportunity that might be helpful in multiplying public funds with private funds.

Nanno Kleiterp:
It is happening already. FMO is doing it. The AfDB is doing it. It could also be scaled up very much. You also see more and more people in the Western world interested in social investments, who agree to accept lower returns in exchange for social returns. I think there will be many more markets to attract private capital to finance projects in developing countries with capital that is willing to take higher risks in exchange for green returns.

What improvements in the banking environment in developing countries are required? On innovative banking and the appetite of banks to take risk: can you introduce more risks instead of cutting rewards?

Peter Blom:
You must differentiate between risk capital that is needed in Africa and other parts of the world, and the readiness of banks to take risks. What we learned is that banks have a certain utility function, also in developing countries. If we want to encourage people to put deposits in the bank in developing countries, those banks should not be taking extra risks. They should take that very seriously and only finance healthy and good entrepreneurs. Having said that, there is a separate need, here as well as in developing countries, for risk investments. For that you need a different channel. So I agree with you that you need risk capital but I would not necessarily put that as a sort of action of local banks. Banks have to be stable factors in society; that is important for the people.

Trevor Manuel:
Across the African continent, you can observe a patchy set of experiences in banking. Across the continent we don't have bank supervision outside the Central Banks. We don't have a FEZ. We tried, but we don't have a FEZ type of body. Supervision is still very much

a function of the Central Banks. So perhaps one of the things that we should ask is to share experiences and that Central Banks or the bank supervision divisions collaborate more closely so that if in a small country you have to deal with a big bank you can act on the basis of shared experiences. This would be possible because these would all be people bound by the same secrecy provisions.

It would also be important that we try and do this because, in the context of the newly established Financial Stability Board and as we get into those discussions, there need to be an unfolding African experience, otherwise we are left off the table again.

In respect of the risk appetite, and I speak here again as a non-banker, isn't there a different kind of problem? Banks still tend to have an asset and liability mismatch: frequently banks tend to borrow short and lend long. If you carry mortgages and those kinds of things, or you have mortgage originatives going off the radar screen and nobody want those any longer, can that be improved? In the absence of that, there frequently is a tendency to take on crazy sorts of risks to make good, which will be wiped out in the context of IFRRS.

The other issue is that we have been dealing with countries that have incredibly low savings ratios. Probably, when that stuff hit the fan in the US, savings ratios were negative. It is not quite the same here in Europe, those kind of ratios, the pool of savings or the impact on the amount of risk appetite, but I think I heard Peter Blom saying consistently that the more transparency you have in the balance sheet, the more it is possible for stakeholders to see through, the easier it is because I think that there is a sense of accountability at the public supervision about the way you run these things. If you are chasing mega bonuses those issues are not in question. So supervision has an important role to play.

Nanno Kleiterp:
I agree very much with Peter Blom: banks have a fiduciary respon-sibility so they have to be very careful with the risks they take. What you need is innovation in financial institutions. Vineet Rai showed that development banks could play an important role investing in seed capital because it is their role to increase access

to finance. That has been done by setting up microfinance institutions, increasing them, scaling them up.

If you have the experience in investing and making money, the risks are lower. But there is always a cut-off from where you cannot invest anymore if you want to see your money back and have a small return. In this sense, you have to spread your risks: not everything is acceptable. Somebody said risk is a black hole, but we try to avoid those black holes and stay with the risks we understand. For equity that is very important.

Let me finish with saying that it is all about people. If we had two million people like Vineet Rai being entrepreneurial and innovative all over the world, then a lot more could happen. There is a limitation in people who really have those capabilities to set up new enterprises with a very good probability of success. That applies as well to capital venture funds, for investment companies: the challenge is to select the ideas and the people together and have confidence in the success of those people.

Conference Summary

Allison Evans

What strikes all of us, I suppose, about this financial crisis has been both its scale and its speed of transmission. We have heard a number of things that reflect that speed. The crisis started off within a very rarefied atmosphere of financial markets and boutique products strange to the real economy. The speed with which this happened, I think, is quite significant and something that perhaps took many of us by surprise. But twelve months on from the failure of Lehmann Brothers, and looking back eighteen months after Bear Stearns and two years after Northern Rock (and even further back), it is an important point in time for us to reflect on what has been the impact of this crisis for developing economies and how, if at all, it has changed our ideas about growth and development strategies.

I suppose we can at least rest a little easy in the sense that the initial panic linked to the crisis is perhaps over or at least underground for the time being. But, talking generally about the early signs of recovery within parts of the OECD and particularly also within emerging economies, one of the things that we have done work on in the Overseas Development Institute (ODI) and that many of you have pointed at today, is that actually the developing economies around the world have been affected quite differently by this crisis.

I think it is an interesting question to ask why that has been the case. Why have some countries weathered the crisis more effectively than others and what can we learn from that? I will come back to that later on, but in terms of where we are in the recovery, one of the things I am thinking about is: do we feel optimistic or do we feel pessimistic? Is the glass half full or is it half empty at this point? I think it depends quite a lot on what matrix of recovery we are looking at.

I am reflecting now on a meeting that we hosted at ODI on Monday this week, where we brought together a number of different perspectives on the financial crisis one year on in developing countries. It was very interesting for those of us who were relatively close to development agencies and to the aid business that there was a general sense of pessimism: this crisis is long and deep, we don't really know yet where we get the bottom out in developing countries and there is a need for more resources and for doubling our efforts.

But for those of us who represented the private sector at the meeting, there was a much more bullish feeling in the sense that there are early signs of recovery, capital is flowing, we can see there are a lot of opportunities and development financing institutions are getting about and doing their business and filling the gaps. It just struck me that the answer to the question of whether one sees the glass half full or half empty at this point of the crisis depends very much on the matrix one is using to assess both its depth and the recovery from it.

That actually connects to another, bigger point that Trevor Manuel made about what matrix we use for measuring societal and economic progress more broadly and the fact that this crisis, but also a lot of broader thinking about development, is beginning to push us in the direction of much more holistic measures that go beyond GDP alone. I think that is a very interesting trend and something that we should take away from this meeting. Our need to get on board some of that thinking about different measures or programmes and, of course, issues around sustainability looms very large there.

Not business as usual

What was very interesting in a number of presentations and discussions around the impact of the financial crisis is how quickly we got to talk about other crises. We talked about the food crisis, and the long arm of the food crisis, in fact, because that crisis is still unfolding in a lot of countries. Shenggen Fan's presentation reiterated why that might be the case, and pointed at the overhang of hunger and malnutrition that has flowed from that. But we also talked a lot about the climate crisis, which has come back time and time again. If Lord Nic Stern were standing here at this moment, he would say: 'Yes, financial crisis, absolutely, very significant, big, important, but nothing compared to the impending climate crisis'.

It leads me to think again about our discussions around the following hypothesis: would the same solutions that we have been talking about today be on the table if we actually had primarily been talking about the climate crisis and not the financial crisis? Would we have a different package? Would the solutions be more radical? Would we be engaging in more talk about paradigm shifts and the rest? It is just a question!

When we talk about crises, which I think is absolutely right – we have to focus on them because crises contain both challenges and opportunities to reflect on – it is really important for us to also reflect on what is going on with some of the other big drivers of growth and development and the extent to which these, combined with crises, are changing the risks, rewards, risk returns and the risk opportunity framework facing many developing economies. What are those long-term drivers? Well, urbanization. Urbanization is big news in Africa. Demographics – the youth bulge – is also a massive issue. The global and regional drivers of security and insecurity are again hugely significant within the development space. And, of course, the thing that overshadows everything in a way is the shift in power from the West to the East. These issues have in many ways changed the framework, the risks, the rewards and the risks opportunity framework that developing economies are now working with to try and shape their future growth and development strategies.

If the combination of these big drivers could speak, they would say it in no other terms: 'Not business as usual'. We have to start thinking differently, thinking radically, and this is a key moment to do it. What I sensed in the room throughout the discussion, particularly this morning, was that there were some very different opinions about how much of a game changer this crisis actually is.

We could shift that around and say: 'How much of a game changer do we want it to be?' That is a question that we should all consider as we leave today.

Diverse approaches to growth and development

That is the backdrop to this conference. What came out of this morning's session? Well, the morning session dealt specifically with diverse approaches to growth and development. I don't know about you, but I did not hear anything in the morning that was paradigm shaking. That is not meant, in any sense, to do injustice to all of the fantastic contributions we heard, but maybe that is where we are in the debate. Maybe this is not about paradigm shifting, but again, a question for us to ponder. What I heard was a whole number of things. You would perhaps have heard other things but let me just summarize them.

The first point that came up time and again was that this was a crisis that had its roots in the financial sector, but actually the financial sector, like it or not, is critical to our recovery. But in being critical we have to change some of the ways of doing business. That was a message that, to my mind, came out loud and clear.

Another key theme from this morning was the theme of interdependence, which Professor Ndulu put squarely on the table. Yes, this financial crisis, perhaps even more so than previous financial crises, and certainly more so than the previous financial crisis but also more than the food and the fuel crises, has demonstrated to all of us the interdependence of welfare in developed countries and in developing countries.

So this is the world we now live in. Interdependence is also crucial to our recovery and that means fighting protection, democratization of capital markets – I love that notion: democratizing credit – insuring that voice is more effectively and more equitably distributed and dealing with the balance between the provision of capital, access to capital and regulation. These are all issues that affect us all and around which we have to take strong collective action.

A third theme was about the need to think about smarter and better ways of doing things. There was quite a lot of emphasis on innovation and technology, on raising our gains, taking the opportunity to not only come out of the crisis, but also moving to where we need to be in order to address future crises, and in particular the climate crisis.

Another theme was about not throwing the baby out with the bathwater. It was said a few times, but in developing economies – and it is a dangerous thing to lump them altogether because they are a very varied set of economies – as a whole there has been a huge improvement in rates of growth, in macro stability, in the productivity of public spending and all of these good things, including the facilitation of markets in a number of developing and poor economies. It is crucial that we hold on to those. Actually, the countries that have done better in response to crises are those that recognized and stuck with these reform gains and are building on them rather than turning their back on them.

Resilient growth and financial deepening

To come back to Mr. Ndulu's point, all said and done, it is crucial not to throw the baby out with the bathwater but to attend to the terms of engagement through which developing economies participate in this globalized economy. In some ways, this is not new as the literature on engaging in the globalized economy is as wide as it is deep. By I wonder whether this current conjuncture of crises makes some of that thinking even more apposite.

There is quite a lot of emphasis on changing the terms, but also on thinking about new resilient growth paths, tackling some of the vulnerabilities of those structurally not fully developed economies. What does a resilient growth path look like? Out of the morning's session, there were a number of elements that came together that I want to summarize here.

The first one is about investing in social protection. Resilience comes in part from making sure that you have protective measures in place for the poorest and most vulnerable. This is not, you know, a drag on growth. It is an investment in future growth. In the short run, the argument against social protection always comes down to affordability, fiscal drivers and so forth, but actually I think the evidence is overwhelming that social protection in and of itself, aside from doing all the good things in terms of protecting people, is actually good for long-term growth. Likewise, investing in girls' education, women's access to capital and so on is also good for long-term growth.

Another big theme is attending to the issue of financial sector deepening and access to finance in developing countries. This seems to be a fundamental issue, and this point about the financial sector being part of the recovery as well as being heavily responsible for the crisis seems absolutely critical and a big theme of today. But I think that perhaps we, certainly from the morning session, did not get a full sense of where to start this deepening of the financial sector in developing economies. Do we focus purely on banks; do we think about stock markets; do we think about a whole range of intermediaries that are necessary to support healthy financial sectors? What do we think about the financial challenges of linking poor producers to supply chains, and what needs to happen to do that effectively?

So there is a whole cluster of issues there, and in a discussion I was just having in the break we concluded that in order to get more functioning, effective financial sectors you may need to start somewhere else and deal with issues such as property rights, contract enforcement and so on. These are interesting questions, but something that is crucial for a resilient growth path has to have a solid financial sector linked in to it.

State–business relations and economic integration

The other question that did not come up very clearly in the morning, but that I want to drag a little bit from Trevor Manuel's discussion in the afternoon, is about another crucial element of a resilient growth path. It is what I call, or what we in ODI call, effective state-business relations, which is the framework around which you negotiate and facilitate the role of business in the economy.

Underpinning that is a capable state. I don't think we can ignore that.

Effective state-business relations seem to me to be a crucial part in which communication, negotiation and the terms of agreement between the state and the business sector is well understood to be a vital tool for more resilient growth.

Another key issue that was raised was integration. The issue of effective regional integration not only in product markets but also in factor markets came up a lot. Also, thinking perhaps more innovatively about supply chains and the need to think both in terms of regional as well as global supply chains came up. I understand there is an active debate at the moment about the fact that quite a lot of suppliers are beginning to retreat a bit from the very complex and long global supply chains because of the added risks linked to the financial crisis, and that they are beginning to concentrate more of their efforts around regional supply chains. I, for one, think that is not a bad development, at least for a number of poorer countries.

The role of aid and states

What we did not talk about much in the morning is how to finance this more resilient growth. One thing that struck me was that there was not much mentioning, if any, of aid and in some ways that may be a very positive thing. But I wonder whether we might not need a stronger message. All of that stuff about the future of growth strategies is very good, but what role did aid play in that and could we possibly be more robust on that, even if we finally concluded that the main role for aid is important and supportive for the provision of global public goods necessary to enable that growth to take place? Nevertheless, where we think aid may have a continuing role in that, it was something we perhaps missed the boat on.

In the afternoon session, Trevor Manuel said that financing for development is not going to sort itself out. It needs active and conscious engagement by capable states as well as responsible funders, whether they are from within the development community or from within the private sector. That seems to me to be a strong message somewhere in the middle of that kind of pendulum swing that was mentioned a few times today between market fundamentalism and the other extreme of state dirigisme. Somewhere in the middle, on the sensible middle ground, is the acknowledgement that, of course, we need states and markets and, of course, they need to be active as well as responsible and capable.

What kind of other steps are required if financing for development is not going to sort itself out? What are some of the recommendations or ideas that came out of the conversation in the afternoon? How are we going to sort this out? I picked up a few ideas.

The first is Trevor Manuel's point of sorting out the global architecture for decision-making and collective action, which is his governance point. We got a proliferation of 'Gs' within the international space at the moment: starting with the G3, then we have the G7 and G8, the G20 and the G 77, and it goes on. We need at some point to put a stop to this and be very clear what the direction around global collective action and decision-making needs to look like.

A second point was about continuing to support capable states, and this reiterates the need to not allow the pendulum to swing too far. But I think it is a fact, and we all need to acknowledge that there are market features and there are coordination features, and that we need capable states to address those.

I was interested to hear what I felt was a kind of rewrite of an old debate in development about the micro-macro paradox being applied to the discussion of what is going on in banking, which is the macro-rationality versus the micro irrationality. But it was also interesting that Trevor Manuel firmly put the point about the need to focus support on capable states at the centre because of continuing failures. But then we also heard that certainly business can play a role in contributing to tackling some of these failures through the new breed of values-driven financial organizations, but those depend on issues like locality and scale and the new thinking about the interdependence between economy, ecology and equity on which Peter Blom focussed in his presentation.

I was also struck by what I heard about applying the talents of the business community to social challenges, which was the clear message coming out around the prospects for social enterprise and harvesting talent from the business community to apply to ongoing and sometimes seemingly intractable development challenges of which issues to do with market failure and so forth are squarely intertwined.

As I said, it was not long ago that a discussion around financing for development would have focussed almost entirely on official flows. It is, in fact, very refreshing to have heard relatively little about that. But at the same time, it is actually not far-fetched to say that we need to be very careful not to completely obliterate the very important goal of improving the quality of ODA as a tool for financing development. We need to keep that pressure on. There is much to be learned from the private sector in terms of transferring lessons of how we might do ODA better. It certainly cannot be business as usual for ODA. There is always a need to review, to replenish and to innovate. But as we focus now on building better, stronger, more regulated and more responsible financial markets, we must not completely loose sight of the fact that there is still a continuing need for effective development assistance. One hopes that that would come to a close very soon and the need to think about exit strategies of course is uppermost in our minds, but let us not loose sight of the continuing significance of what I think are still a significant number of poor economies.

Now, if any of you knew my predecessor at ODI, Simon Maxwell, you will know that he always finishes off with three bullet points. Well, there are a lot of things that Simon and I have been changing at ODI, but I will keep hold of this tradition because I think it is quite useful. So let us finish with three bullets:

First: the panic is over. There are early sign of recovery from this financial crisis, but I think, listening and hearing the debate here, that we do have a long way to go in terms of building back better from this crisis. I think it is inevitable that a massive shock of this scale leads us to think much more around shock proofing and resilience than perhaps we were thinking about before. One of the things I take away from this is really trying to think through what a crisis-resilient growth path really looks like and what we are we trading off in the process of trying to deliver that.

Much of what we ultimately try to do in development will be hindered or helped by sorting out some of these global governance issues. The fact that the global community has now stepped up with a strong contra-cyclical instrument in the wake of the financial crisis just hints to think that this should have been done a long time before, and we need to reinforce that as good practise and to encourage more of it. That applies both to the international and also to the regional level. As well as thinking about crowding in private capital and using the World Bank to do that, we also need to sort out how we are going to crowd in the sort of public goods that developing countries need to develop effectively and grow effectively.

At a national level, developing economies' strategies are probably going to be somewhat different as a result of the financial crisis, and those economies that were able to be very proactive in their response to the crisis, in many respects, have weathered the crisis reasonably well. I think there are a number of quite good examples from the African continent – countries that were proactive so that actually we are going to see now some very green sheets of recovery. But there are big challenges ahead, and the danger is that in recovering from this crisis we do not see the train coming along, coming in our direction, which of course is the climate crisis, if it is not with us already. So diversify, integrate, sort out some of the institutional rules of the game to actually support stronger markets that connect poor people to regional supply chains, that crowd in private capital, that is responsible and that is focussed on values and long-term development outcomes.

Contributors in Order of Appearance

Bernard Berendsen is member of the Advisory Council on Foreign Relations of the Ministry of Foreign Affairs in the Netherlands. He started his international career at the Central Bank in Sudan in 1969. In 1970 he joined the United Nations Economic Commission for Asia and the Far East in Bangkok, Thailand. He completed his PhD thesis at the Erasmus University in Rotterdam in 1978 on the subject of regional models of trade and development dealing with issues of international trade, economic development and integration. He joined the Ministry of Foreign Affairs in the Netherlands in 1975. After various assignments in The Hague he became Director for Africa in 1994, was posted in Jakarta from 1997 until 2000 and became Netherlands ambassador in Tanzania before retiring in 2005. He was editor of the two precious volumes in the series published by SID in coorperation with KIT Publishers.

Rick van der Ploeg is Professor of Economics at Oxford University. He is Deputy Director and Senior Research Fellow of the Oxford Centre for the Analysis of Resource Rich Economies (OxCarre), and also Research Fellow of New College and Associate Member of Nuffield College, Oxford. He is Research Fellow in international macroeconomics at the Centre for Economic Policy Research and is a Council Member and Coordinator of the public sector economics programme at CESifo, Munich. He is Adjunct Professor of Political Economy at the University of Amsterdam and a Research Fellow of the Tinbergen Institute and member of the Editorial Board of Netspar at Tilburg University. He is former Chief Financial Spokesperson in the Dutch Parliament and State Secretary of Education, Science and Culture of the Netherlands, and has been on the board of various commercial and non-profit organisations. Published books include *Foundations of Modern Macroeconomics* with B.J. Heijdra (OUP, 2002), the edited *Handbook of International Macroeconomics*, and several other books in the English and Dutch language.

Michael Spence is Chairman of the Commission on Growth and Development, Senior Fellow at the Hoover Institution and Philip H. Knight Professor Emeritus of Management in the Graduate School of Business at Stanford University. In 2001, he was awarded the Nobel Memorial Prize in Economic Sciences. He served as Philip H. Knight Professor and dean of the Stanford Business School from 1990 to 1999. Since 1999, he has been a partner atOak Hill Capital Partners in Menlo Park. From 1975 to 1990, he served as professor of economics and business administration at Harvard University. Spence was awarded the John Kenneth Galbraith Prize for excellence in teaching in 1978 and the John Bates Clark Medal in 1981 for a significant contribution to economic thought and knowledge. Spence was named chairman of the economics Department at Harvard in 1983 and served as the dean of the Faculty of Arts and Sciences from 1984 to 1990.

Martin Wolf is associate editor and chief economics commentator for the Financial Times, London. In 2004 he published *Why Globalization Works* (Yale University Press) and in 2008/2009 *Fixing Global Finance*, in which he explains why global imbalances cause financial crises – including the recent crisis in the US – and outlines the steps for ending this destructive cycle. Mr Wolf is also associate member of the governing body of Nuffield College, Oxford; honorary fellow of Corpus Christi College, Oxford University; honorary fellow of the Oxford Institute for Economic Policy (Oxonia); and a special professor at the University of Nottingham. He has been a forum fellow at the annual meeting of the World Economic Forum in Davos since 1999 and a member of its International Media Council since 2006.

Sylvester Eijffinger is Professor of Financial Economics at Tilburg University and Board Member of the European Banking Center in Tilburg, as well as Visiting Professor of Economics at Harvard University in Cambridge, MA during the Spring semester of 2008. He held, amongst others, Visiting Professorships at University of Johannesburg, Universidade Catolica Portuguesa, and the University of Munich. Professor Eijffinger has published widely in prestigious economics journals

Hans Schlaghecke is journalist and editor at the Dutch Newspaper Het Financieele Dagblad. He is a former employee at the Dutch Ministry of the Interior and Kingdom Relations.

José Edgardo Campos is since April this year Advisor to the Vice-President of the World Bank Institute. Before taking up this position he was Governance Adviser for Bangladesh at the World Bank. Prior to this appointment, he was Lead Public Sector Specialist and the Coordinator of the Bank's Governance and Anticorruption Thematic Group. Dr Campos also worked at the Asian Development Bank as a Senior economist and spent two years as senior strategy adviser for public sector reforms at the Department of Budget and Management (DBM), Government of the Philippines. Prior to joining the World Bank, Dr Campos was an assistant professor of public policy and management at the Wharton School of the University of Pennsylvania. Dr. Campos completed his Ph.D in the Social Sciences at the California Institute of Technology and his M.S. in Agricultural and Applied Economics at the University of Minnesota. He has co-authored four books and numerous papers on issues pertaining to political economy, governance, and corruption.

Diane Elson is Professor of Sociology at the University of Essex, UK. Previously, she worked for the United Nations Development Fund for Women (UNIFEM) and for Manchester University where she was Chair in Development Studies. Her current research and teaching interests are in global social change and the realisation of human rights with a particular focus on gender inequality. She served as a member of the Millennium Project Task Force on MDG 3.

Geske Dijkstra studied economics and sociology at the University of Groningen, where she also obtained her Phd in Economics in 1988. Currently she is associate professor in economics in the Programme of Public Administration. She combines research and teaching with carrying out studies and consultancies for organizations involved in development cooperation, such as the World Bank, the Swedish International Development Agency (Sida) and the Dutch Ministry of Foreign Affairs. She is the (co-)author or (co-) editor of eight books, and published extensively in international journals.

Luc Soete is director of UNU-MERIT, the United Nations University – Maastricht Economic and social Research and training centre on Innovation and Technology. UNU-MERIT emerged after the integration of UNU-INTECH and the University of Maastricht research institute MERIT, for the latter of which Professor Soete was founding director since it was set up in 1988. Luc Soete is also Professor of International Economic Relations (on leave) at the Faculty of Economics and Business Administration at the University of Maastricht, and is member of the Dutch Advisory Body for Science and Technology Policy (Adviesraad voor Wetenschaps- en Technologiebeleid (AWT)). Before coming to Maastricht in 1986, Luc Soete worked at the Department of Economics of the University of Antwerp (previously known as UFSIA), the Institute of Development Studies and the Science Policy Research Unit both at the University of Sussex, and the Department of Economics at Stanford University. Professor Soete completed his first degrees in economics and development economics at the University of Ghent, Belgium, before obtaining his DPhil in economics at the University of Sussex. His research interests cover the broad range of theoretical and empirical studies of the impact of technological change, in particular new information and communication technologies on employment, economic growth, and international trade and investment, as well as the related policy and measurement issues.

Vijay Paranjpye is currently a Chairman of Gomukh Environmental Trust for Sustainable Development in Pune, India, as well as Chairman of Blue-Cross-Society of Pune and he teaches Environmental Science at the School of Environmental Studies at the University of Pune, India. Mr. Paranjpye is also involved in several environment and rural development projects such as for example: Rural Development Programme covering 20 villages in Kolwan Valley near Pune with a major objective to lift 330 households above the poverty line, to implement schemesto enhance the hygiene in these villages and to set up projects for the empowerment of women; and "River Basin Management: A Negotiated Approach", a project by DGIS (Dutch Ministry of Development Cooperation) where comprehensive River Basin Planning for social upliftment, with poverty elimination, water security and foodsecurity as the basic objectives, will be studied.

Cor van Beuningen is the Director of SOCIRES, a Dutch-based thinktank specializing in governance, democracy and civil society organizations in the public domain. He holds Masters degrees in regional planning and in public administration. Mr van Beuningen has twenty years of experience in international cooperation, including ten years of field experience in Latin America, Africa and Asia, being employed by both governmental and non-governmental development agencies. He is advisor to the Netherlands Institute for Multiparty democracy, and to several other public and private institutions involved in non-commercial public-private partnerships, both in the Netherlands, in Eastern Europe and elsewhere.

Ad Melkert is currently UNDP Associate Administrator at the UN Envoy in Iraq. Before this post from 2005 to July 2009, he served as Under-Secretary-General, and Associate Administrator of the United Nations Development Programme (UNDP). From 2002-2005 Mr.Melkert was Executive Director and a member of the Board of Directors at the World Bank. Mr. Melkert joined the World Bank after a long and prominent political career in the Dutch Labour Party (PvdA). He was member of the Dutch Parliament and Minister of Social Affairs and Employment, and in 2001 was elected party leader.

Nancy Birdsall is President of the Center for Global Development, a policy-oriented research institution that opened its doors in Washington, DC in October 2001. Prior to launching the Center, Ms Birdsall served for three years as Senior Associate and Director of the Economic Reform Project at the Carnegie Endowment for International Peace. Her work at Carnegie focused on issues of globalisation and inequality, as well as on the reform of the international financial institutions. From 1993 to 1998, Ms Birdsall was Executive Vice-President of the Inter-American Development Bank, the largest of the regional development banks, where she oversaw a $30 billion public and private loan portfolio. Before joining the Inter-American Development Bank, she spent 14 years in research, policy, and management positions at the World Bank, most recently as Director of the Policy Research Department.Ms Birdsall is the author, co-author, or editor of more than a dozen books and monographs. Ms Birdsall holds a PhD in economics from Yale University and an MA in international relations from the Johns Hopkins School of Advanced International Studies.

Jan Kees de Jager is an IT entrepreneur and politician in the Netherlands. He was state secretary of finance for the Christian Democratic Party from 2007 until the fall of the government in February 2010, after which he became minister of finance in the resigning cabinet. Before his appointment as state secretary he worked for an internet company which he co-founded en he was active in many organizations and boards. Including as deputy secretary general of the European youth organizations YEPP and as a member of the founding council of the Scientific Institute of the CDA and he was member of the Executive Board of the CDA. During the 2008 G20 in Washington Summit he represented The Netherlands because of the absence of the Prime-Minister and the Minister of Finance.

Shenggen Fan was appointed general secretary of the International Food Policy Research Institute (IFPRI) at the beginning of 2010. Since joining IFPRI in 1995, Dr. Fan served as Director of the Development Strategy and Governance Division, Senior Research

Fellow and led IFPRI's program on public investment. Prior to IFPRI, he held positions at the International Service for National Agricultural Research (ISNAR) in the Netherlands and the Department of Agricultural Economics and Rural Sociology at the University of Arkansas. He received his Ph.D in applied economics from the University of Minnesota, and his bachelor's and master's degrees from Nanjing Agricultural University in China. Dr. Fan's major research includes pro-poor development strategy, pro-poor investment, and rural-urban linkages in developing countries, focusing mainly on Asia, Africa and Middle East. He currently directs a research division that works on governance, development strategy, public investment, and rural-urban linkages; and country strategy support in China, Ethiopia, Ghana, Malawi, Mozambique, Nigeria, Uganda, Vietnam, and other countries.

Benno Ndulu is currently serving as the Governor of the Bank of Tanzania. He is best known for his involvement in setting up and developing one of the most effective research and training network in Africa, the African Economic Research Consortium. He served first as its Research Director and later as its Executive Director. He received an honorary doctorate from the ISS in the Hague in recognition of his contributions to Capacity Building and Research on Africa and supporting preparation towards democratic transition in South Africa. He has since closely been involved in the drafting of MAP, NAI and NEPAD. Following his PhD degree in economics from Northwestern University in Evanston, he taught economics and published widely on growth, adjustment, governance and trade. He has been involved in policy advisory roles world wide and has served in a wide range of Boards and committees internationally, including IMF Board of Governors.

Alfredo G.A. Valladão is a Professor at the Institut d'études politiques de Paris (Sciences Po), in charge of the Mercosur Chair and Coordinator of the Working Group on EU-Mercosur Negotiations and of the International Conference of Forte Copacabana on "Defense and Security European-South American Dialogue". Senior Researcher Fellow at the Instituto de Estudos Estratégicos e

Internacionais (IEEI – Lisbon). Journalist, specialized in international politics, editorialist for collaborates with Radio France International, he also contributes regularly to the BBC and CBN (Brazil). Former diplomatic and defense correspondent for the daily Libération (France). Member of the Editorial Board of the quarterly reviews on international affairs Questions Internationales (France) and Res-Publica (Portugal). Founder and former member of the Editorial Board of the economic and geopolitical yearbook L'Etat du Monde (France). Author of documentary films for French television networks. He has written extensively on issues of international security, diplomacy, and international trade.

Jan Willem Blankert works for the European Commission in Jakarta, as the Special Adviser for the relations between the EU and ASEAN. From 2003 to 2007 he worked in the Commission's Headquarters in Brussels on the relations between the EU and China. He is an economist (from the University of Amsterdam, 1975) and a veteran of economic and political reform and economic integration. With the European Commission since 1985, he worked many years on European integration issues, first in Brussels (Internal Market and macroeconomic convergence) and after that in Poland (1994-1998), Bosnia (1999) and Serbia (1999-2003). Before 1985 he worked for the governments of Tanzania and Suriname and for UNICEF. He has been teaching at the University of Amsterdam (1975) and the Amsterdam Higher Economic School (1984). He wrote his book when he was the EU Fellow at the Lee Kuan Yew School of Public Policy in Singapore, during the academic year 2007/08

Nanno Kleiterp is the Chairman of the Management Board of the Netherlands Development Finance Company (FMO). Since joining FMO in 1987 Mr Kleiterp served in various positions: Chief Investment Officer FMO (2000-20008), Chief Finance Officer FMO (1996-1999), Manager Latin America FMO (1994-1995), Manager SME FMO (1987-1992) and Investment officer (1987-1992). Before joining FMO he worked as Investment officer, FNI (National development bank Nicaragua) (1983-1987); in a rural development project Adult

Education, Patzcuaro, Mexico(1981-1983) and as a research on the effect of innovations on small farmers in San Martin,Peru (1979-1981). Mr Kleiterp is associated to a number of professional bodies, institutes and charitable organisation such as for example: European Development Finance Institutions (EDFI) where he is Member of the Supervisory Board; Fund for Tuberculosis (KNCV)as Vice chairman Supervisory Board and Chairman Audit Committee; De Waal Foundation, Board member; and Royal Institute for the Tropics (KIT), Council member.

Trevor Andrew Manuel is a South African politician, currently serving in the Cabinet of South Africa as Minister in the Presidency in charge of the National Planning Commission. Previously he was the Minister of Finance from 1996 to 2009, during the presidencies of Nelson Mandela, Thabo Mbeki and Kgalema Motlanthe; he was one of the country's longest-serving finance ministers. In May 2009, he was re-assigned to head up a National Planning Commission by President Jacob Zuma shortly after the latter's inauguration.After the unbanning of the African National Congress (ANC), Manuel was appointed as deputy co-ordinator in the Western Cape Province. At the ANC's first regional conference in 1990 Manuel was elected publicity secretary. At the ANC's 1991 national conference Manuel was elected to the National Executive ommittee. In 1992 Manuel became head of the ANC's Department of Economic Planning. Manuel was elected as an ANC Member of Parliament in 1994 and was appointed by President Nelson Mandela as Minister of Trade and Industry; two years later, in 1996, he was moved to the post of Minister of Finance.

Peter Blom has been CEO of Triodos Bank since 1997. Born in Leiden in the Netherlands he studied economics at Vrije Universiteit in Amsterdam and was jointly responsible for establishing one of the first centres in the Netherlands for organic food, including an organics shop, restaurant and information center in Amsterdam. He then worked at Triodos Bank as a Senior Business Banking Account Manager, before becoming Joint Managing Director, until he took up his current role as CEO and Chairman of the Executive Board in 1997. Peter Blom is also Chair of the Global Alliance for Banking on Values, Member of the Board of The Dutch Banking Association, Chair of the Organic Food and Agricultural Council of the Netherlands and Deputy Chairman of the Multifunctional Agriculture Taskforce by order of the Dutch Ministry for Agriculture. Peter Blom was awarded the Dutch Royal distinction of Knight of Oranje Nassau in 2008 for his contribution to social banking and sustainability. Triodos Bank won the Financial Times and IFC Sustainable Bank of the Year Award 2009.

Vineet Rai has over 15 years of experience in leading innovative interventions in Social Development, Venture Capital, Micro Enterprises and Microfinance Investments. Founder of Aavishkaar (and related companies), Vineet is the Co-founder and Director – Intellecap, a pioneer and leader in the multiple bottom line investment advisory industry. He is also the Co-founder and Director – Rural Innovations Network, a Chennai-based Non Profit company that creates networks for rural innovations. In several of his advisory functions, Vineet is on the advisory board of Lemelson Recognition and Mentoring Program at IIT Chennai. Vineet has been awarded Ashoka Fellowship in recognition of his contribution to the field of Social Entrepreneurship and Life Membership of XLRI Alumni Association He holds a Post-Graduate diploma in Forestry Management from Indian Institute of Forest Management, Bhopal.

Alison Evans became ODI Director in May 2009. She is an economist working on poverty, public policy, institutional change and the role of international development assistance. Practical policy experience, including six years at the World Bank, covers poverty reduction strategies (PRSPs), budgetary processes, aid modalities and aid effectiveness, plus evaluation. Other interests include fragile states, policy coherence and social protection. Extensive experience in Southern and Eastern Africa, Western Balkans and shorter assignments in SE Asia.